IMAGES
of America

HAM LAKE

ON THE COVER: Pictured is the 1905 family reunion of the first permanent settlers of Ham Lake, the Mads Gilbertson family. For more information, please see page 12. (Courtesy of the Anoka County Historical Society.)

IMAGES
of America

HAM LAKE

Melvin Aanerud with the
Ham Lake Chamber of Commerce

ARCADIA
PUBLISHING

ISBN 978-1-4671-1403-5

Published by Arcadia Publishing
Charleston, South Carolina

Printed in the United States of America

Library of Congress Control Number: 2015939525

For all general information, please contact Arcadia Publishing:
Telephone 843-853-2070
Fax 843-853-0044
E-mail sales@arcadiapublishing.com
For customer service and orders:
Toll-Free 1-888-313-2665

Visit us on the Internet at www.arcadiapublishing.com

Contents

ACKNOWLEDGMENTS

Thanks go to the following people and organizations for their contributions to the production of this book: Eric Aanerud for technical assistance; Kathleen Dipprey Aanerud for proofreading; Lois Titterud Anderson for photographs and history; Anoka County Surveyor's Office for maps; Todd Mahon, of Anoka County Historical Society, for photographs and encouragement; Sharon Ashford, who kept the Ham Lake history on the city website; Richard Braastad for a photograph; Janette Braastad for a photograph; Lisa Bauer for photographs and history; Cindy Birkeland for photographs; Marvin Buchholz for photographs; Cathleen and Ted Elwell for photographs; Dan Gillund for artwork; Glen Cary Lutheran Church for photographs; Ham Lake Chamber of Commerce for sponsorship; Ham Lake Senior Center for history and also photograph identification; Hoffman Sod Company for a photograph; Chris Mickman for photographs; *Minneapolis Star Tribune* for a photograph by Jack Gillis; Minnesota Historical Society for photographs; Minnesota State House of Representatives office for photographs; Minnesota State Senate office for photographs; Ronnie and Marylou Moore for photographs; Rose Nelson for photographs; Doris Nivala, the City of Ham Lake, for photographs and information; Our Saviour's Lutheran Church for photographs; Betty Moe Sannerud for photographs; Susan Saverese for photographs; Lorraine Soderquist for photographs and history; and Twin Cities Gateway for photographs by Wayne Adams.

People were generally very generous in allowing me to use their precious historical documents—I am very grateful.

All courtesies at the end of captions in the book deal strictly with the images.

Letter from the Ham Lake Chamber of Commerce

A community is many things; it is not only its people, its churches, its schools, and its recreation, but it is also its businesses.

As pioneers came to Ham Lake, their first occupation was agriculture. It went from subsistence to cattle, turkeys, potatoes, and sod, and the most profitable subdivision of property went to housing. Timber had to be removed to create farmland, and there was business in felling trees and selling the wood. To support their agricultural pursuits, farmers of the area began the first business, a creamery on Lake Netta. This led to the need for ice, and an ice business began.

With the establishment of Highway 65, transportation became more than Indian trails, and it brought people to and through Ham Lake. Cabins and resorts were built on Coon Lake, and the area became a destination for city people. A garage was built on Highway 65; it was the only one between the Twin Cities and Cambridge. A commercial center developed around it. This inspired the county to create Crosstown Boulevard to connect the city of Anoka to this location, which became known as Soderville because of the entrepreneurial spirit of the Soderquist family. A real main street was developing until the expansion of Highway 65 in 1958 changed the look and feel of the area.

Ham Lake is quickly changing from rural to exurban to suburban. Businesses are welcome, and since 1982 the Ham Lake Chamber of Commerce has encouraged, promoted, and represented them. We are most pleased to sponsor the writing of this pictorial history of our community. A very special thanks to Mel Aanerud, a Ham Lake resident and a member of the Ham Lake Chamber of Commerce Board of Directors, for his dedication of abundant time and energy writing this book for so many to enjoy.

—Al Stauffacher, president, and Wendy Renner, executive director

2015 Ham Lake Chamber of Commerce Executive Board

Pres. Al Stauffacher, Twin Cities Gateway
Vice Pres. Ellen Christopherson, Sjoberg & Associates

Board of Directors
Tim Holtz, Holtz Landscape & Irrigation
Sarah Jordahl, 21st Century Bank
Mel Aanerud
Ben Bina, American Family Insurance
Scott Summerbell, Edward Jones Investment

Introduction

Between anywhere and somewhere is a place we call community. There were hunters who came to the Ham Lake area, but they had no desire to stay and took their game and moved on. There were even some names of people who made claims; after all, land could be homesteaded after the Homestead Act of 1862. But, some earliest names never actually came, and those who did certainly did not stay.

The people who started the settlement of Glen Cary intended to make a community. A major fire, however, convinced them to move on. It took hardy Scandinavians who were looking for a better life for themselves and their posterity to make Ham Lake a community. To those early settlers, a community was a place where they lived, worked, worshipped, married, had families, and were buried. In the process of those lives, they farmed, built houses of worship, houses of learning, and houses of commerce. None knew they were city builders, but they understood about community, self-resilience, and reliance on others.

We had some dream not covered in this book. One was to move the Minneapolis–St. Paul International Airport to Ham Lake, and this dream increased land values for a while; however, it was decided not to make that move. There was a group that wanted to transform part of the city into a Scandinavian village not unlike Renaissance fairs, but it would be Scandinavian in character and held in the winter. It never happened. There was a developer who wanted to produce a neighborhood for airplane owners with a runway through the center so people really could fly to and from their homes. This was another dream unfulfilled.

The early settlers would have never thought that their land would be used to sell grass, yet for about a decade Ham Lake was the largest producer of landscape sod in the state. They would never have believed that the city would dedicate over 352 acres to public parks or that the major city celebration would be held in the middle of a city lake in February.

This book tracks the city from its agricultural roots, from rural to exurban to suburban.

Those early settlers did develop a community where they lived, worked, worshipped, married, had families, and were buried, and we are all the better for it.

One

Early History

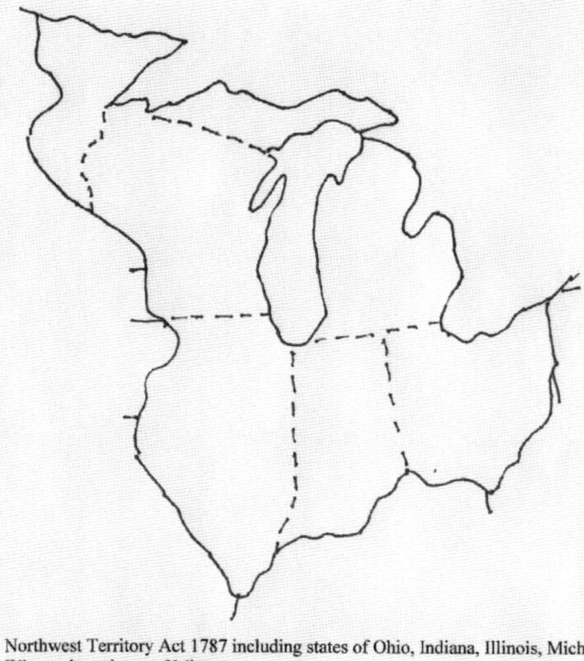

Northwest Territory Act 1787 including states of Ohio, Indiana, Illinois, Michigan, Wisconsin and part of Minnesota

The Northwest Ordinance (formally An Ordinance for the Government of the Territory of the United States, Northwest of the River Ohio) was an act under the Articles of Confederation of the United States and was passed on July 13, 1787. This was created prior to the US Constitution and the federal government as it is known today. (Author's collection.)

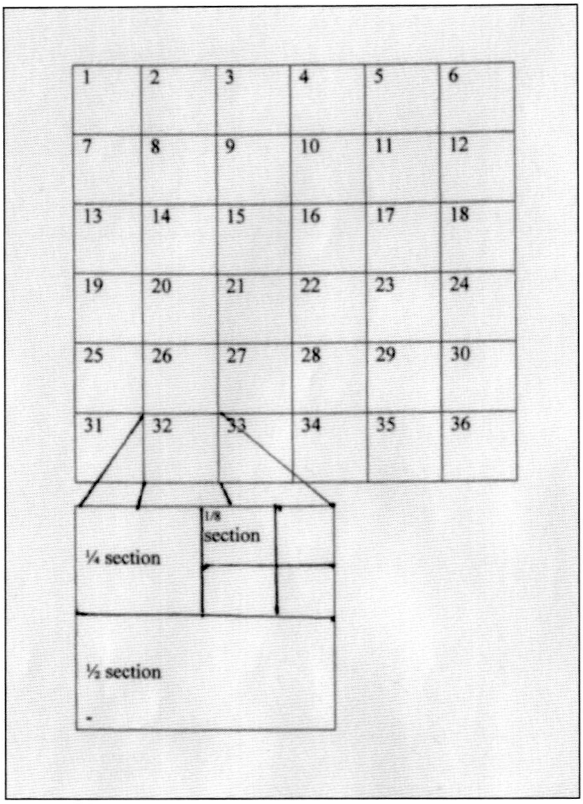

The Land Ordinance of 1785, along with the Northwest Ordinance, established the system used to determine land ownership. Every 36 square miles a township was established, and all land within the township could be determined by a system of halves and quarters. All property descriptions come from this system. Ham Lake is a perfect geographical township under this system: six miles by six miles square. (Author's collection.)

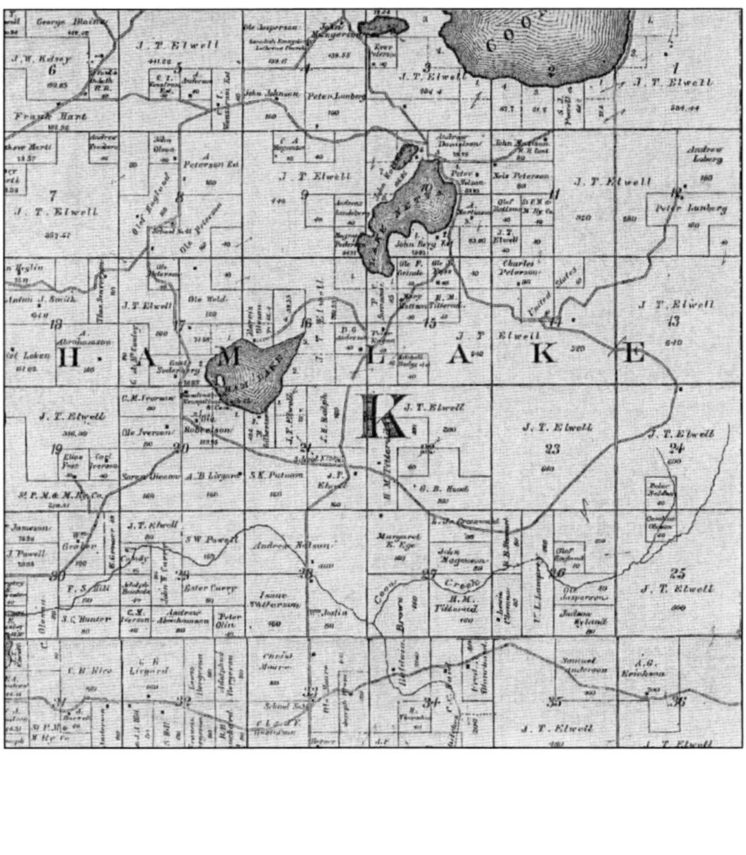

This 1888 plat map is the first one that includes Ham Lake. The township lies in the center of Anoka County, with a chain of lakes from Coon Lake in the north, Lake Netta in the center, and the southern-most lake that looks exactly like a slice of ham with an island as the ham bone—Ham Lake. (Courtesy of Anoka County.)

The next existing plat map is from 1904. This one shows some changes in ownership of the different sections, caused by the Panic of 1893. (Courtesy of Anoka County.)

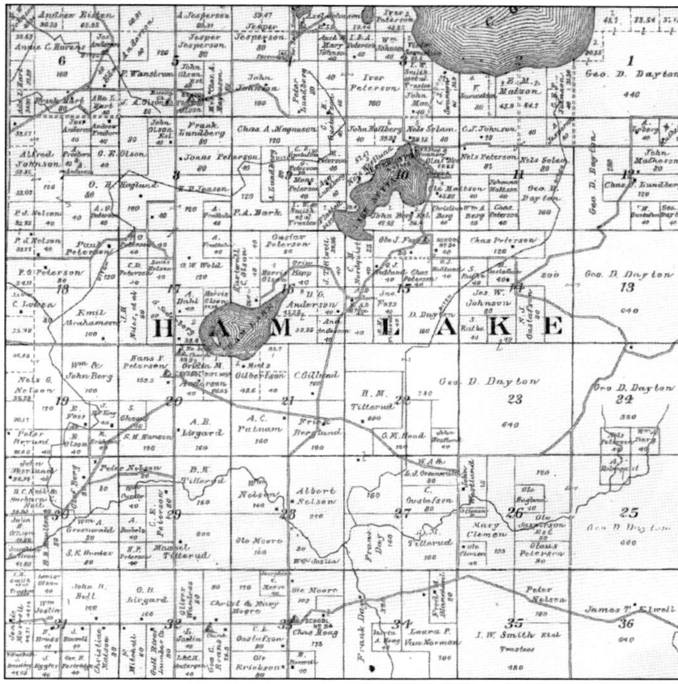

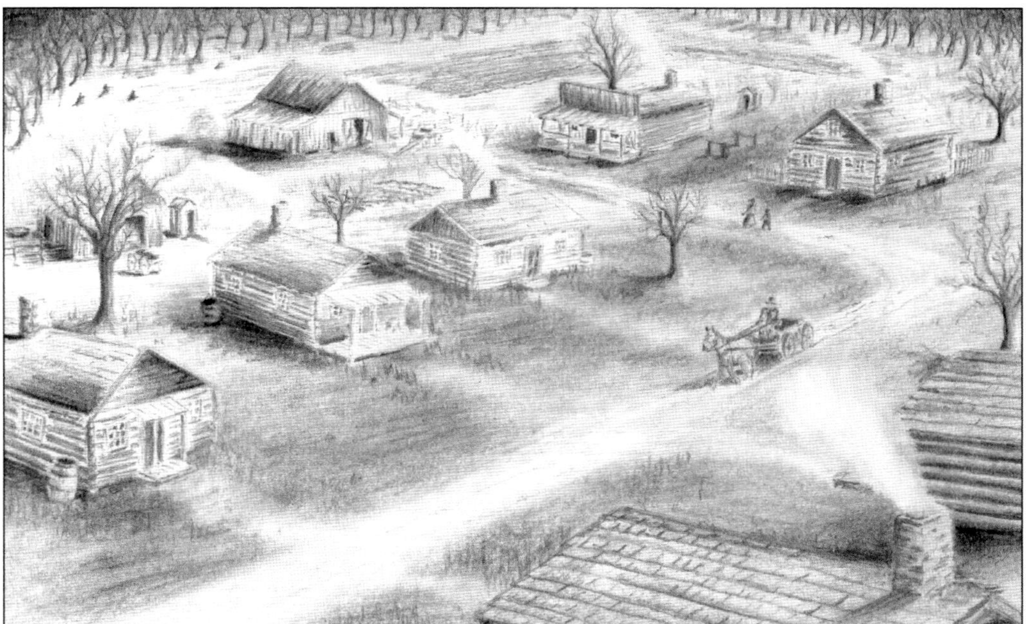

The earliest record of settlers in the Ham Lake area goes back to 1855, and in 1856 settlers established a town located just south and west of the lake shaped like a ham. These settlers platted and sold lots for a community named Glen Carey, a Scottish name meaning "beautiful valley." It was alternately spelled Glencarie and Glen Cary. The location was widely advertised as a future city. With only seven or eight cabins built, a bill to move the Anoka County seat to Glen Carey was placed in the Minnesota Legislative hopper, but timely opposition by a delegation of citizens from the city of Anoka killed it. (Courtesy of Dan Gillund.)

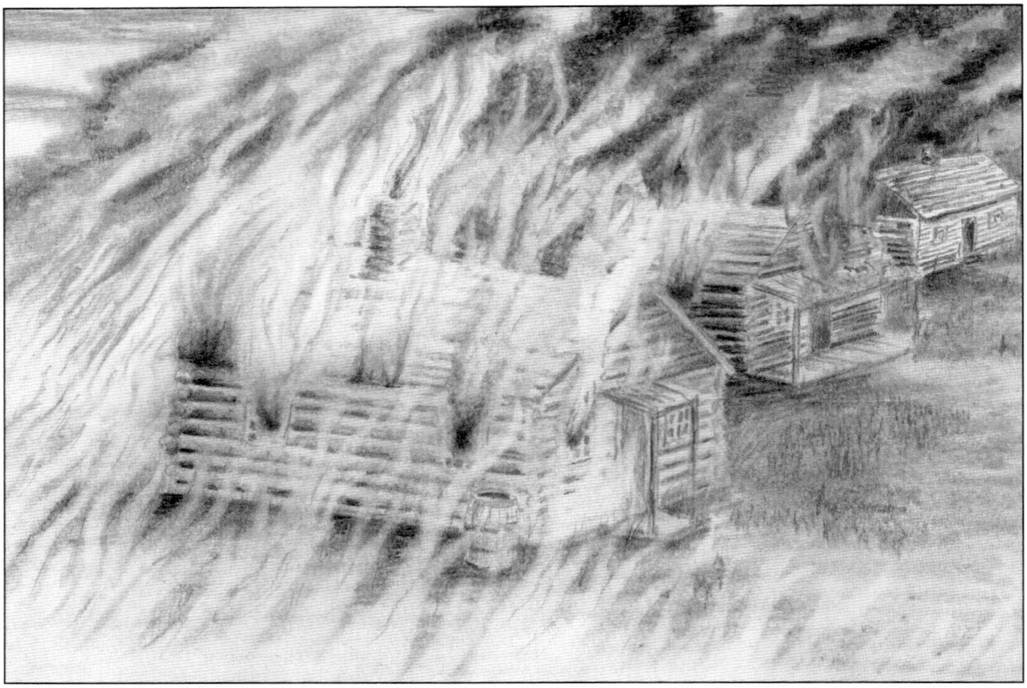

In 1857, a prairie fire destroyed all of the houses in the community. Some of the inhabitants barely escaped with their lives, saving only very few household goods. These settlers left the area. (Courtesy of Dan Gillund.)

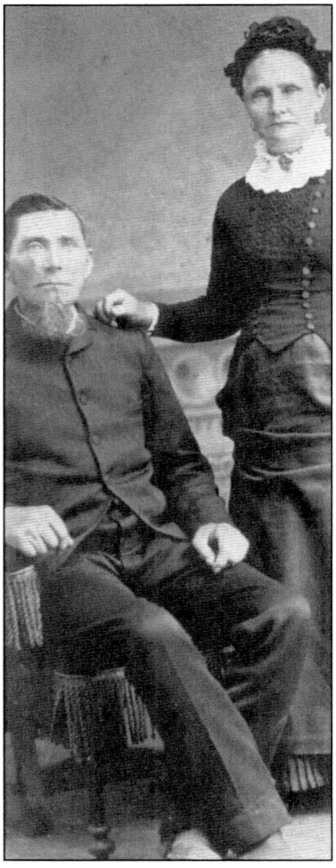

The first permanent settlers in Ham Lake were Norwegians Mads (sometimes spelled Mats) Gilbertson and his wife, Olena (Christopherson). It took them three days by team and wagon in 1866 to travel from St. Anthony (near what is now Minneapolis) to Ham Lake. Mads was already 48 years old at the time. They settled in Section No. 20. The first church service and the first day school were held in their cabin. They also provided the land for the Glen Cary Church when it was built. They had six children: Karen (Mrs. Arnie Livgard), Olia (Mrs. Olaf Moore), Ellen (Mrs. Edward Abrahamson), Martin, John, and Laura (Mrs. Even Larson). Mads and Olena were followed by other Scandinavians, H.M. Titterud and A.B. Livgard. Other early settlers were Nels Peterson, Ole Moore, Iver Peterson, Ole Foss, Ole Peterson, Thomas Olson, and Ole Heglund. (Courtesy of the Anoka County Historical Society.)

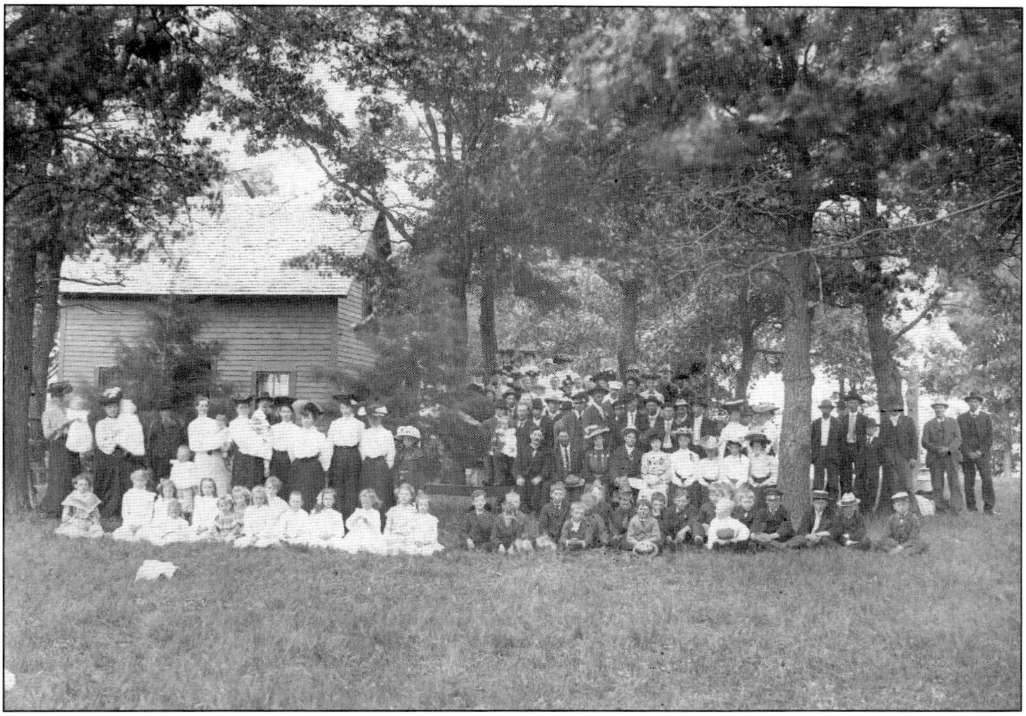

Travel was not easy at the turn of the century, so families lived close to each other. This is a 1905 reunion of the Mads Gilbertson family. (Courtesy of Ronnie and Marylou Moore.)

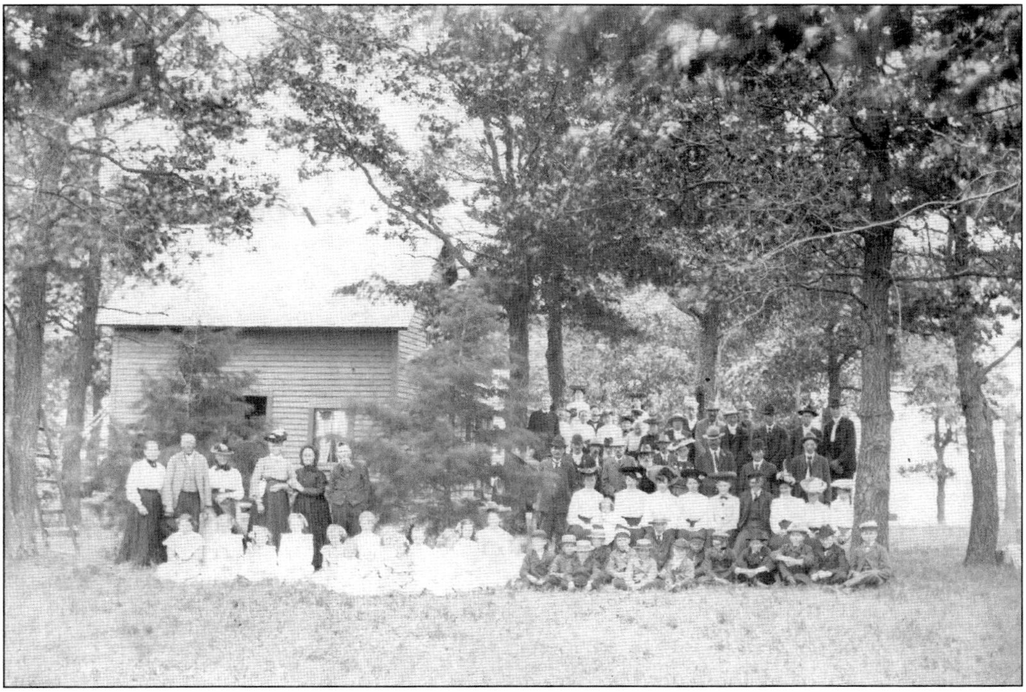

Families not only lived near each other, but they had get-togethers that were far more formal occasions than in later years. Take note of the Sunday best of the Mads Gilbertson family at the 1906 reunion. (Courtesy of Ronnie and Marylou Moore.)

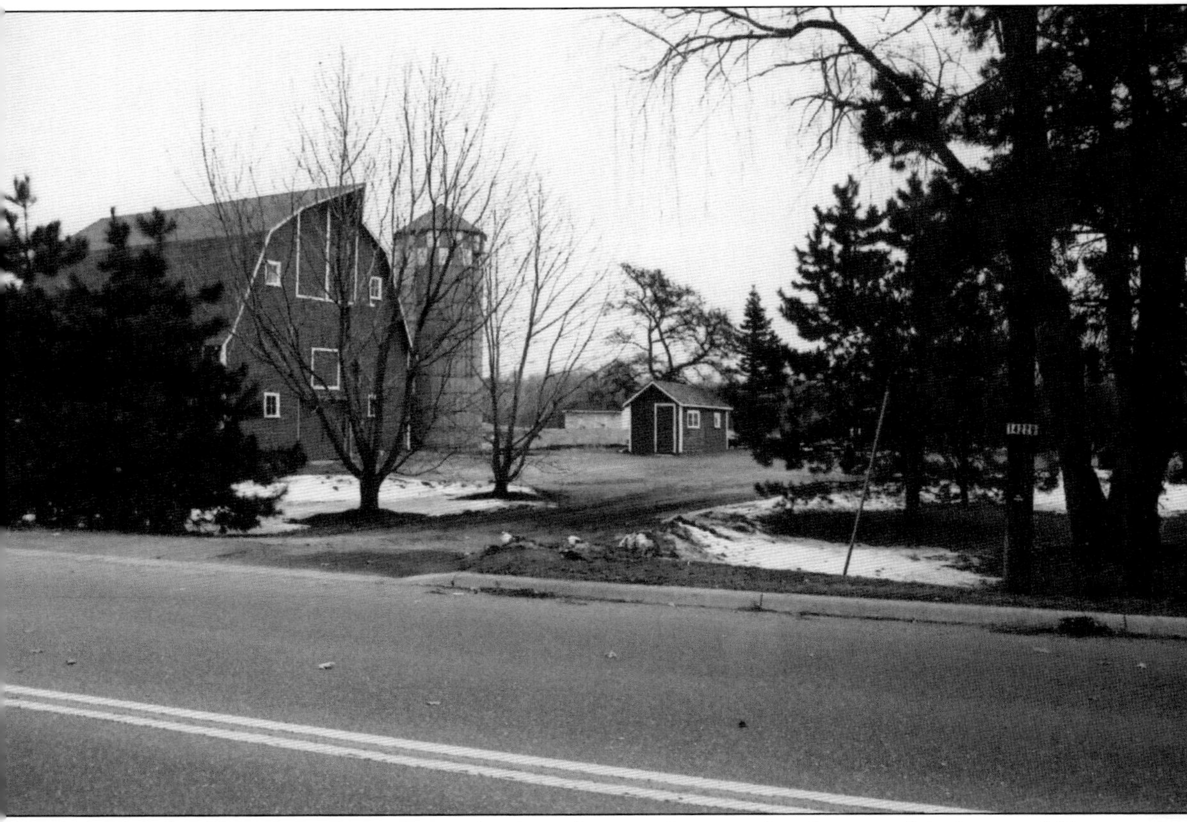

Anoka County recognizes farms that have been in the same family ownership for over 100 years as Century Farms. Six Century Farms are in Ham Lake, and one of those is the Livgard/Ganter Farm. A.B. "Arnie" Livgard, a native of Norway who came to America in 1865, started the farm by purchasing land in September of that year. His wife was Karen Gilbertson, the oldest daughter of Mads and Olena Gilbertson, the first settlers in Ham Lake. The Livgards lived for a time with the H.M. Titterud family. Karen Titterud was Arnie's sister. Arnie and Karen had 11 children: Ovidia (Mrs. Louis Anderson and after Louis's death Mrs. Nels Hagen), Andrina (Mrs. John Ganter), Emelia (Mrs. Gust Bonde), Benedict, Cornelia (Mrs. Olaf Wold), Alvida (Mrs. Andrew Johnson), Alfred, Clarissa (Mrs. Sabin Smith), Oliver, Oscar, and Gina (Mrs. Albert Horgan). Andrina married John Ganter, and their son Clarence Ganter and his wife, Margaret, took over the property in 1947. The farm straddled Highway 65, and some land was taken when the highway was expanded. Braastad Nursery (now Holtz Nursery) was part of the property, and Aker Door (now The Hope Chest Bridal Boutique) came out of the triangle on the other side of the highway. (Courtesy of the Anoka County Historical Society.)

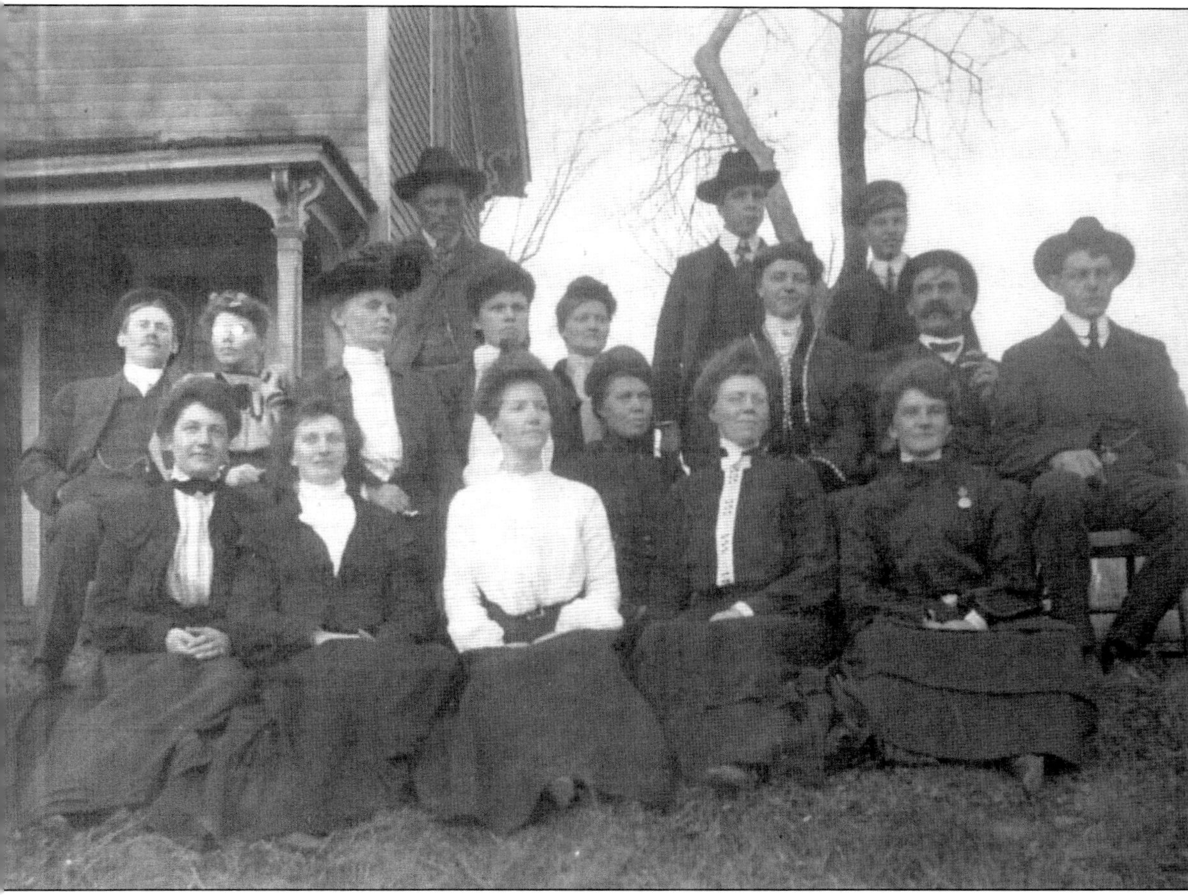

Halvor and Karen (Livgard) Titterud came to America from Norway in 1866 but lived for a time in St. Francis in Anoka County. They moved to Ham Lake and homesteaded in 1868. On February 27, 1869, Maxel Titterud was the first white child born in Ham Lake. His parents took him by oxen and wagon to what is now the Twin Cities to be baptized at Trinity Lutheran Church. The round-trip took the better part of a week. On the way home, when they came to Rice Creek in what is now Fridley, the oxen decided they were hot and tired and went to the middle of the creek and refused to go farther. Karen left Halvor and the oxen and, with the baby in arms, walked the 15 miles to the Gilbertsons in Ham Lake since there were no other houses north of Rice Creek. Halvor and Karen had nine children: Maxel; Berger; Anna Gustava, who died as an infant; the second Anna Gustava (Mrs. Otto Hogda), as it was not unusual for families to use the same name for later children; Ovidia (Mrs. Pater Jasperson); Oscar; Hoakon; August; and Clara, who died as a child. (Courtesy of the Glen Cary Church.)

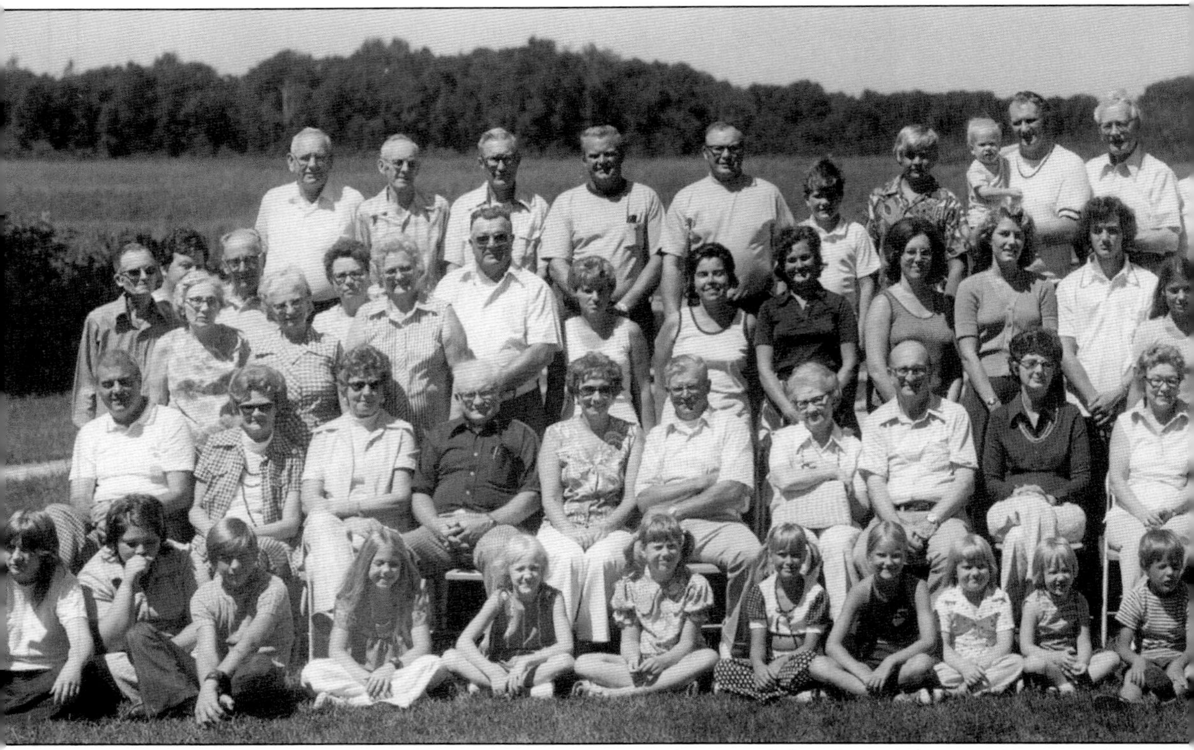

Pictured is the Titterud family reunion in 1974. Note how much less formal they are 68 years after

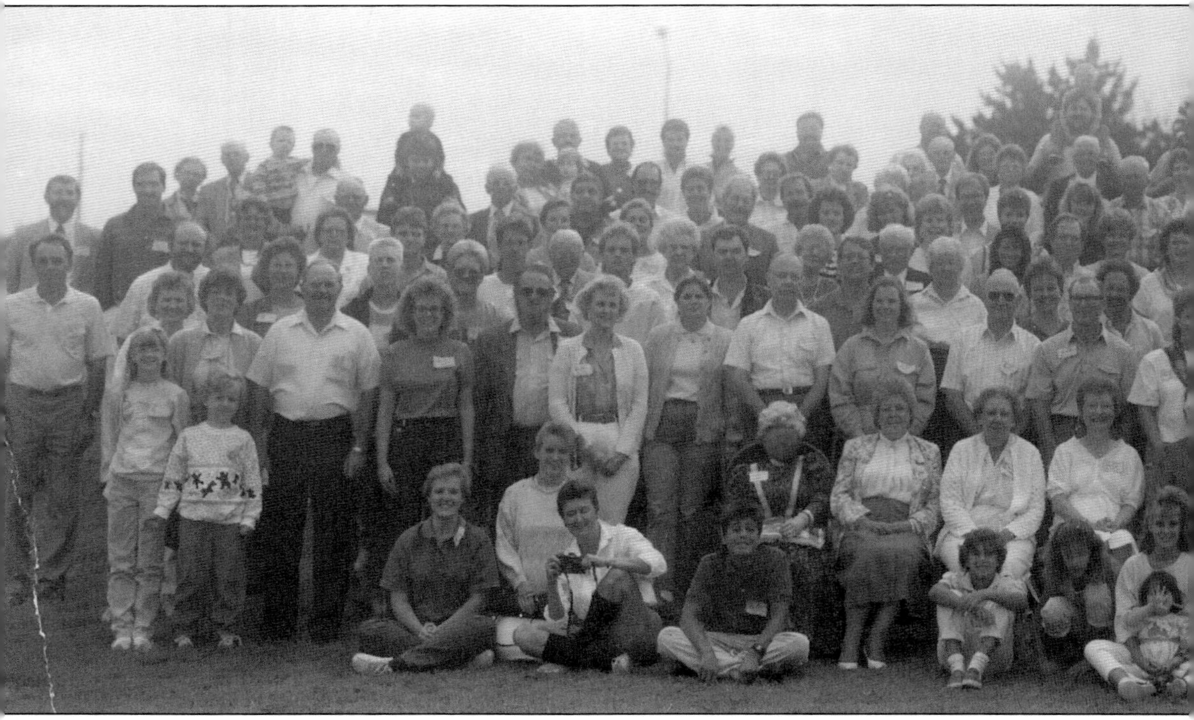

This is the 1988 Titterud family reunion. People at Glen Cary Lutheran Church state that nearly half their congregation is part of the Titterud family in one way or another. (Courtesy

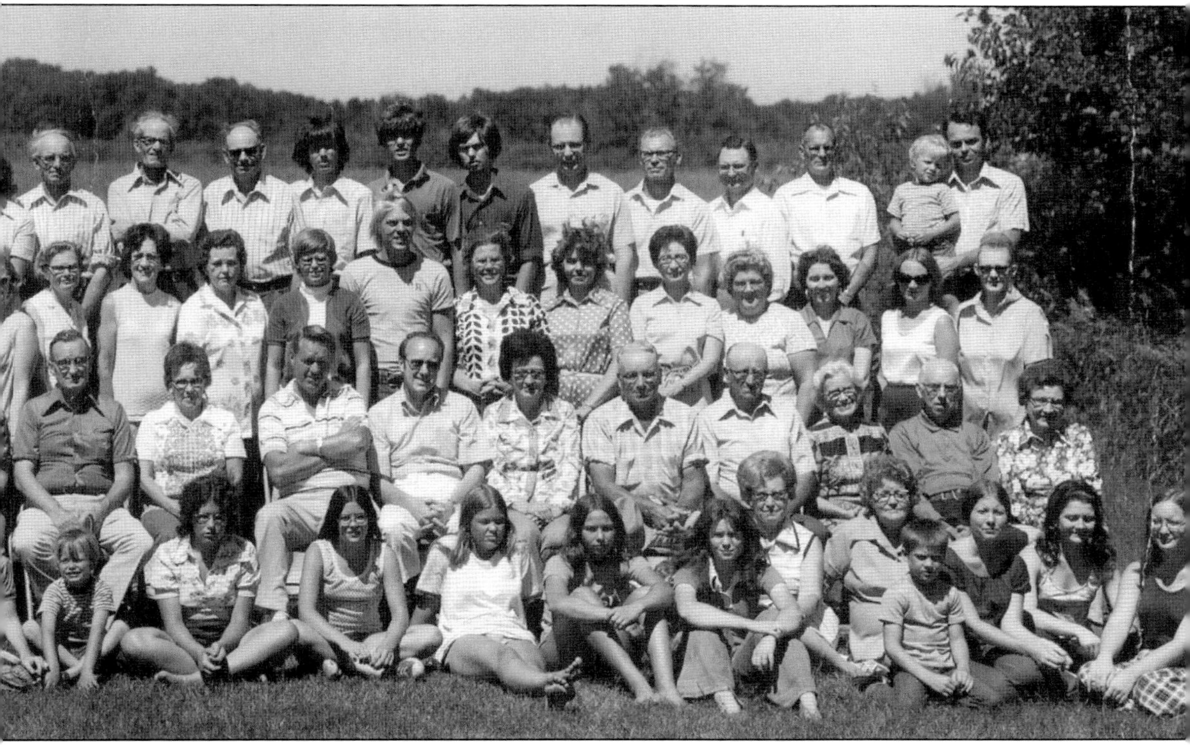

than the Gilbertson family reunions in 1905 and 1906. (Courtesy of Lorraine Soderquist.)

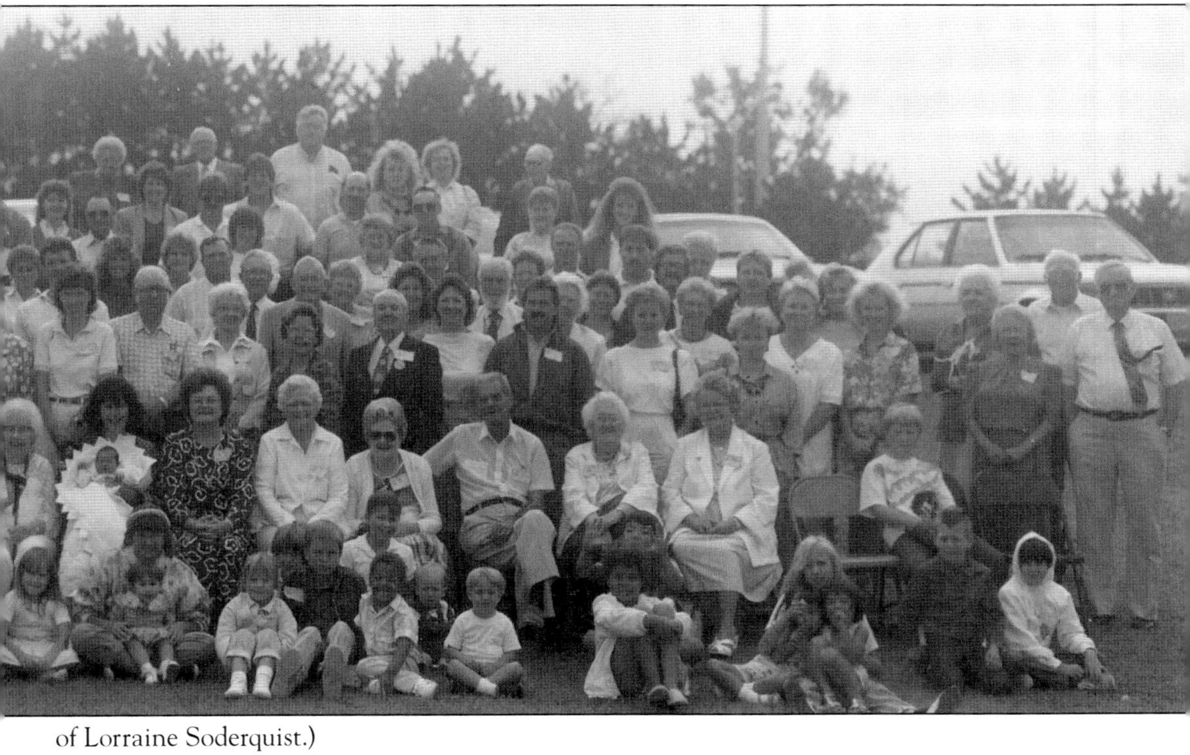

of Lorraine Soderquist.)

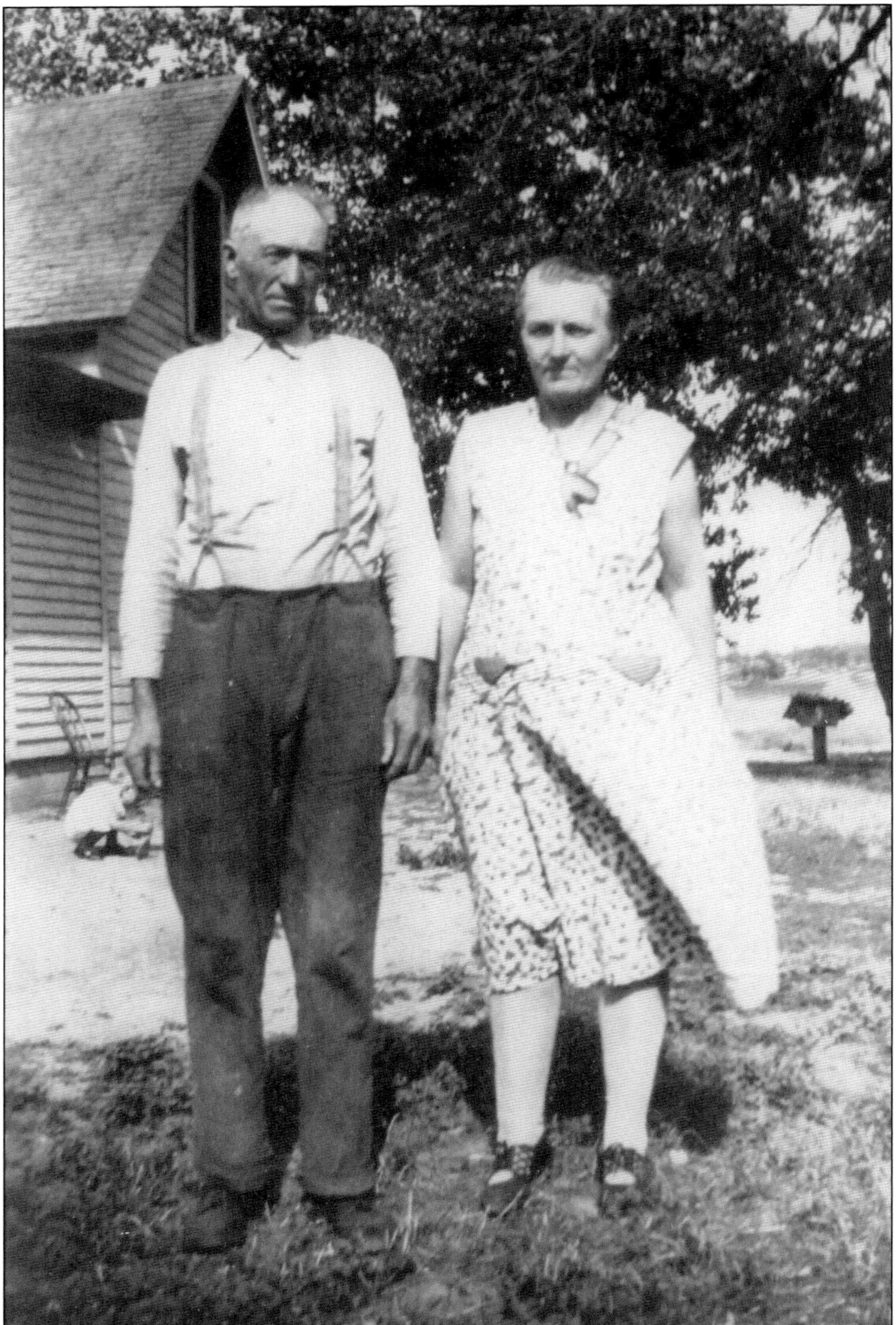

Adolph and Mary Buchholz brought their family from Germany in 1882 and bought property in April 1885. They sold the property to their son Otto Buchholz in 1908. Otto called square dances, the family held basket socials, and people tobogganed on the biggest hill in Ham Lake on the Buchholz farm. At the Christmas programs at the Redbrick School, bricks were heated and wrapped in Buchholz potato sacks to keep feet warm. (Courtesy of the Buchholz family.)

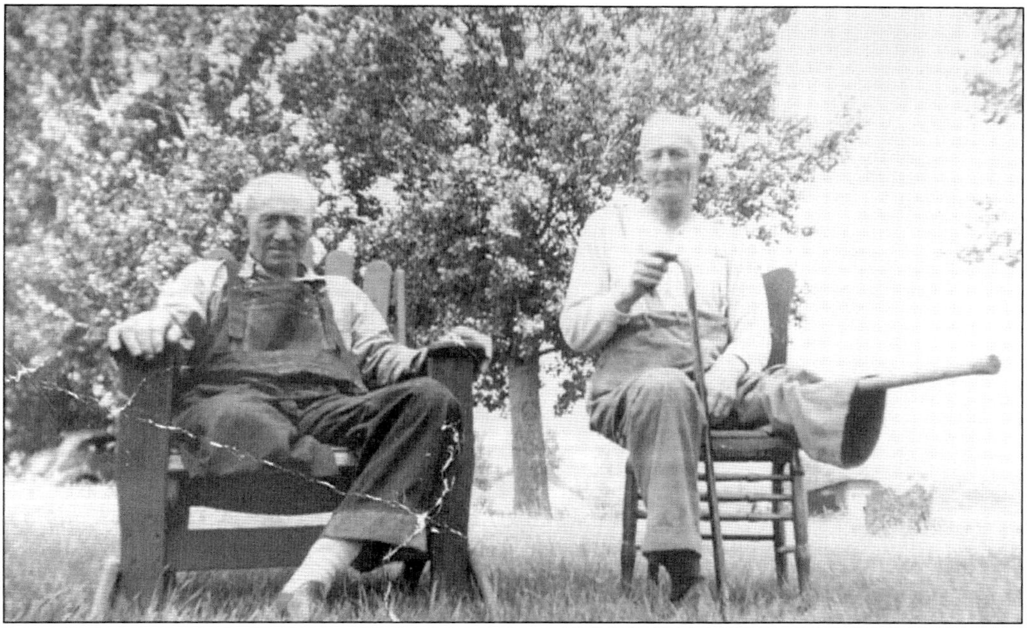

On the Buchholz farm, the family raised cattle and grain to feed the cattle. They also cut wood and grew hay and potatoes to sell. The potatoes were taken to market in Anoka, and the Elwell farms bought some of the hay. In 1949, the property went to Otto and Mary's son Walter when Otto lost his leg in a farming accident. Pictured is Otto (right) and Gust Buchholz in 1941. (Courtesy of the Buchholz family.)

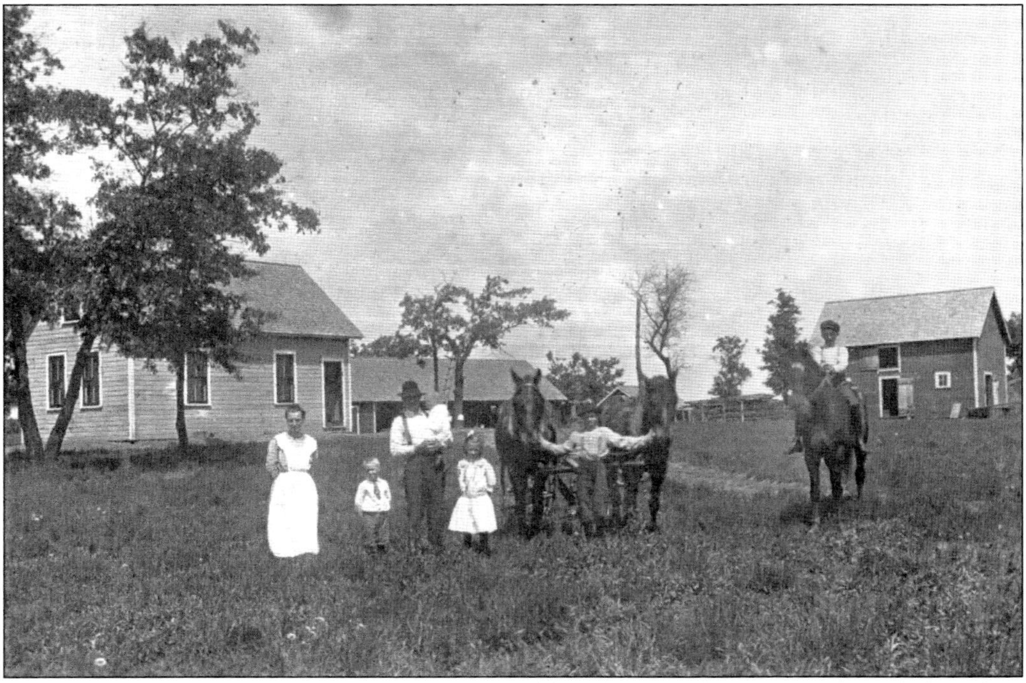

This is the Buchholz family farm in 1904. Pictured from left to right are Mary (Sproske), Walter, Otto, Violet, Hazel, Raymond, and Irving on the horse. (Courtesy of the Anoka County Historical Society.)

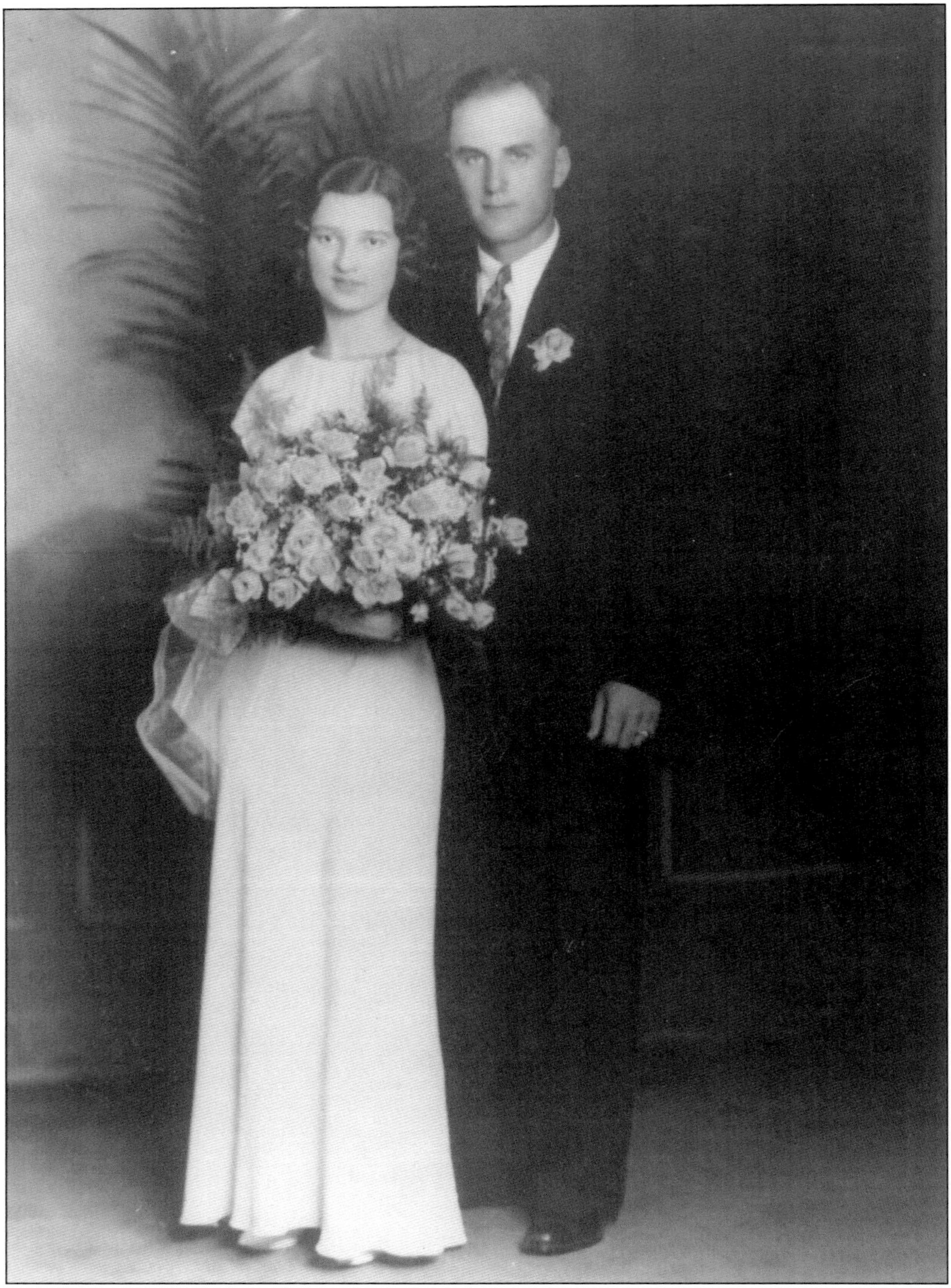

Otto and Mary's son Walter Buchholz, pictured here with is wife, Mildred, inherited the property. Their son Marvin received the property by inheritance in 1989. (Courtesy of the Buchholz family.)

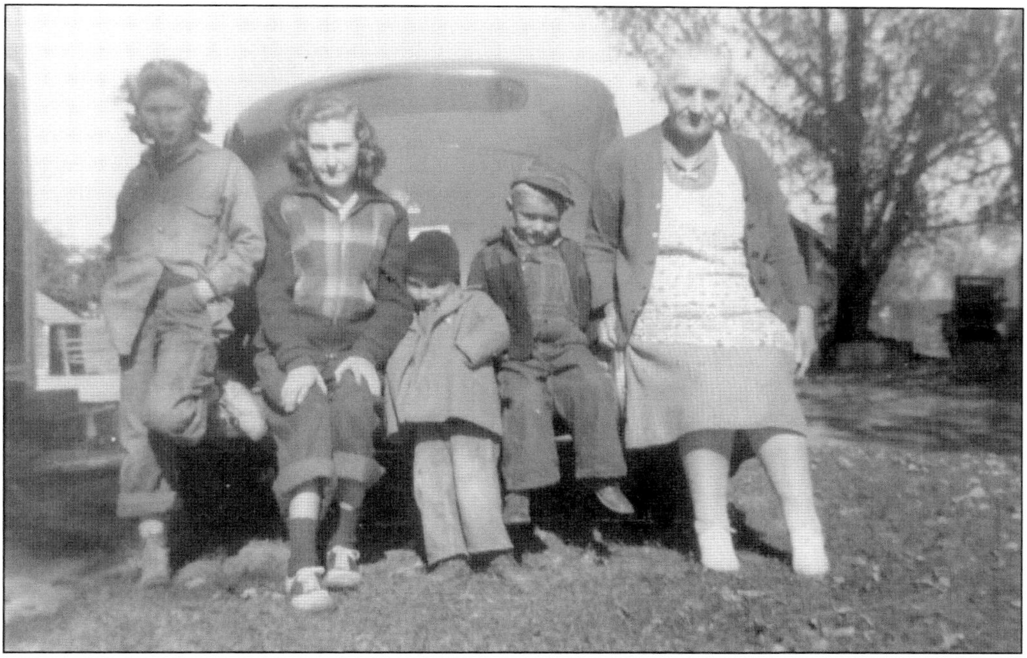

Here is the Buchholz family in early 1945. From left to right are grandchildren Charlotte, Florence, Marvin, and Paul with their grandmother Mary Buchholz. (Courtesy of the Buchholz family.)

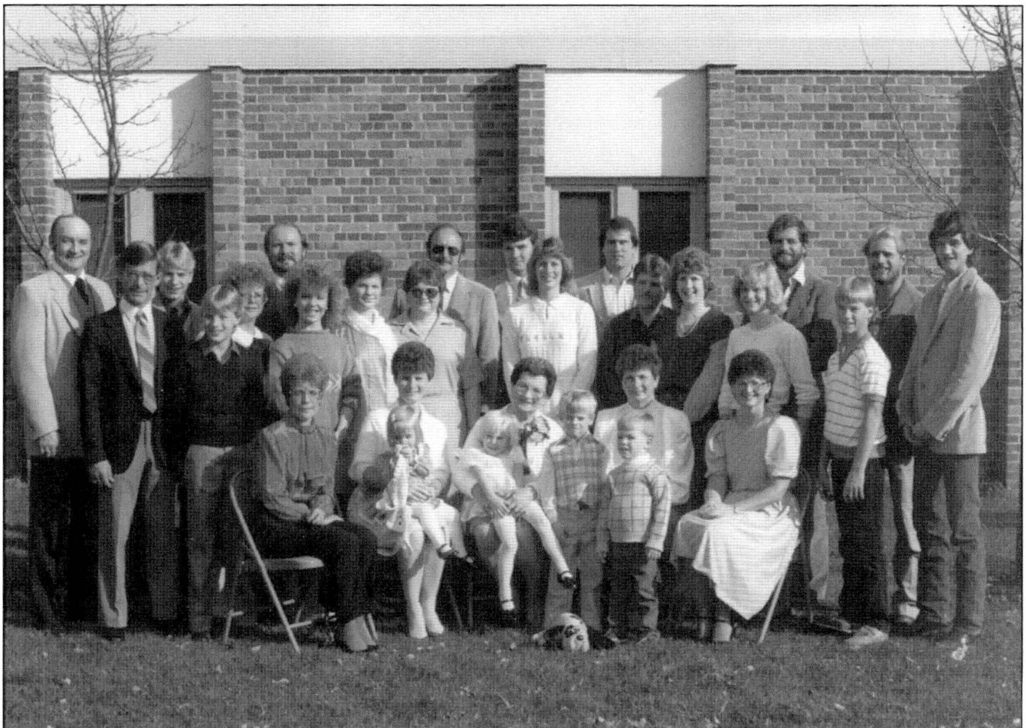

This is a Buchholz family gathering in 1985. Marvin is in the sunglasses in the back center. He was one of the founding members of the Ham Lake Volunteer Fire Department. (Courtesy of the Buchholz family.)

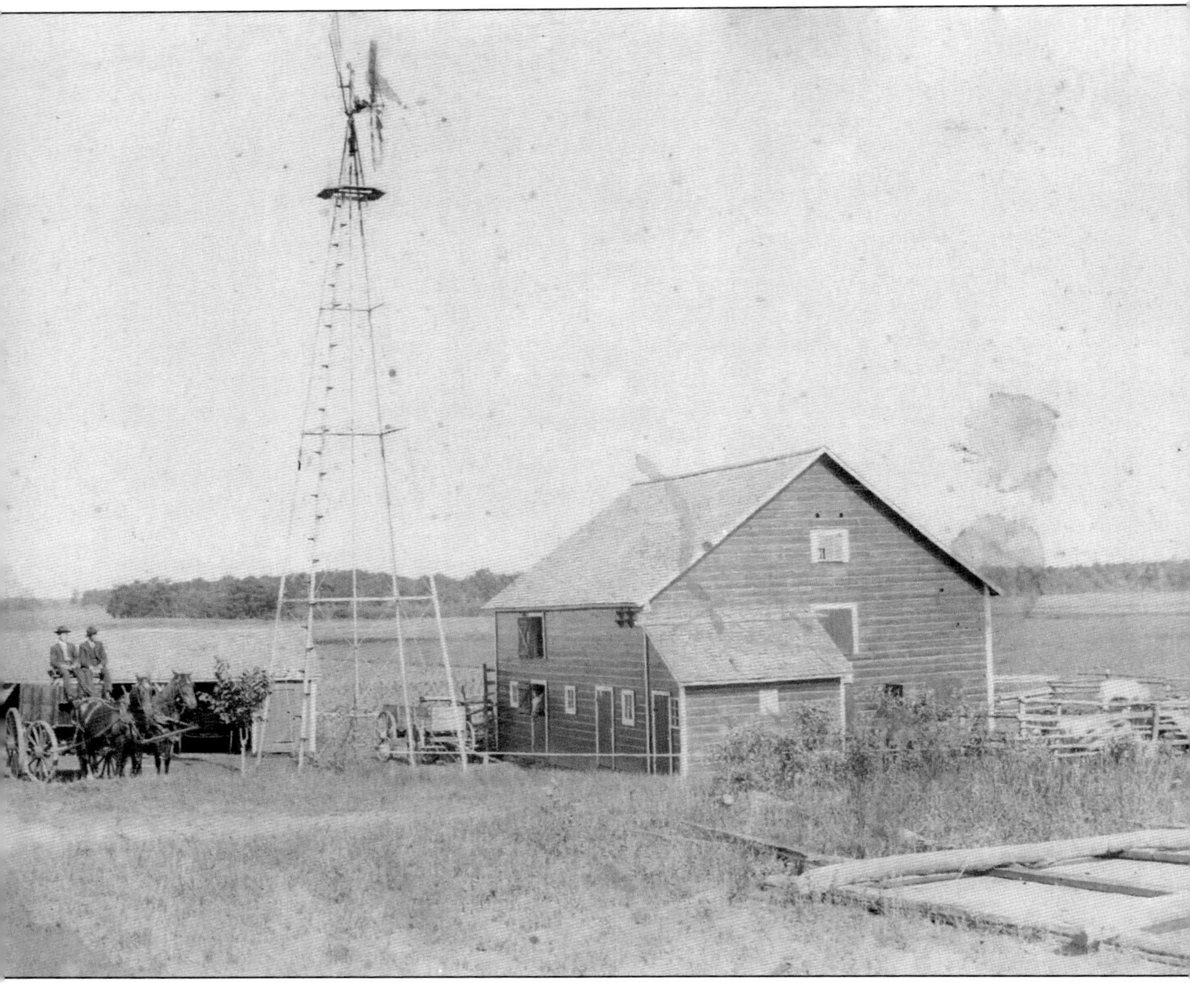

John Olson emigrated from Norway and purchased land in Ham Lake in 1885. Pictured is the Olson family farm in 1906. (Courtesy of the Anoka County Historical Society.)

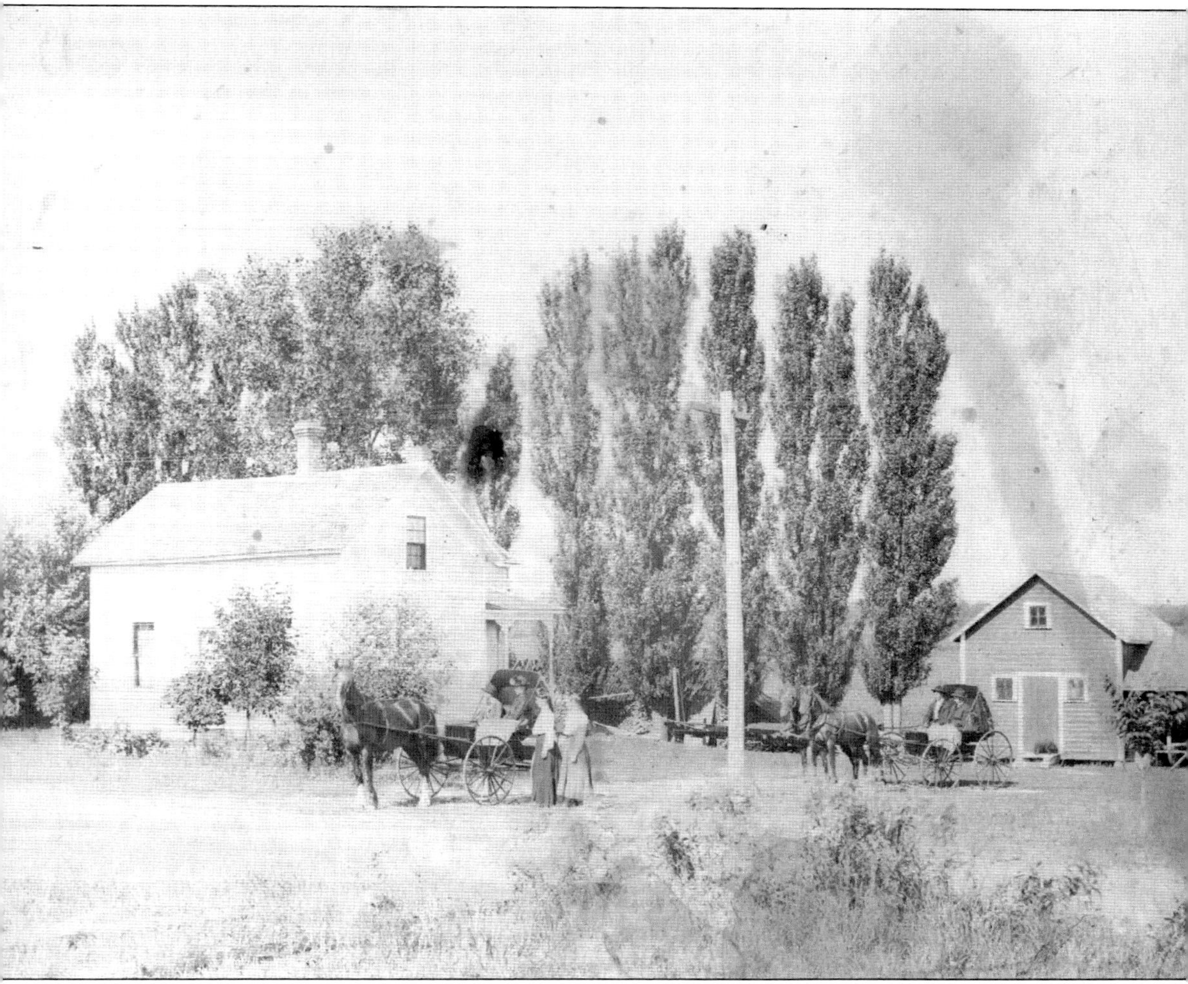

Here is another view of the Olson family farm in 1906. This farm was in Sections Nos. 5 and 8 of the township. (Courtesy of the Anoka County Historical Society.)

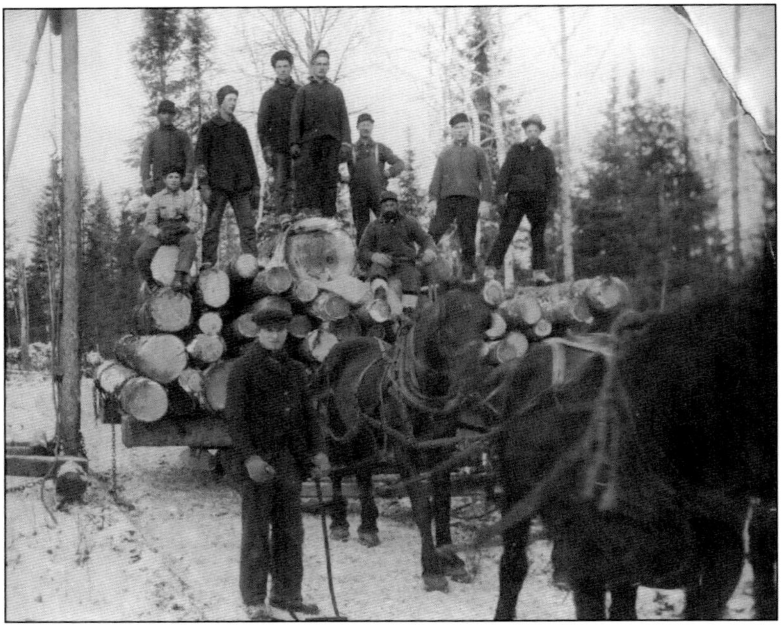

John Olson's grandson Adolph inherited the Olson/Manthye property in 1967. Logging the land was an early way farmers made money off the land. Pictured are Adolph Olson and a group of men harvesting logs from the property. (Courtesy of the Anoka County Historical Society.)

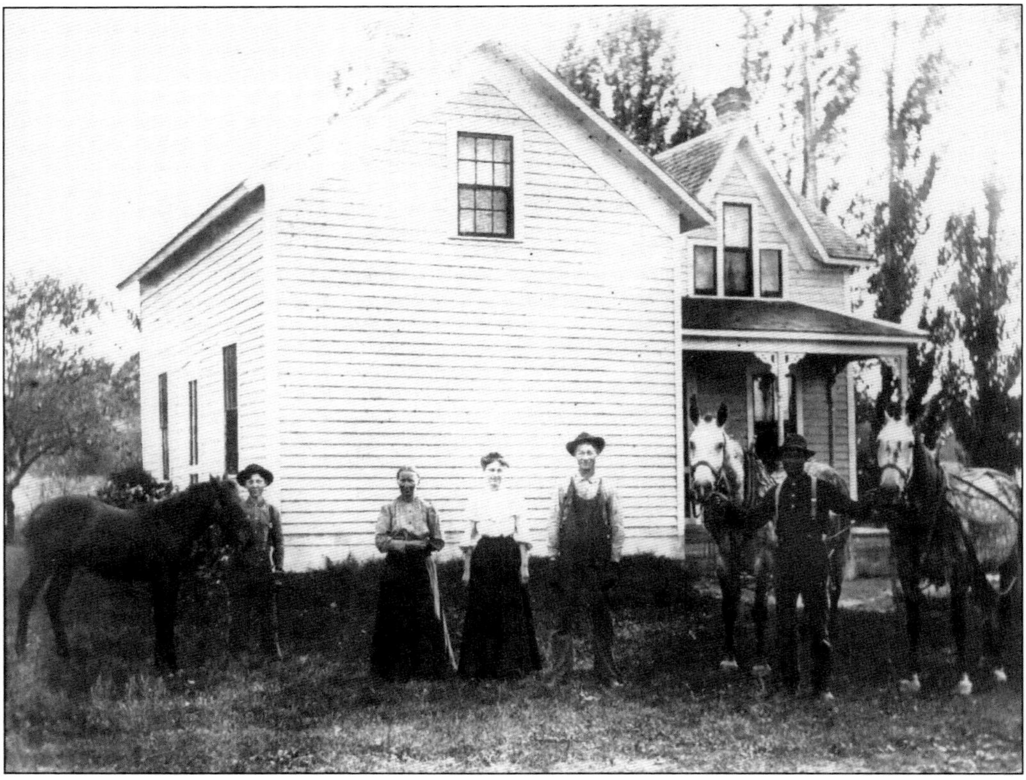

Pictured is the Olson family farm in 1914. Joyce Manthye and Jean Nixon, the adopted daughters of Adolph and Effire Olson, are presently taking care of the farm. (Courtesy of the Anoka County Historical Society.)

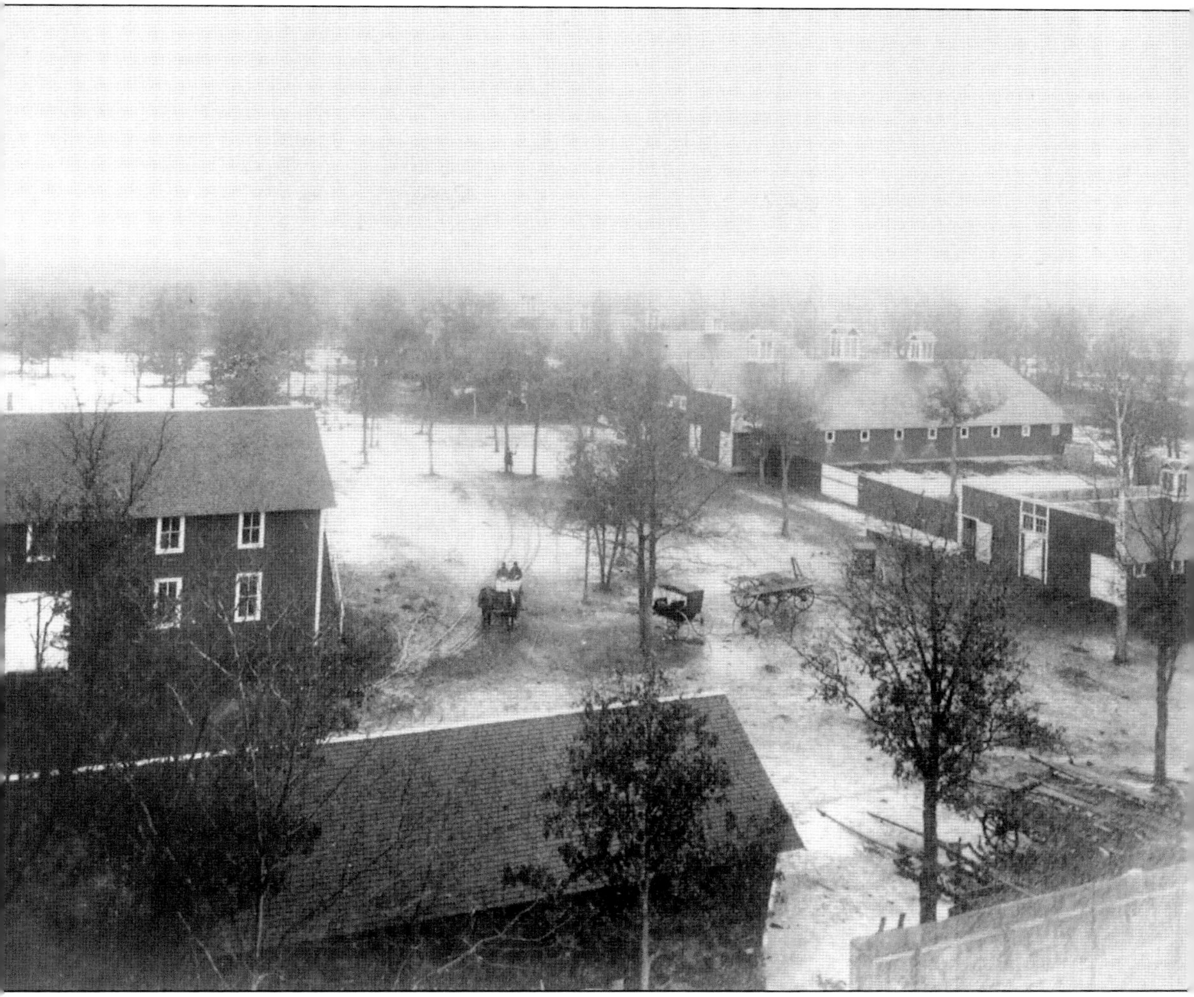

James Elwell was a successful manufacturer and land investor in Minneapolis. He purchased large tracts of marshland in Anoka County, eventually totaling 52,700 acres. This image depicts Oak Leaf Farm. (Courtesy of the Elwell family.)

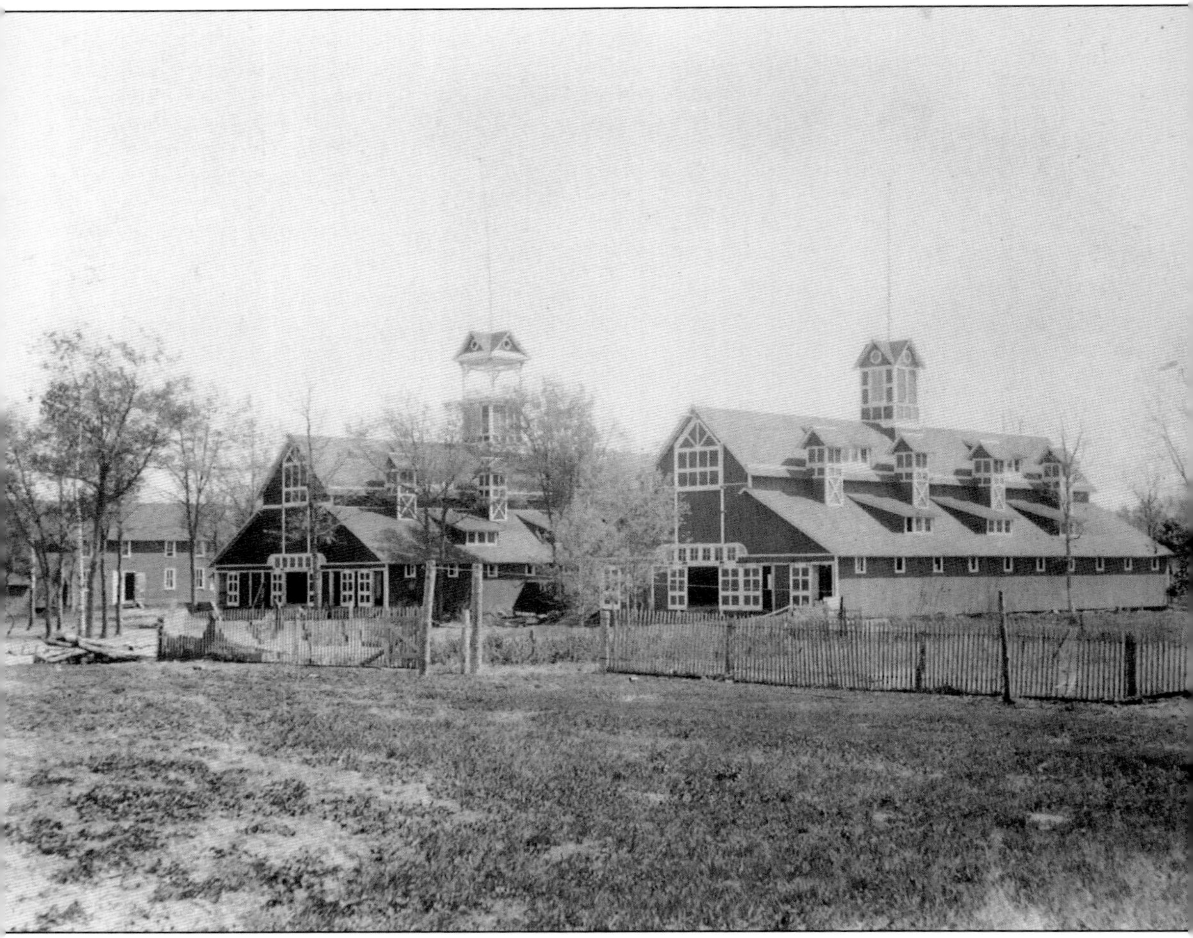

James Elwell created two stock farms in 1888: Golden Lake Farm in present-day Blaine and Oak Leaf Farm in Ham Lake. Elwell bred award-winning cattle and horses on these two farms and built grand buildings in the 1880s and 1890s. (Courtesy of the Elwell family.)

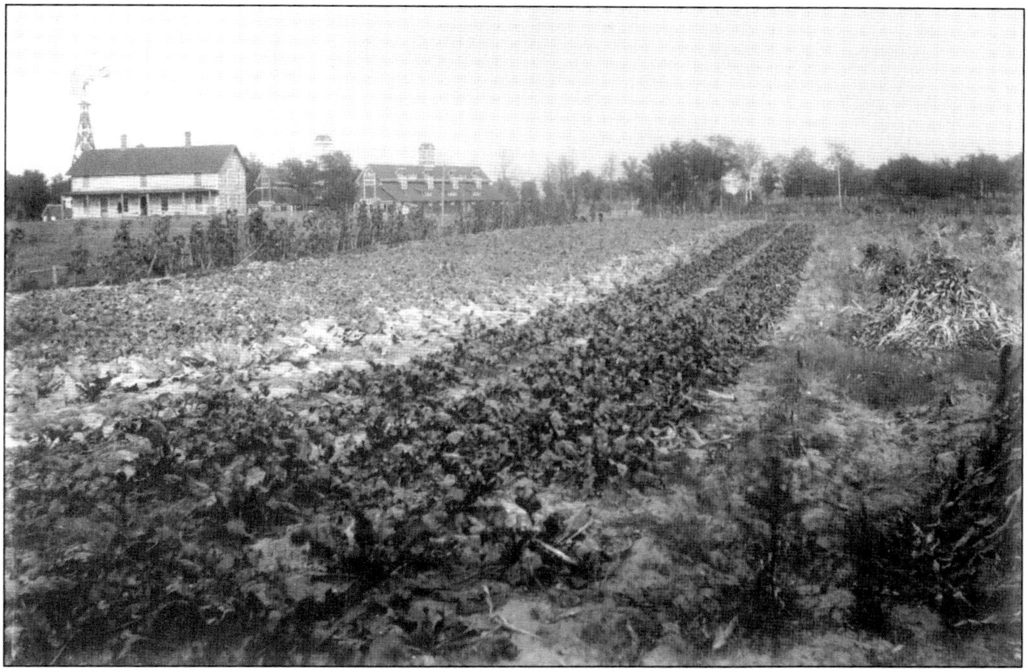

The Ewell farms were major dairy operations. The Elwells were principal shareholders in Elwell Dairy, Inc. and Northland Milk and Ice Cream Company. James also raised turkeys and was a shareholder in Anoka Turkey Farms and the Anoka Farm Corporation. (Courtesy of the Elwell family.)

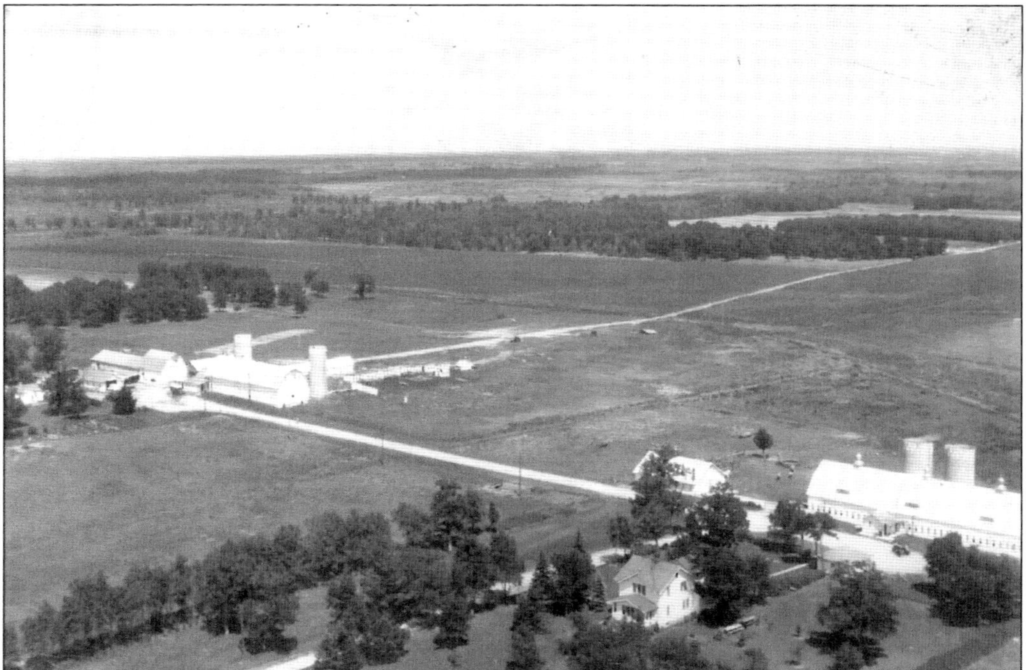

Catherine Elwell, the wife of James's grandson Phillip, and her son Ted currently own the Oak Leaf farm. They raise sod and other farm products. (Courtesy of the Elwell family.)

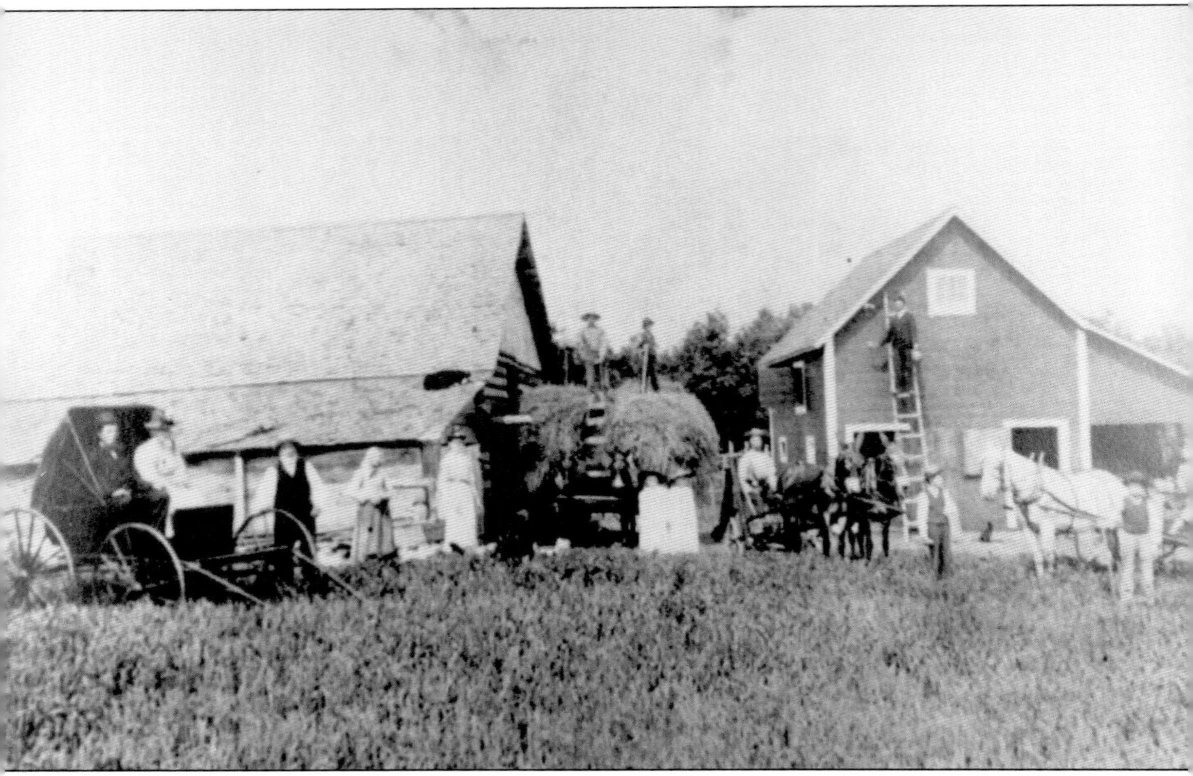

John and Martha Esberg homesteaded property in Ham Lake in 1869. They had two daughters, Christine and Anna. Christine married Olaf Peterson, and they homesteaded on another parcel of land. The farm later went to an Anton Smith. (Courtesy of the Anoka County Historical Society.)

In 1902, Peter, the fourth son of Olaf and Christine Peterson, purchased back the land homesteaded by his grandfather. When Peter died in 1923, his wife, Lillie, and their twin sons, Chester and Lester, continued to farm the land. Both sons married in the 1930s. Chester purchased other land, but Lester continued on the same land. Pictured are Peter and Lillie Peterson with Pearl, Lester, Chester, Edyth, and Florence. (Courtesy of the Anoka County Historical Society.)

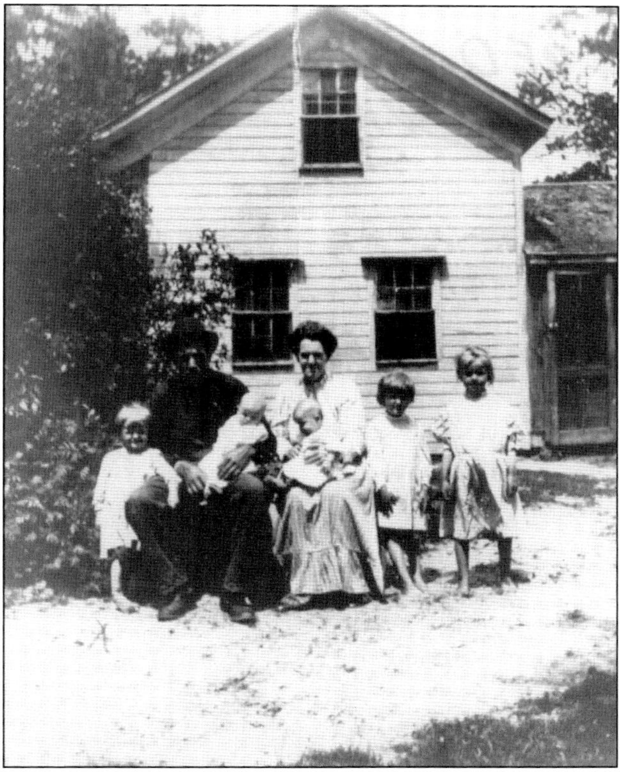

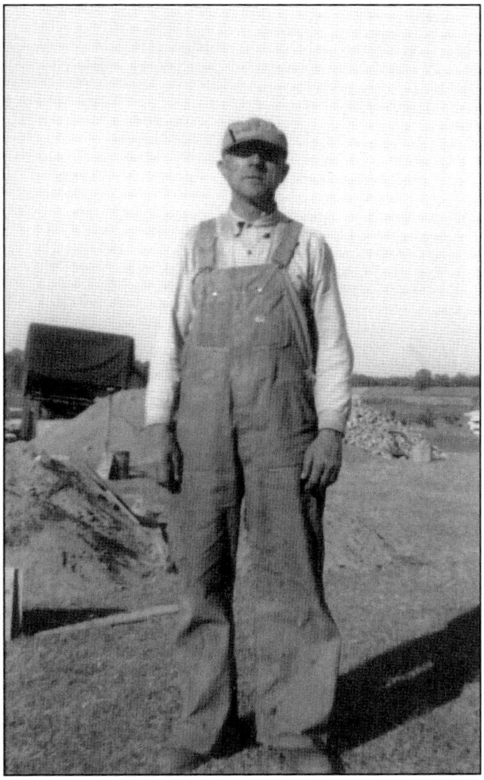

Lester Peterson married Lillie Olson, who had worked for 10 years in a harness factory in Minneapolis and had saved enough money to keep the property. Pictured here is Lester. (Courtesy of the Anoka County Historical Society.)

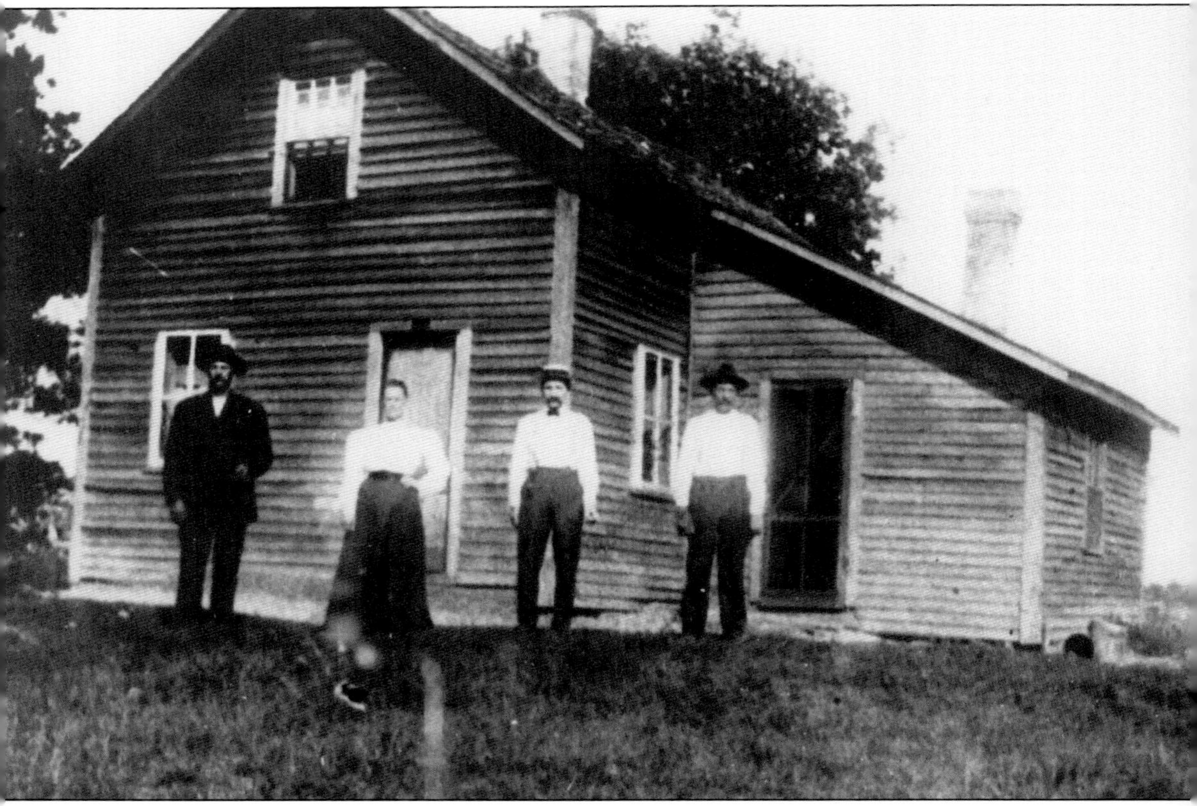

This is the Andrew Peterson family. Standing from left to right are Matt, Betsy, Peter, and Jonas. The house was built in 1870. In 1969, Lester and Lillie's son Willis took over the property. Although he was a professor of economics at the University of Minnesota, he continued to raise cattle and cut hay. (Courtesy of the Anoka County Historical Society.)

Two

AGRICULTURE

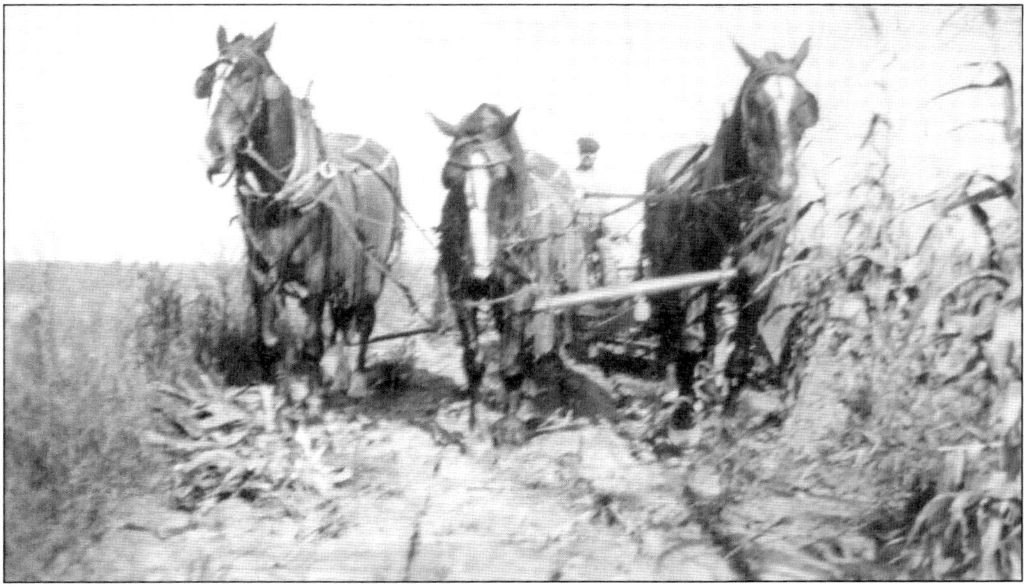

Early settlers found the soil well suited to farming, as it was not as rocky as they had been accustomed to in Scandinavia. The agricultural statistics of 1880 show that 677 acres were under cultivation in the township, with the crops being wheat, 4,639 bushels; oats, 2,103 bushels; corn, 2,990 bushels; beans, 64 bushels; sugarcane, 105 gallons; cultivated hay, two tons; wild hay, 122 tons; apples, 24 bushels; tobacco, 30 pounds; wool, 250 pounds; and butter, 12,600 pounds. Pictured is the horsepower used by farmer Charlie Moore. (Courtesy of Ronnie and Marylou Moore.)

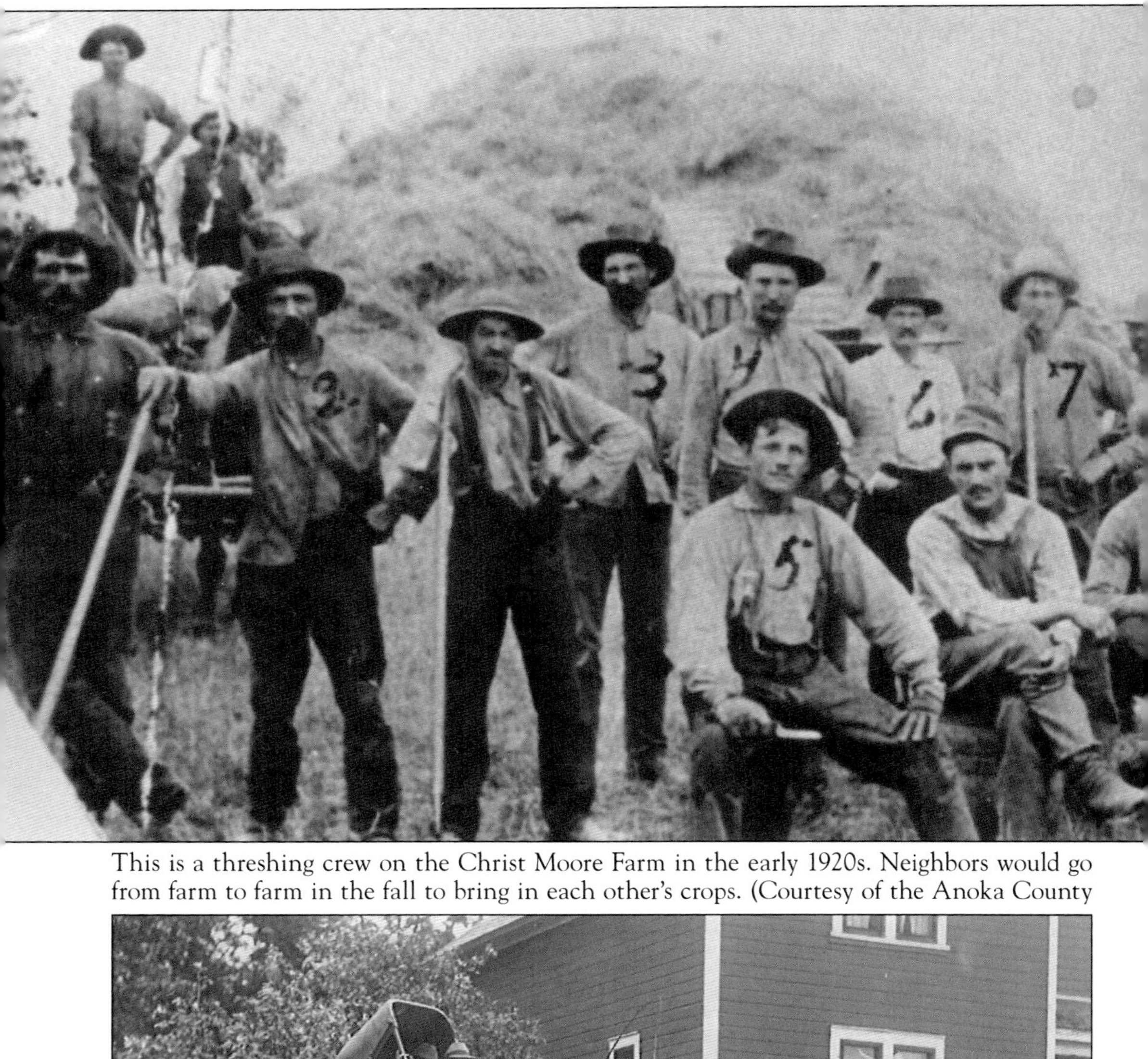

This is a threshing crew on the Christ Moore Farm in the early 1920s. Neighbors would go from farm to farm in the fall to bring in each other's crops. (Courtesy of the Anoka County

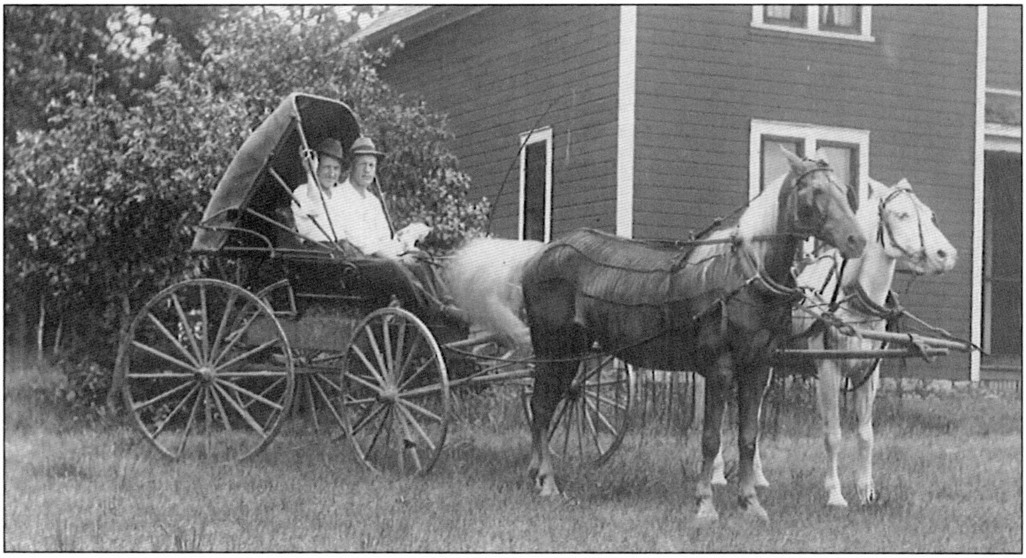

Transportation at this time was still by horse. This is Charlie Moore's country buggy. (Courtesy of Ronnie Moore.)

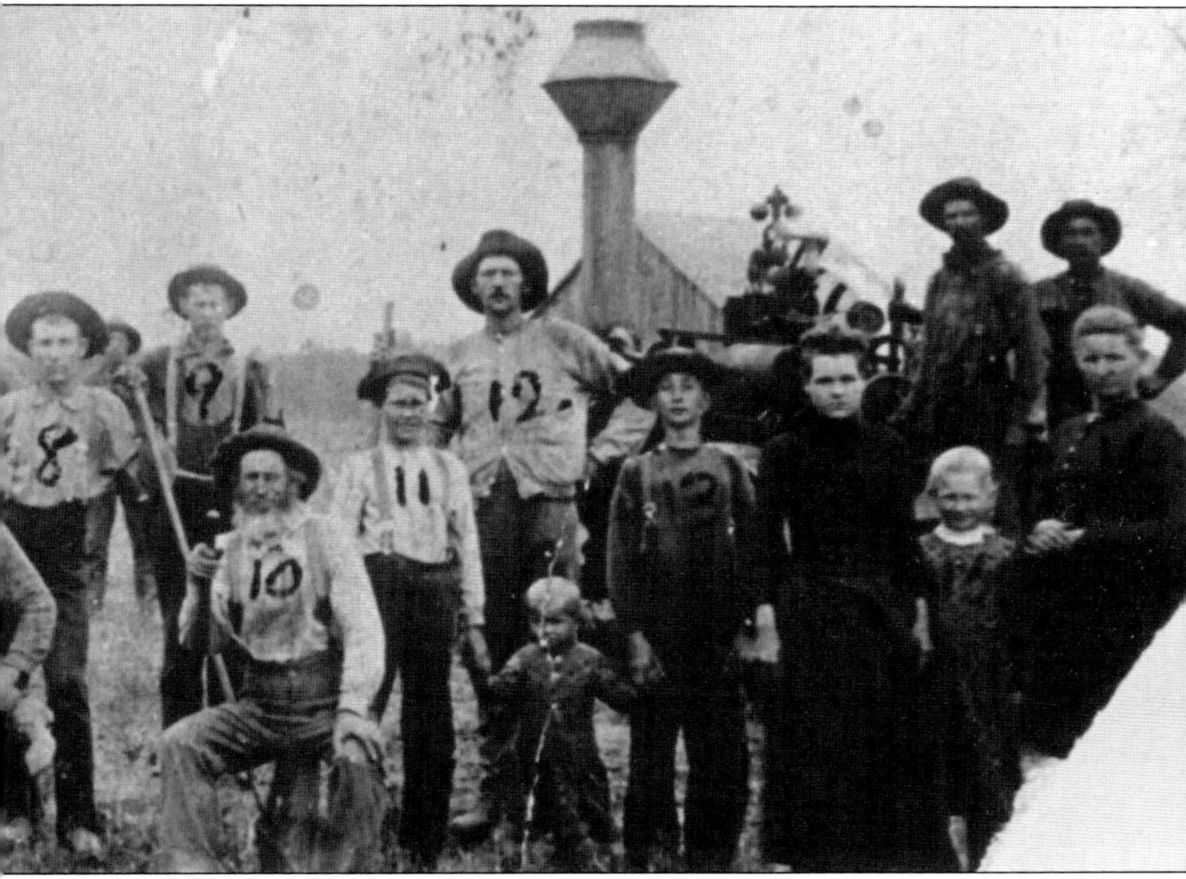

Historical Society.)

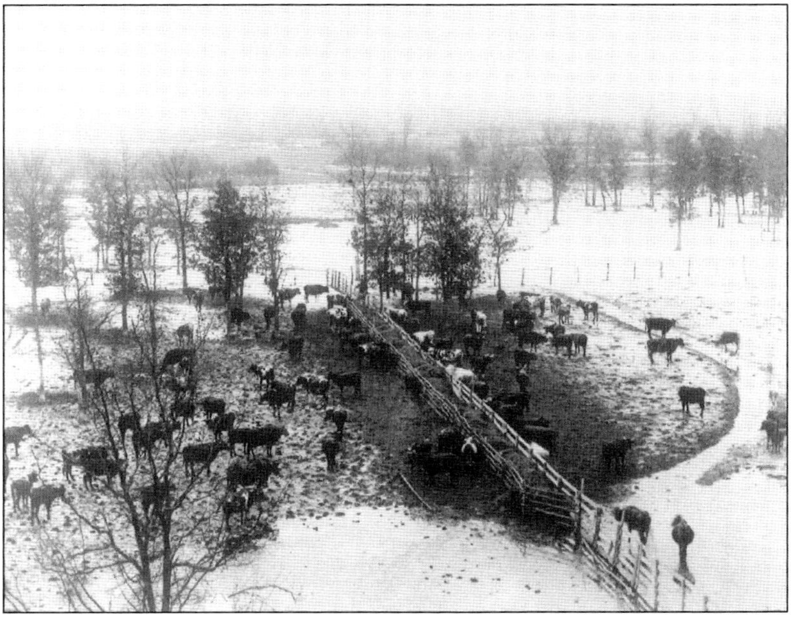

Through the years, dairying became an important industry. Pictured are the Oak Leaf Farm cattle in an 1880s winter. (Courtesy of the Elwell family.)

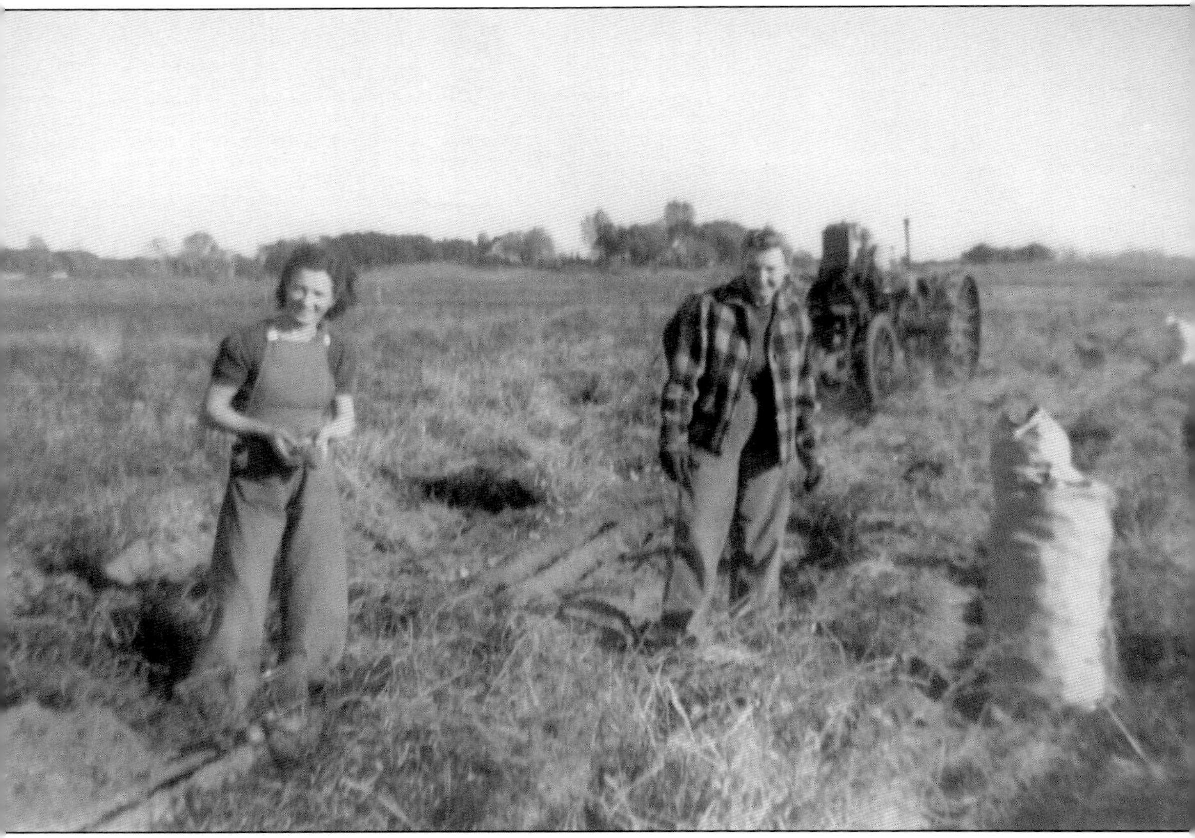

Pictured are Mildred (left) and Violet Buchholz helping with potato planting in 1932. Potatoes became a major cash crop for farmers in Ham Lake. (Courtesy of the Anoka County Historical Society.)

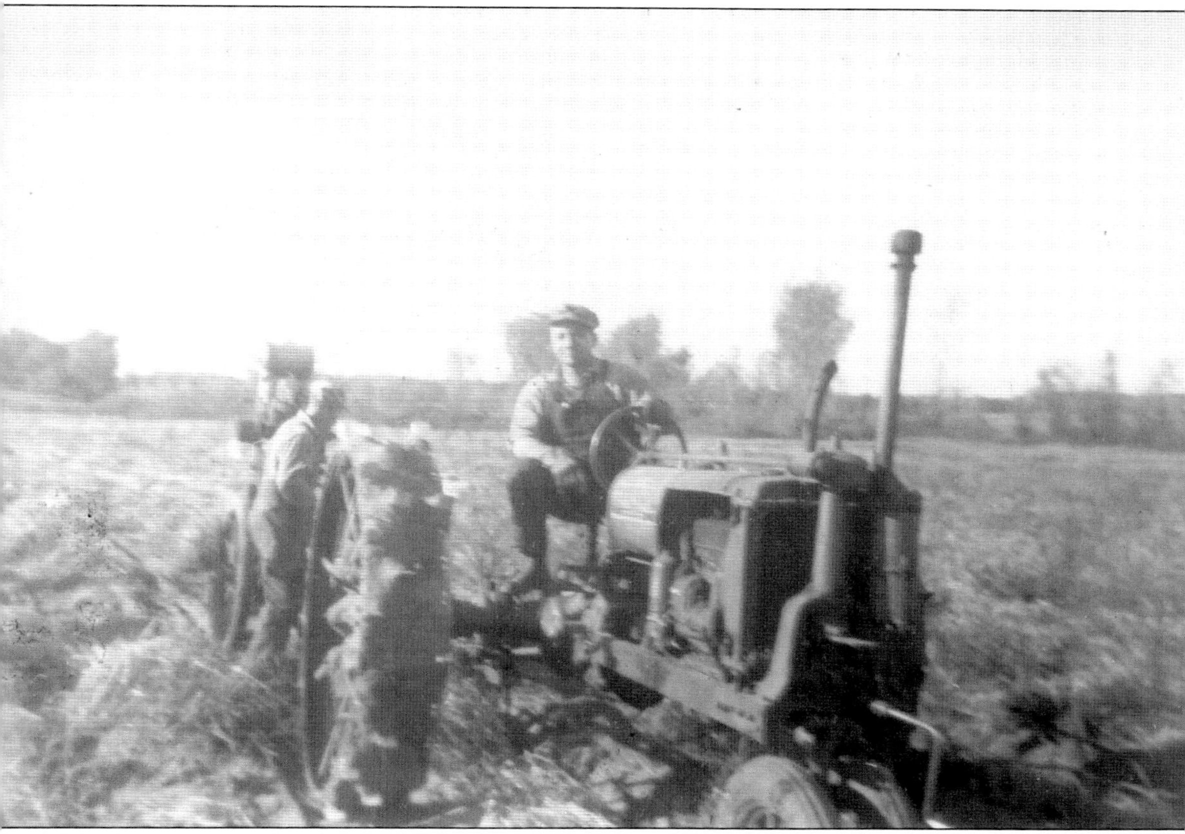

Fall plowing is seen here on the Buchholz farm in 1932. Walter (left) and Irving Buchholz pose for the camera. (Courtesy of the Anoka County Historical Society.)

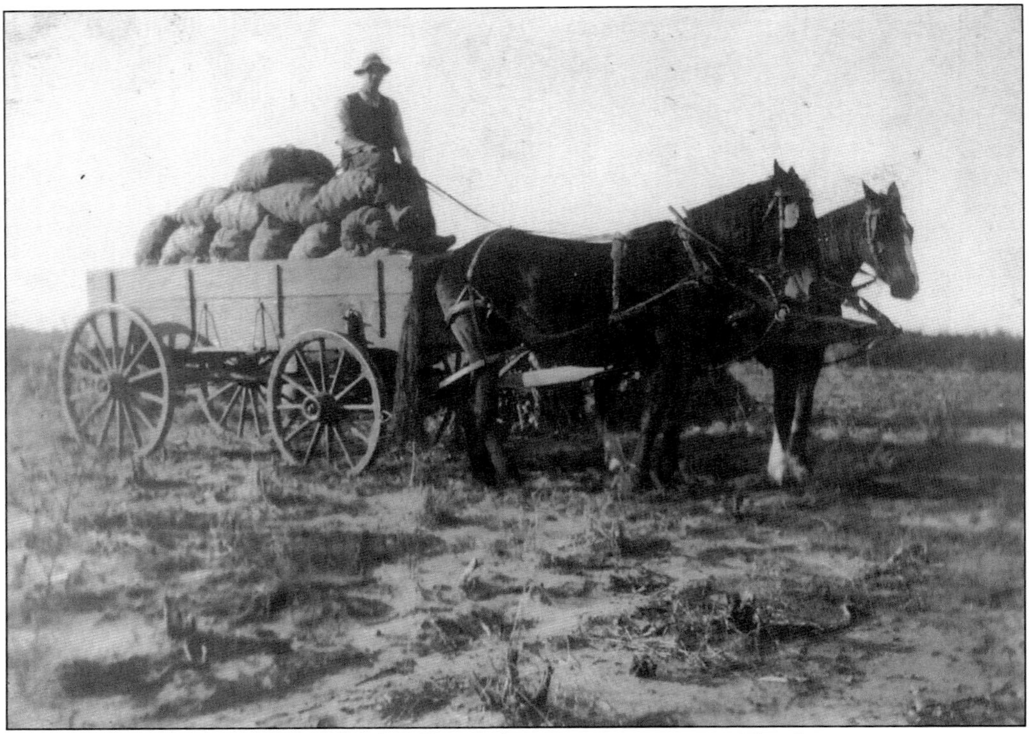

Pioneer farmers soon found the soil well suited to growing potatoes. This became an important commodity for both cash sales and trading. Pictured is potato farmer Charlie Moore. (Courtesy of Glen Cary Church.)

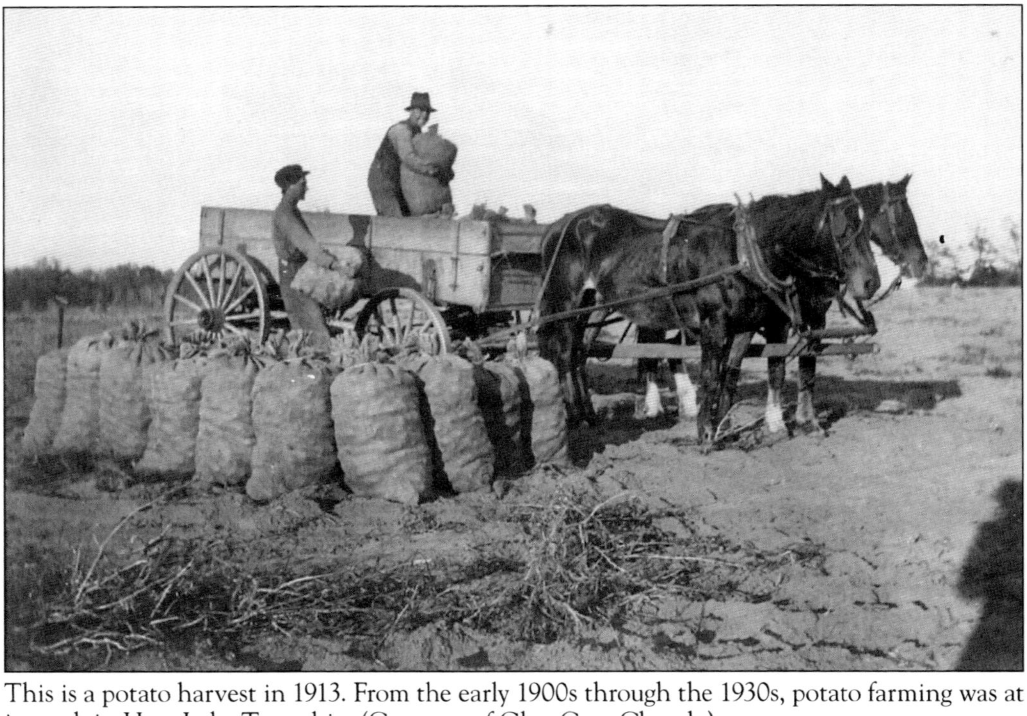

This is a potato harvest in 1913. From the early 1900s through the 1930s, potato farming was at its peak in Ham Lake Township. (Courtesy of Glen Cary Church.)

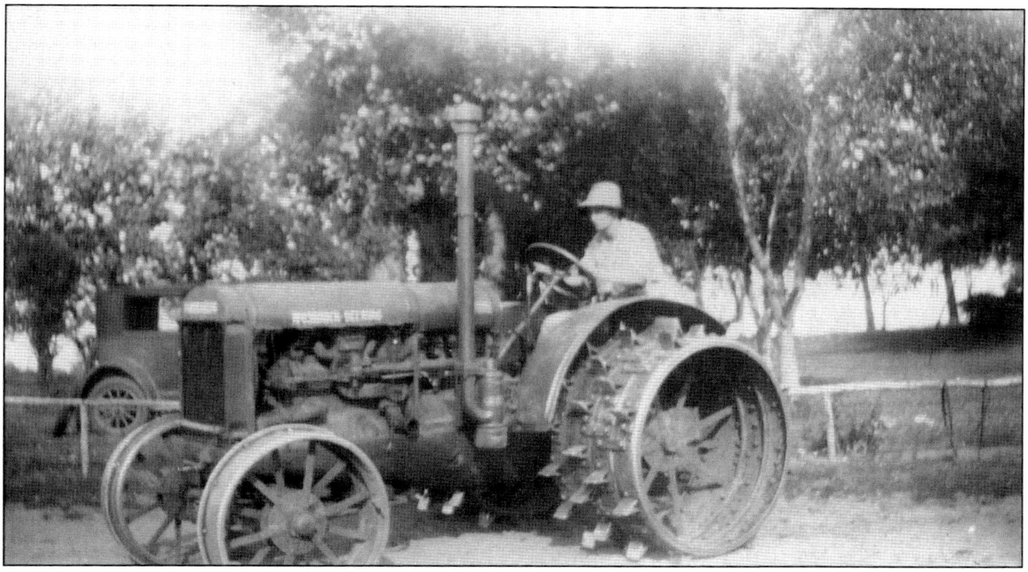

As the years went by, there were many changes in the area with regard to agriculture. With the invention and introduction to farming of the internal combustion engine, horsepower gave way to tractor power. (Courtesy of Glen Cary Church.)

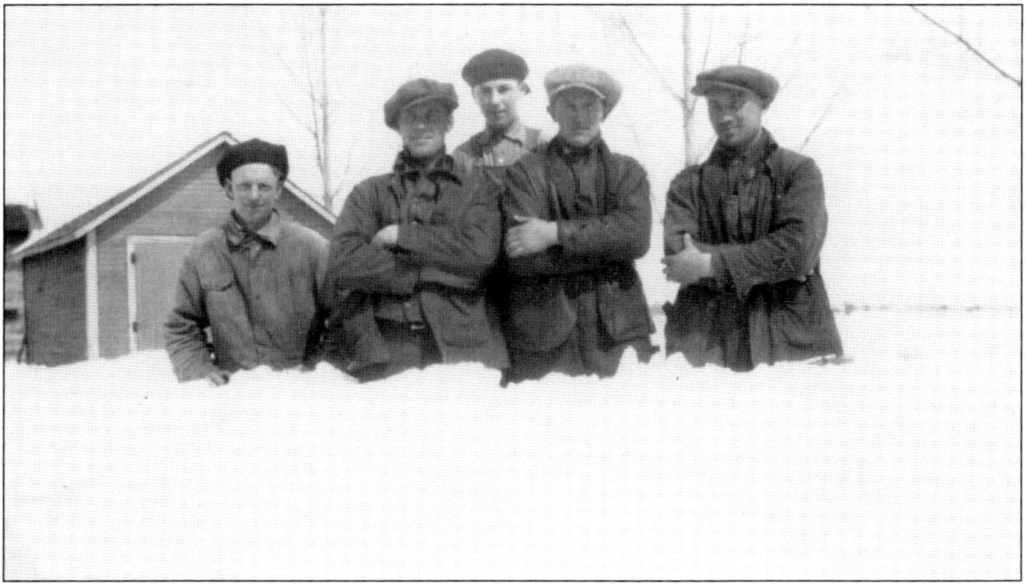

Settlers had to endure harsh weather at times. Even waist-deep snow did not deter hardy boys from getting the needed farmwork done. (Courtesy of the Buchholz family.)

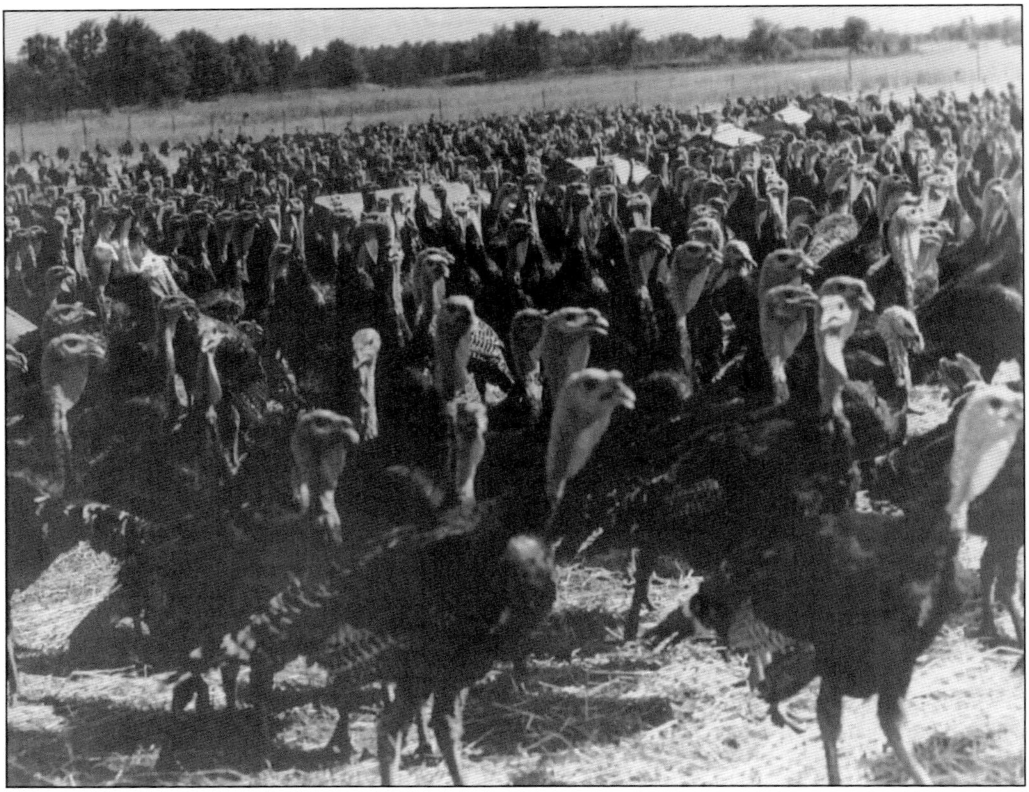

Although turkey farming was not a major industry in Ham Lake, it was for the Elwell family. In 1929, they produced over 1,600 turkeys. (Courtesy of the Elwell family.)

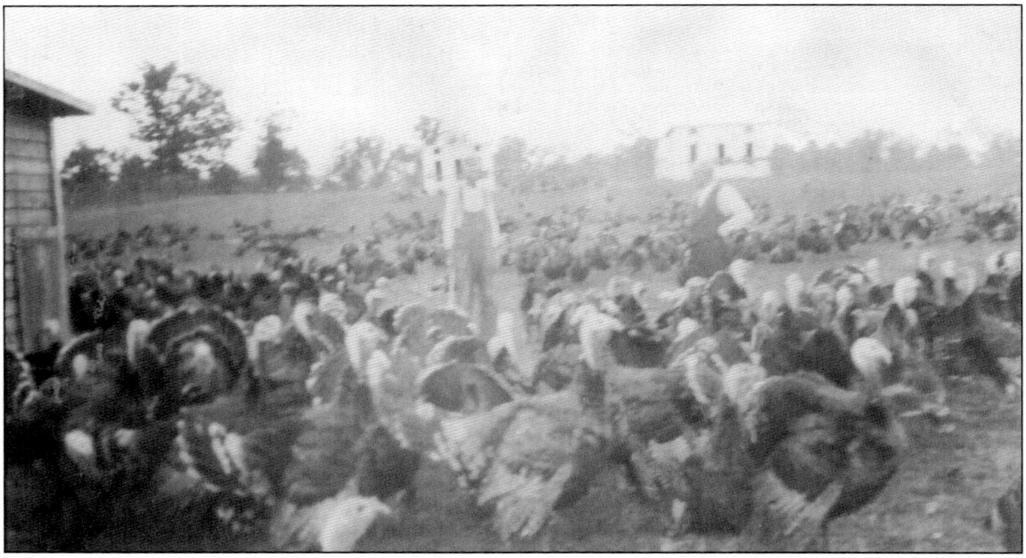

Turkey farming became a major industry in Minnesota, but it had a limited success in Anoka County. These were the years of growing more wild turkeys rather than the domestic, meatier, white turkeys of today. (Courtesy for the Anoka County Historical Society.)

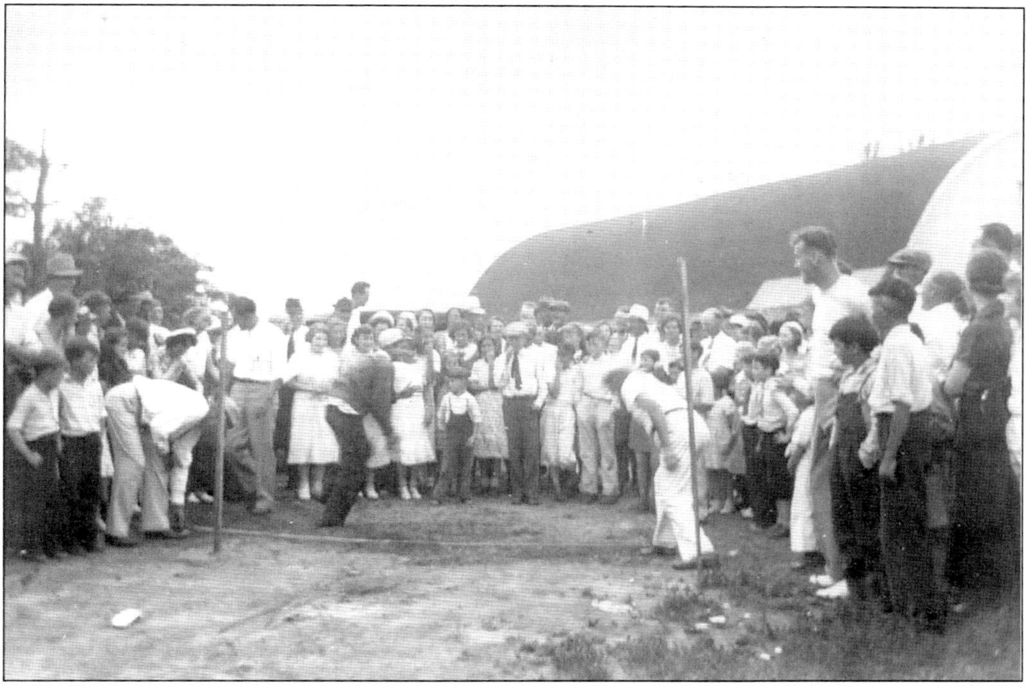

As farming became more modern, organizations began to bring farmers together to promote themselves. Pictured is the annual Farm Bureau and 4-H Club picnic in Ham Lake 1937. (Courtesy of the Anoka County Historical Society.)

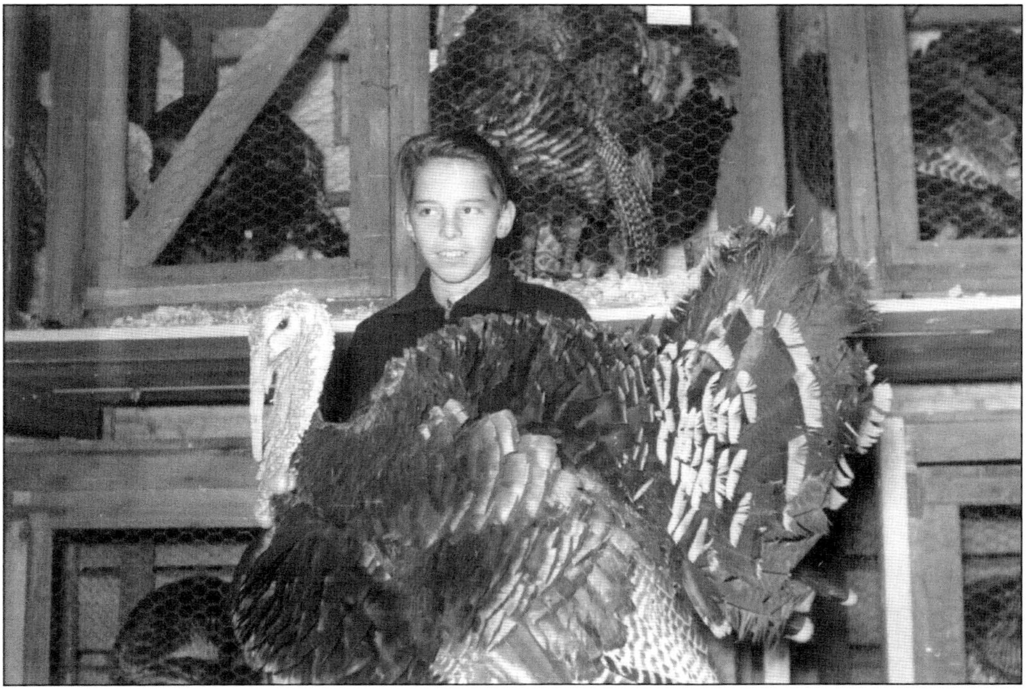

Judging livestock became part of farming culture. Here is Norman Dyck of Ham Lake with one of his three prizewinning turkeys at the Junior Livestock Show in 1941. The three winning turkeys weighed in at a total of 84 pounds. (Courtesy of the Anoka County Historical Society.)

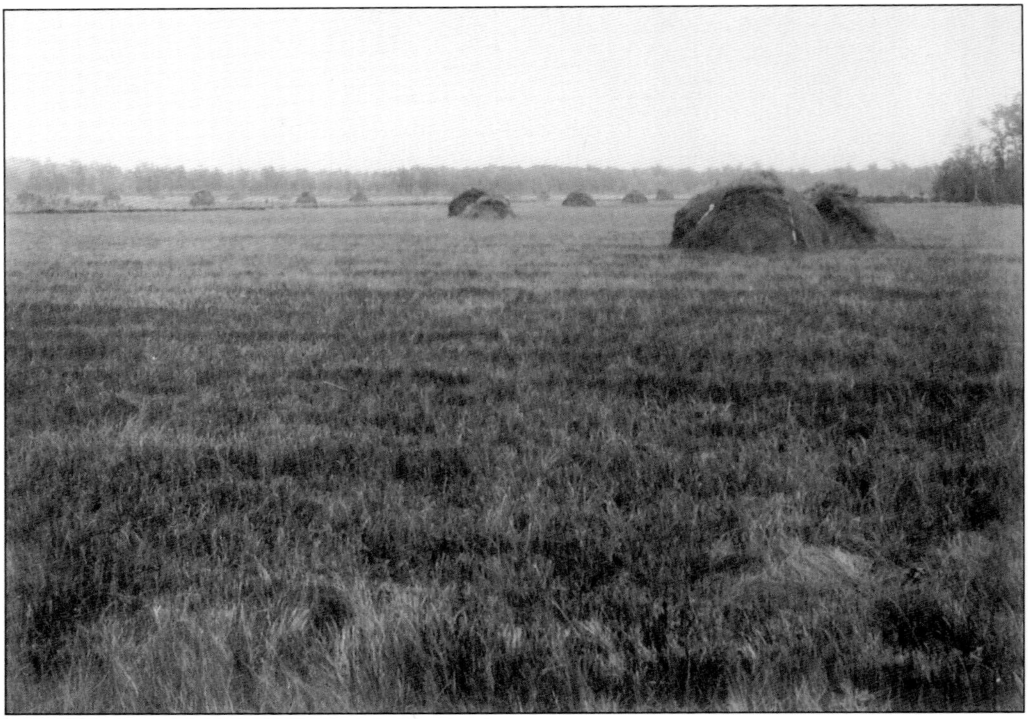

Hay was always a salable item. It grew well in the Ham Lake soil, and there was usually a market for it. (Courtesy of the Elwell family.)

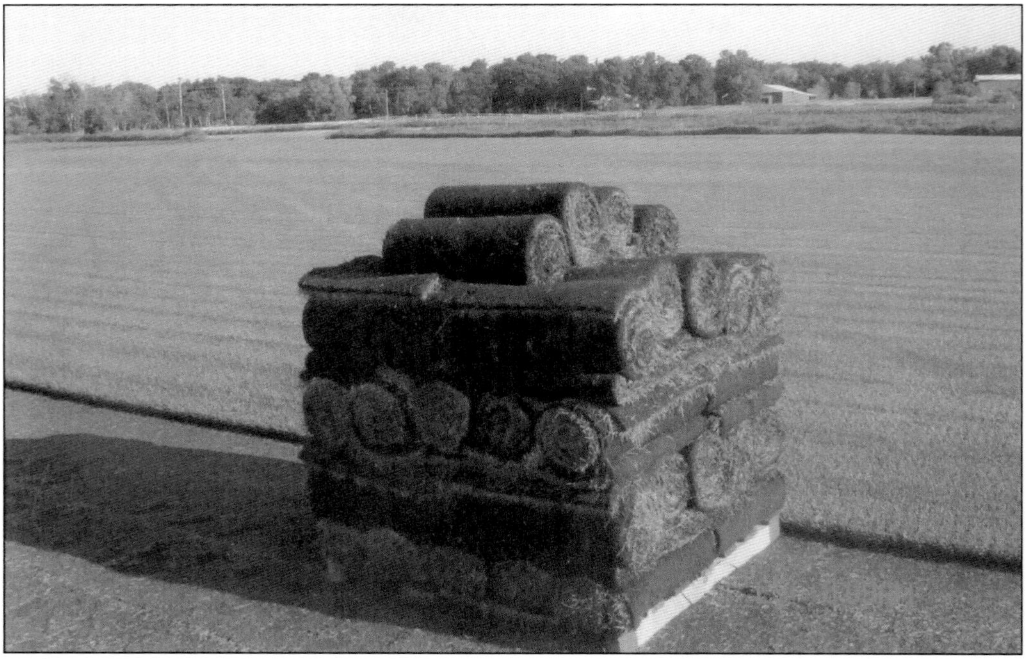

In the 1950s through the 1980s, landscaping sod farming became dominant in the southeastern part of Ham Lake. There, the ground is low and the soil black and heavy, making it well suited to this crop. For a number of years, Ham Lake produced more sod than any other township in the state. (Courtesy of Hoffman Sod Company.)

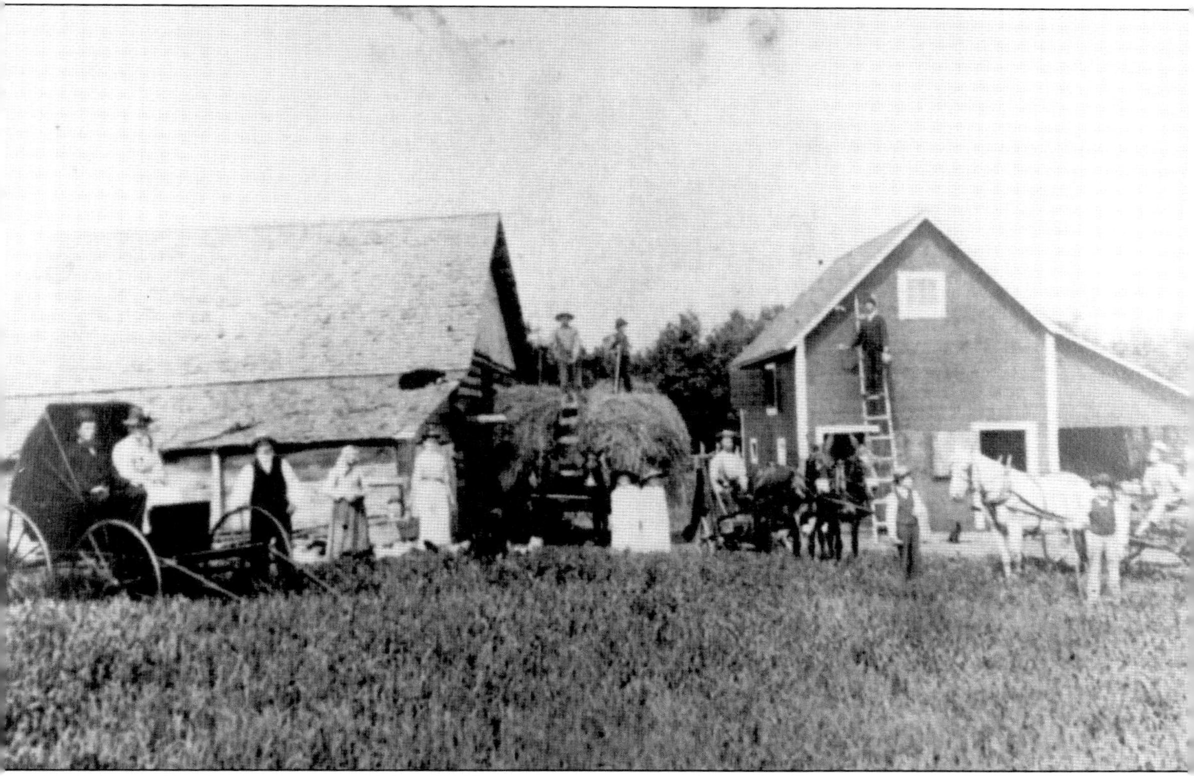

Every area farm has a history, but not all could be included in this book; therefore, the Peterson/Moe/Sannerud farm will serve as a representative story of many in the area. Pictured here (and on page 28) is the Olaf Peterson farm off Highway 65 near Constance Boulevard. Olaf married Christine Esberg in Sweden and came to the United States in 1866. In 1870, they homesteaded property in Section No. 8 of what would become the city of Ham Lake. He worked in Anoka and walked to and from work, totaling 24 miles each day, carrying whatever was needed for the homestead on his back. He helped form three churches: Zion Lutheran in Anoka, Glen Cary in Ham Lake, and Our Saviour's Lutheran Church in Ham Lake. (Courtesy of the Anoka County Historical Society.)

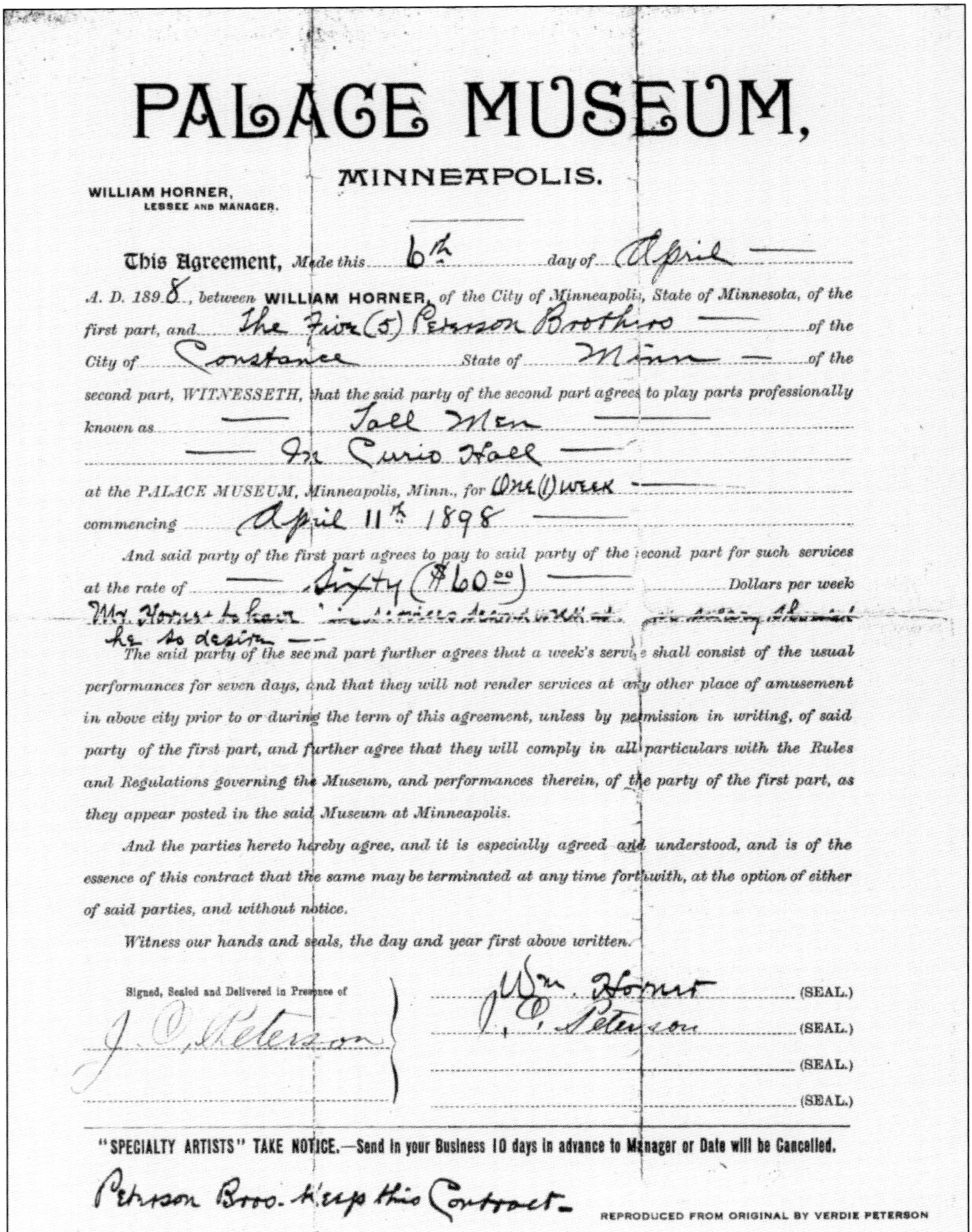

PALACE MUSEUM,

MINNEAPOLIS.

WILLIAM HORNER,
LESSEE AND MANAGER.

This Agreement, *Made this* 6th *day of* April —

*A. D. 189*8*, between* **WILLIAM HORNER,** *of the City of Minneapolis, State of Minnesota, of the first part, and* The Five (5) Peterson Brothers — *of the City of* Constance *State of* Minn — *of the second part, WITNESSETH, that the said party of the second part agrees to play parts professionally known as* — Tall Men — — In Curio Hall —

at the PALACE MUSEUM, Minneapolis, Minn., for One (1) week — *commencing* April 11th 1898 —

And said party of the first part agrees to pay to said party of the second part for such services at the rate of — Sixty ($60.00) — *Dollars per week*

Mr. Horner to have [illegible] should he so desire —

The said party of the second part further agrees that a week's service shall consist of the usual performances for seven days, and that they will not render services at any other place of amusement in above city prior to or during the term of this agreement, unless by permission in writing, of said party of the first part, and further agree that they will comply in all particulars with the Rules and Regulations governing the Museum, and performances therein, of the party of the first part, as they appear posted in the said Museum at Minneapolis.

And the parties hereto hereby agree, and it is especially agreed and understood, and is of the essence of this contract that the same may be terminated at any time forthwith, at the option of either of said parties, and without notice.

Witness our hands and seals, the day and year first above written.

Signed, Sealed and Delivered in Presence of

J. O. Peterson

Wm. Horner (SEAL.)

J. O. Peterson (SEAL.)

(SEAL.)

(SEAL.)

"SPECIALTY ARTISTS" TAKE NOTICE.—Send in your Business 10 days in advance to Manager or Date will be Cancelled.

Peterson Bros. Keep this Contract—

REPRODUCED FROM ORIGINAL BY VERDIE PETERSON

In the spring of 1898, Olaf and Christine's five oldest sons were hired by the Palace Museum in Minneapolis to appear on stage as the "Tall Men." The youngest, Oscar, did not appear because he was only six feet tall. Pictured is a poster from the Palace Museum. (Courtesy of Lorraine Soderquist.)

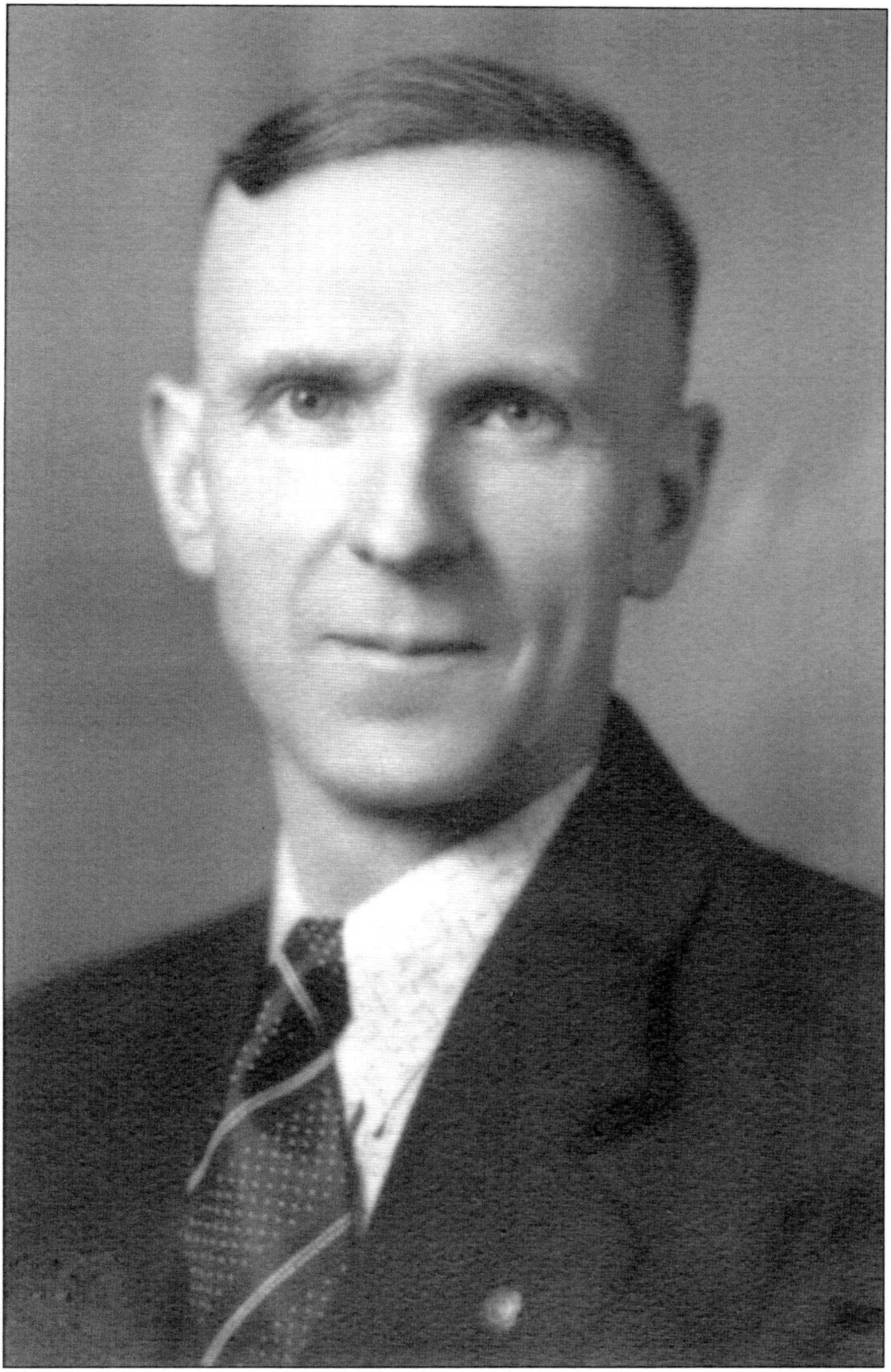

Pictured is Hans Moe (1889–1985). The Hans and Emma Moe family bought a farm in 1936. Among their children was Margaret (Betty) Moe, who went to Glen Cary School, graduated from Anoka High School, and after attending Augsburg College and St. Cloud Teachers College came back to teach at that same Glen Cary School. She married Al Sannerud, and the farm property was used to launch Sannerud and Saverese, an award-winning accounting firm. (Courtesy of Betty Moe Sannerud.)

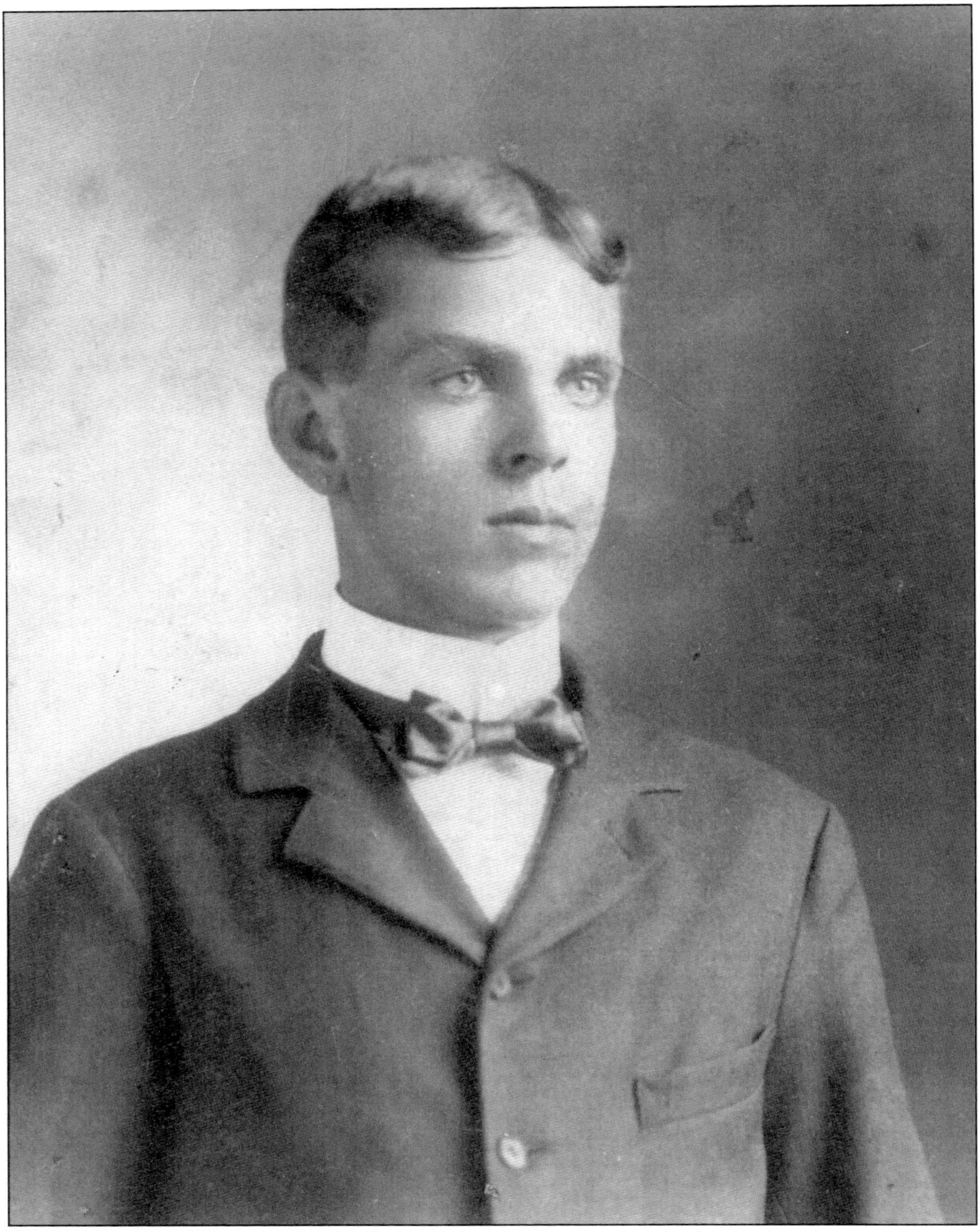

August Peterson, son of Olaf and Christine Peterson, moved to Columbia Heights and became an Anoka County commissioner. He married Clara Carlson, and they had three children before she died. August later married Sigrid Severson, and among their children was Lorraine Peterson, who married Donald Soderquist. For many years, Lorraine and Donald Soderquist managed the Soderquist grocery store. (Courtesy of Lorraine Soderquist.)

Three

Churches

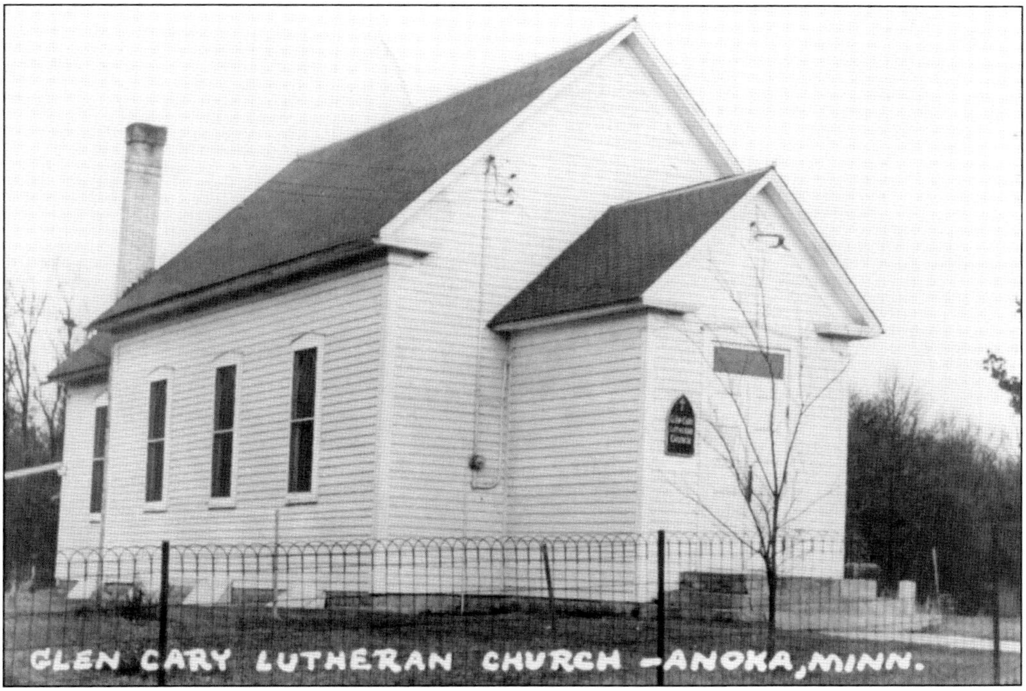

Early religious meetings were held in residents' homes. Because of language differences, Norwegian and Swedish pioneer families decided to build their own separate churches. It is reported by each church that someone complained, "I tink ve should only speak in church the language Yesus spoke when he valked the earth." Of course, the Norwegian church says it was one of theirs, and the Swedish church claimed it was one of theirs. The old Glen Cary Church had its first meeting in 1870 at the home of Mads Gilbertson. Services continued to be held in residents' homes until Mads Gilbertson donated land and a church was built. (Courtesy of the Anoka County Historical Society.)

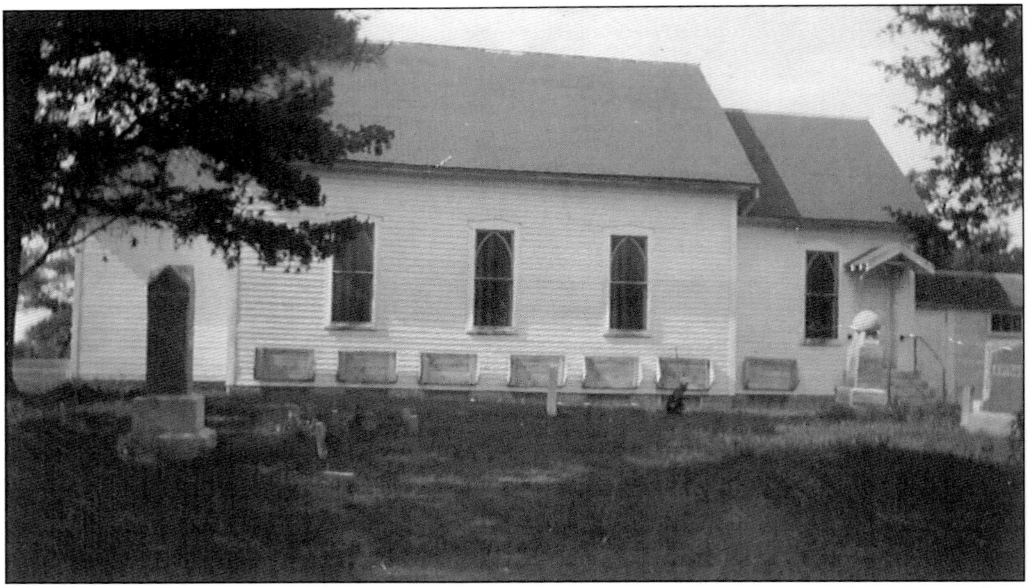

The old Glen Cary Church was only used seasonally from 1875 to 1880, when it was then completed. Church members broke ground on a new church south of their cemetery in 1959 and moved into the new church in 1960. The old Glen Cary Church sat within the cemetery. (Courtesy of Ronnie and Marylou Moore.)

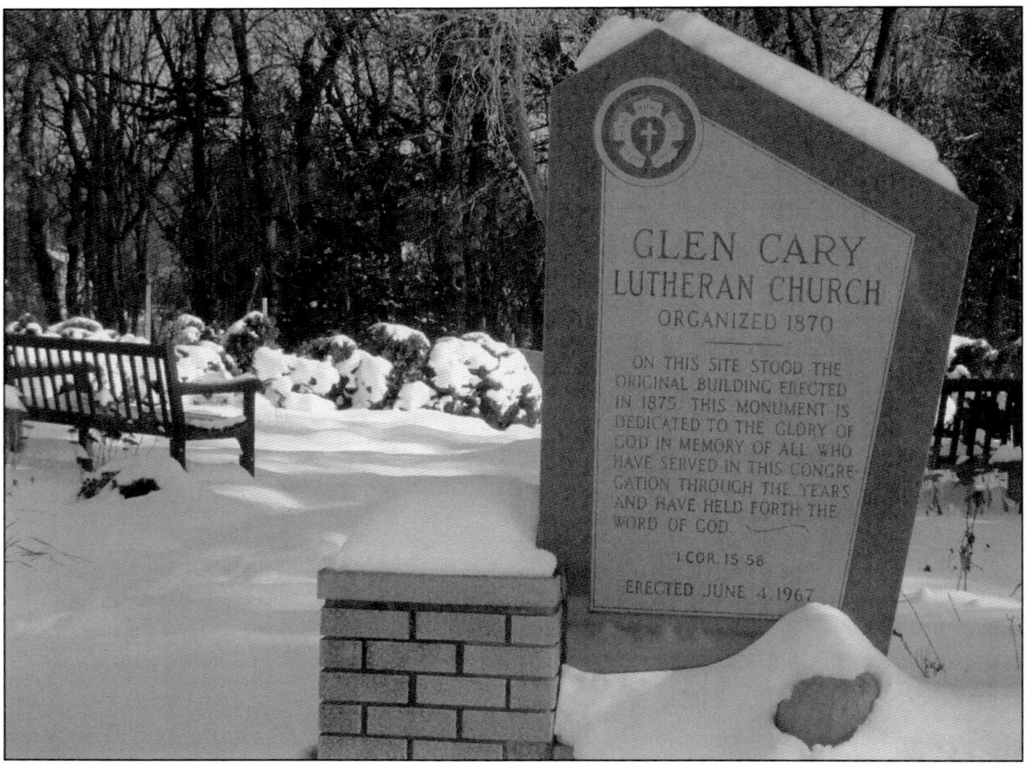

The old Glen Cary Church was torn down in 1965. A memorial plaque was installed in 1967 where the front of the old church stood, which is in the middle of the cemetery that is still in use today. (Author's collection.)

In 1928, a basement was put under the church, and a big wood- or coal-fired furnace was installed. The church went to oil heat in 1949. Electricity replaced candles and oil lamps in 1938. This is the interior of the Glen Cary Church. (Courtesy of Ronnie and Marylou Moore.)

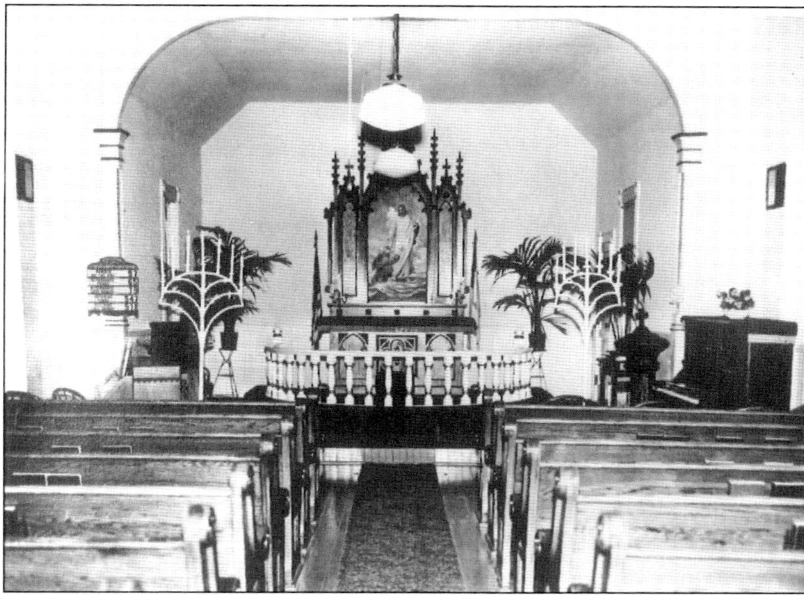

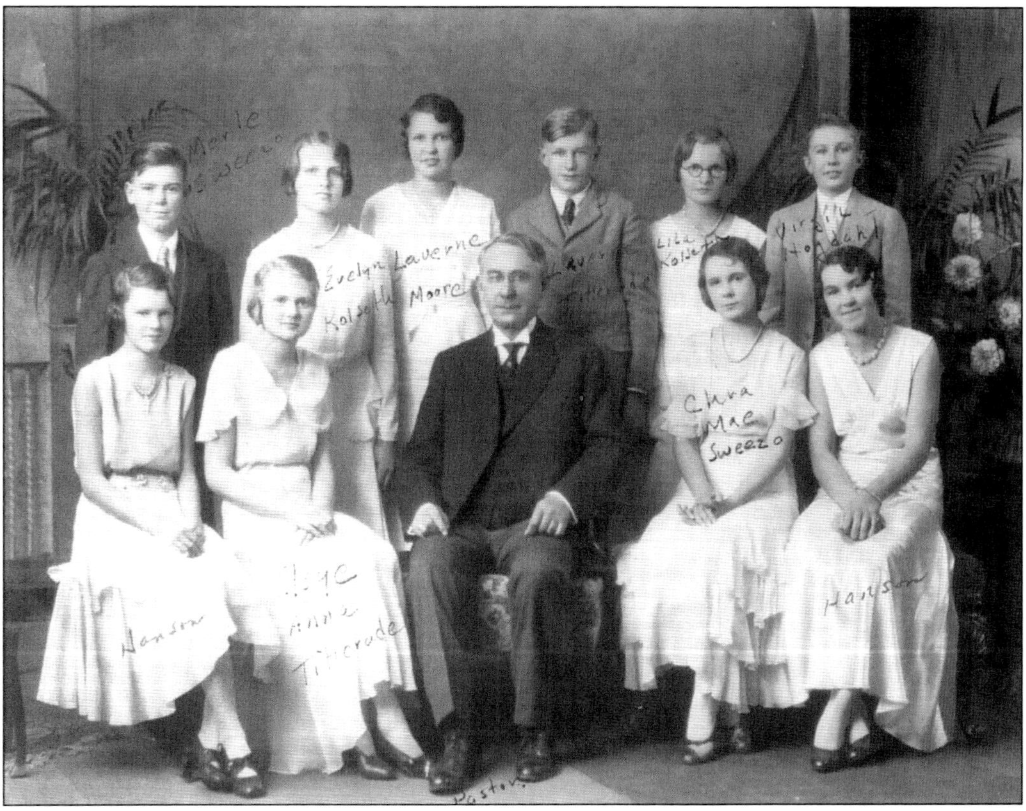

Confirmation was a time for pictures to be taken. Here, the 1931 confirmation class of Glen Cary Church includes, from left to right, (front row) Laura Hanson, Elsye Ann Titterud, the pastor, Clara Mae Sweezo, and Patricia Hanson; (back row) Merle Sweezo, Evelyn Kulseth, Laverne Moore, Laverne Titterud, Lila Kolseth, and Virgil Hogdahl. (Courtesy of the Anoka County Historical Society.)

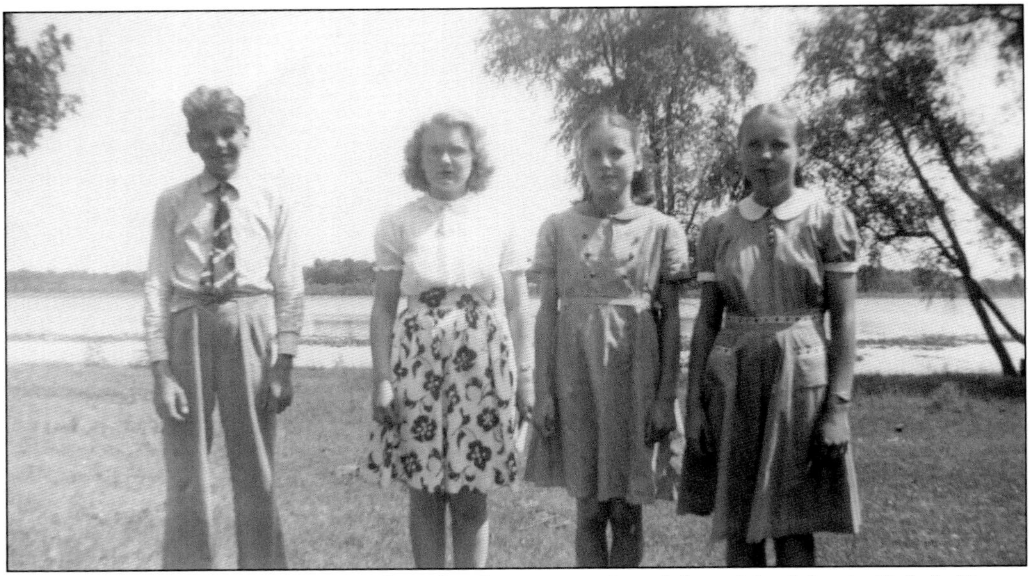

Pictured at the 1942 Glen Cary Sunday school picnic are, from left to right, Marvin Toft, LaVonne Benson, Betty Gillund, and Betty Moe. (Courtesy of Betty Moe Sannerud.)

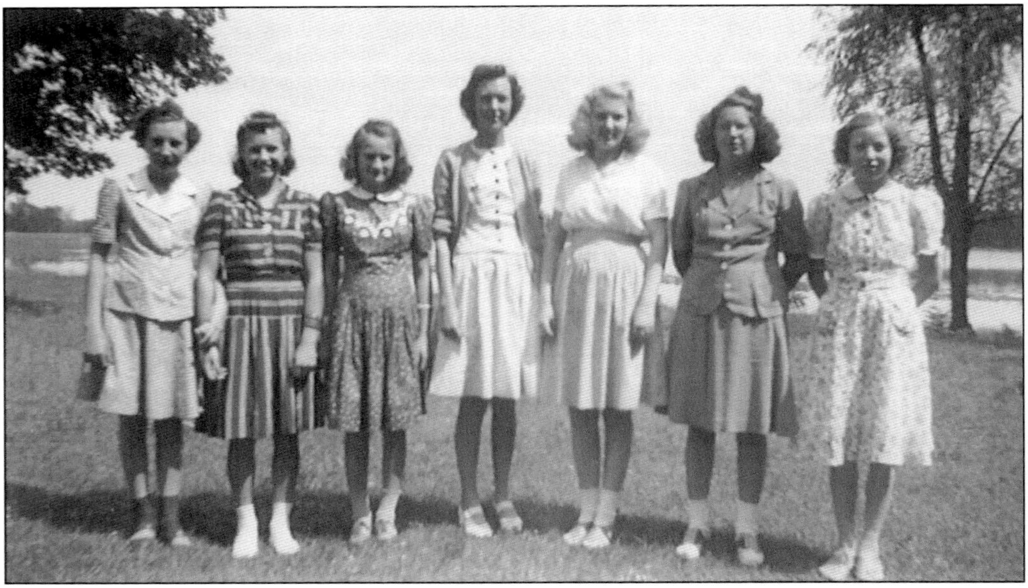

Also posing at the 1942 Glen Cary Sunday school picnic are, from left to right, Ovis Erickson, Lorraine Dukman, Margaret Moore, Arlene Moose (teacher), Marilyn Benson, Juliet Peterson, and Claris Gillund. (Courtesy of Betty Moe Sannerud.)

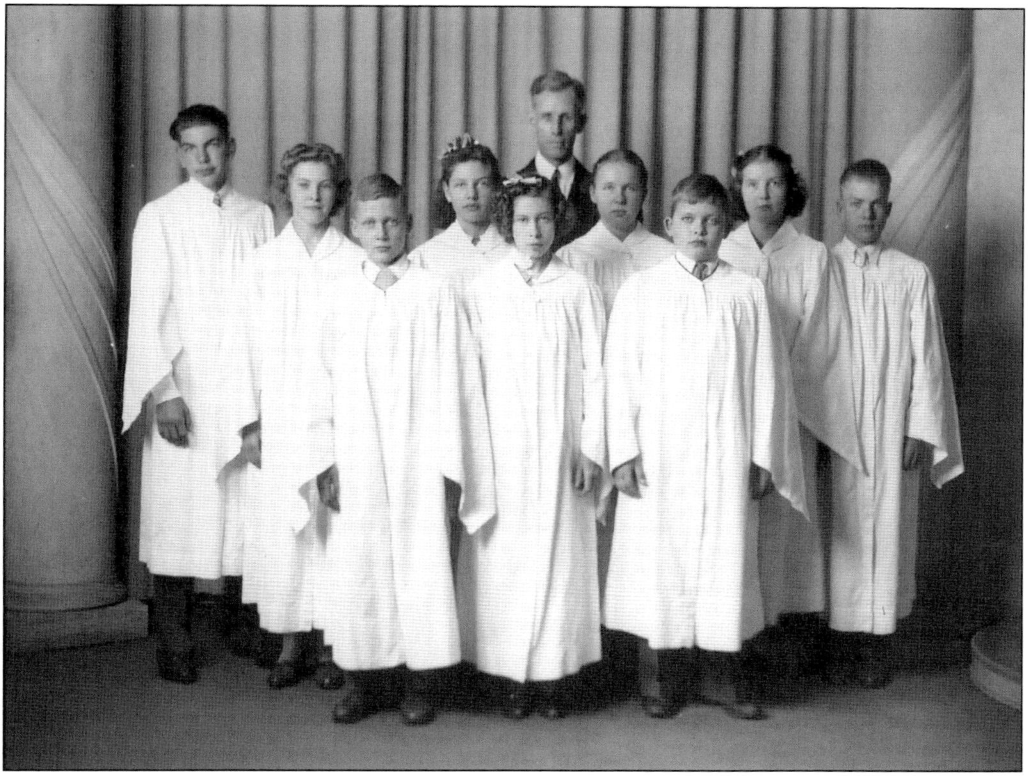

As the years went by, confirmation class became more formal. Posing for the camera at confirmation at Glen Cary Church are, from left to right, (first row) Norman Peterson, Audrey Pearson, and unidentified; (second row) Marvin Toft, Jeanette Widell, Sylvia Toft, Betty Moe, Betty Gillund, and Hilmer Widell with Pastor Selmer Framstad. (Courtesy of Betty Moe Sannerud.)

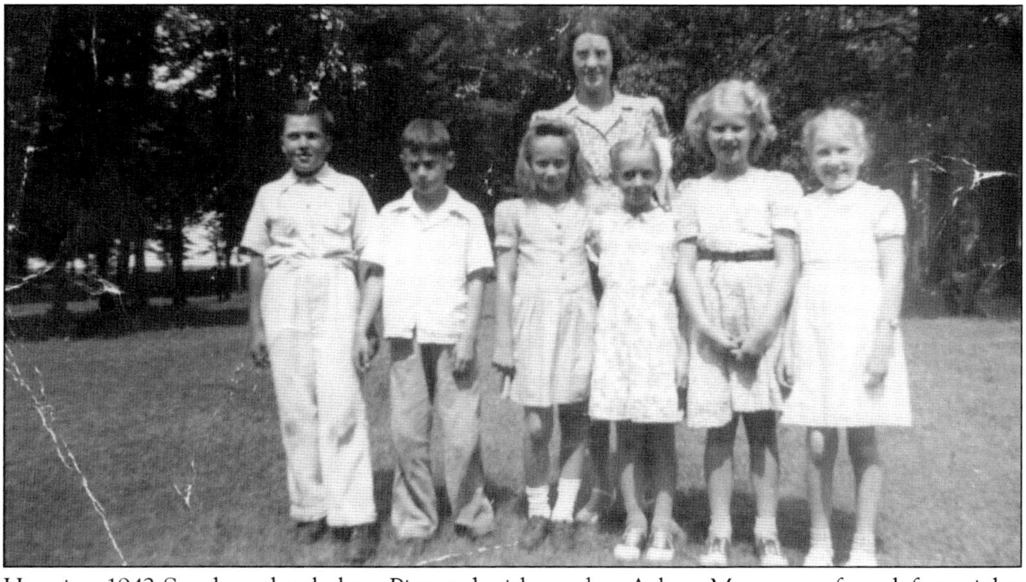

Here is a 1942 Sunday school class. Pictured with teacher Arlene Moore are, from left to right, Dwight Hamm, Ronnie Moore, Ruth Moore, Doris Sauter, Joyce Solie, and Beverly Benson. (Courtesy of Ronnie and Marylou Moore.)

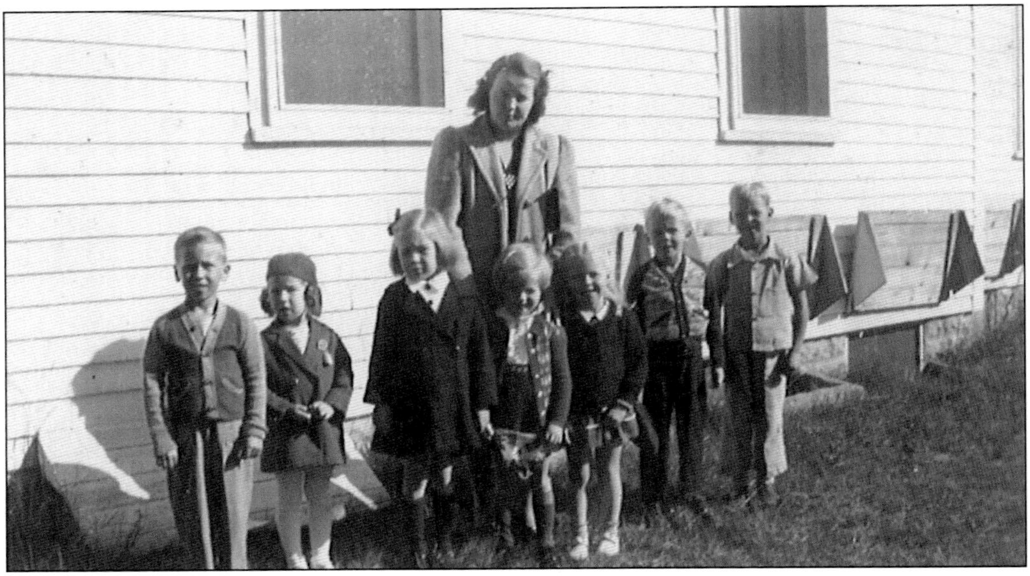

This is another photograph of the Glen Cary Sunday school. Seen here are, from left to right, Dennis Hamm, Ardith Bonde, Karen Mattson, Evelyn Titterud, an unidentified teacher, Loretta Peterson, an unidentified student, and Alvin Peterson. (Courtesy of Ronnie and Marylou Moore.)

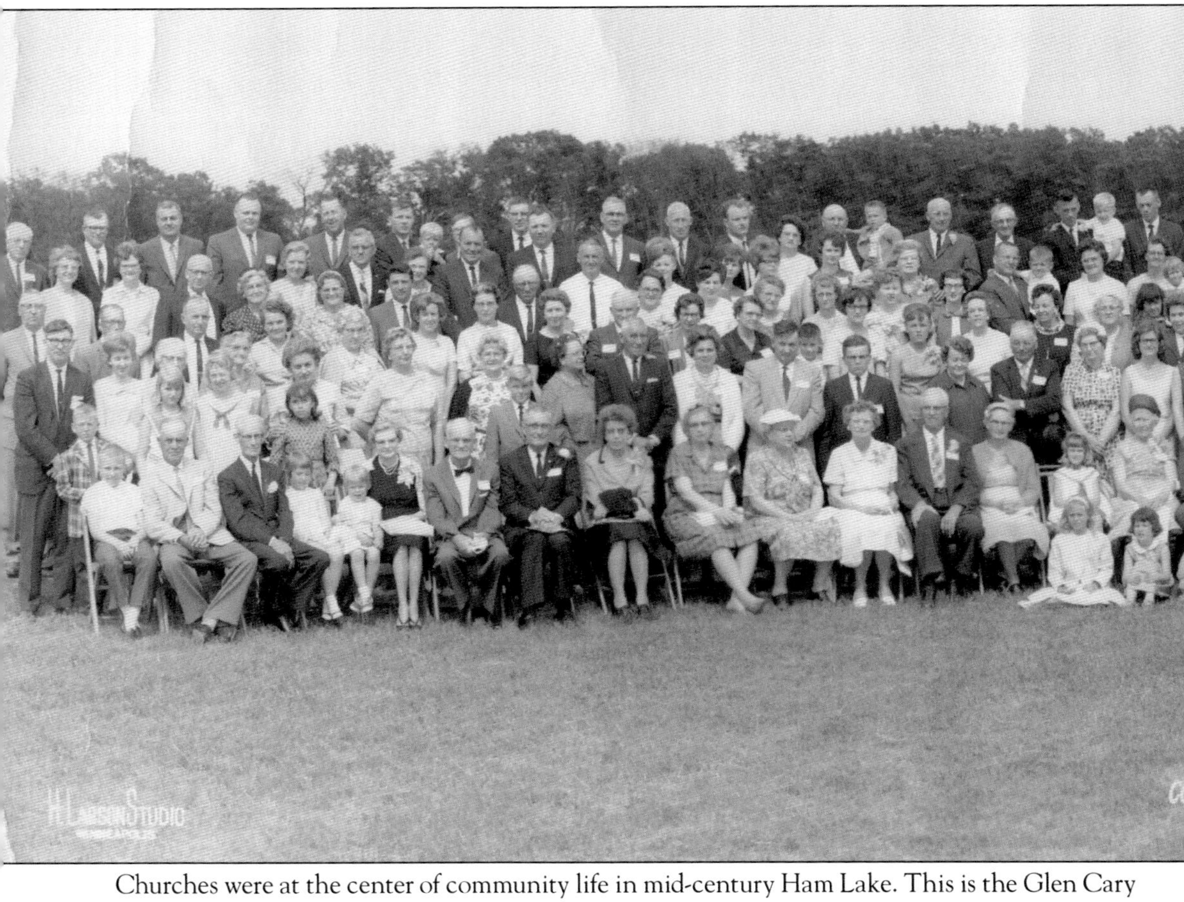

Churches were at the center of community life in mid-century Ham Lake. This is the Glen Cary

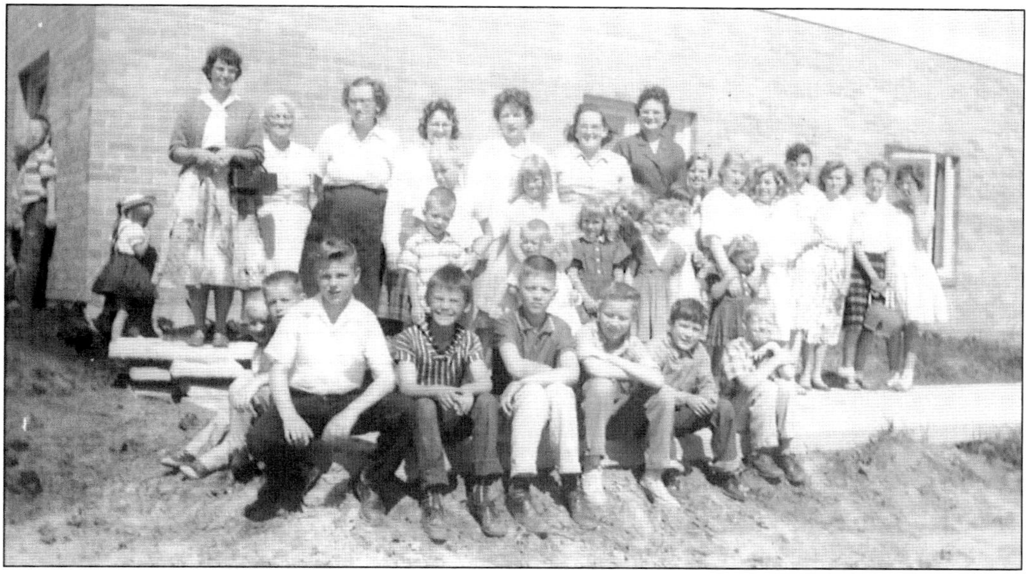

In this photograph is the first Bible school at the new Glen Cary Church. (Courtesy of Betty Moe Sannerud.)

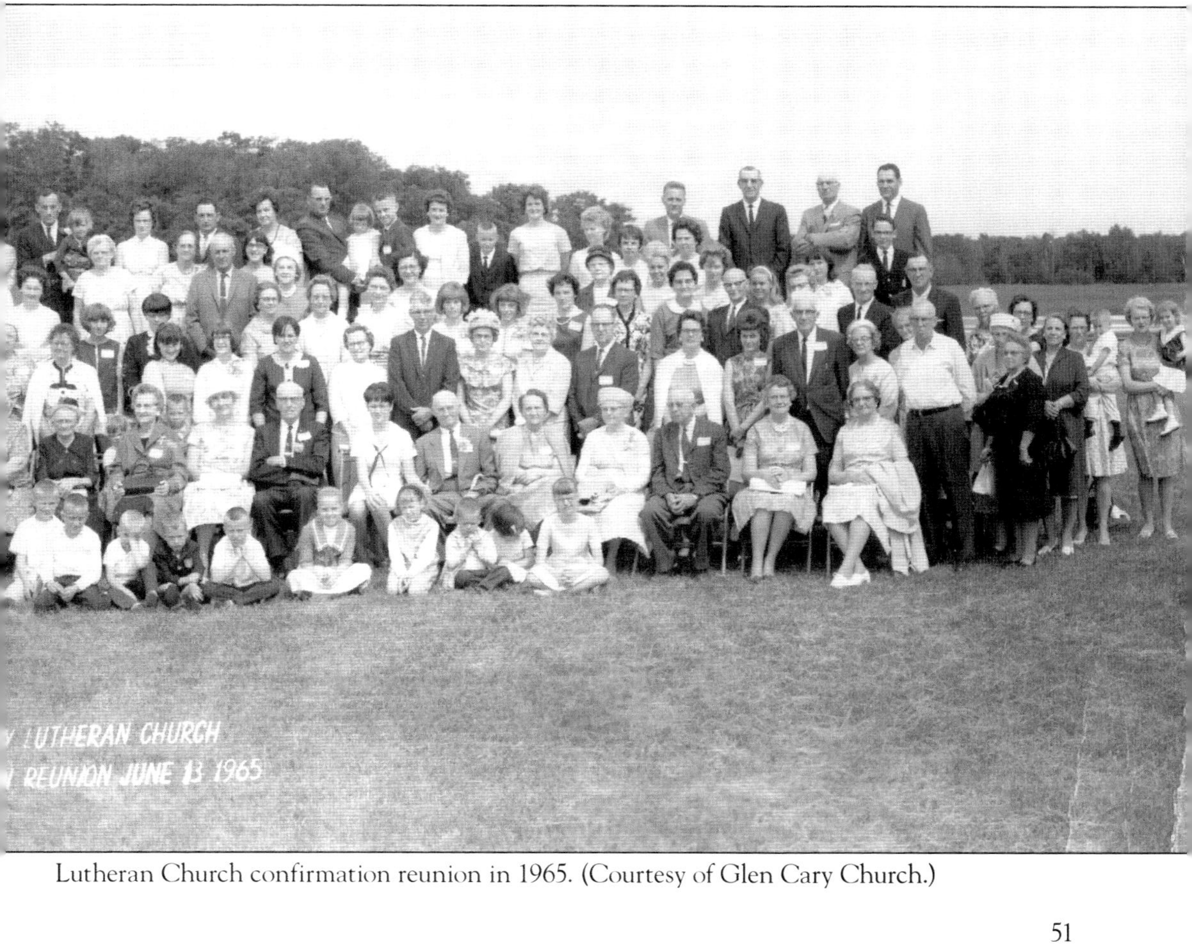

Lutheran Church confirmation reunion in 1965. (Courtesy of Glen Cary Church.)

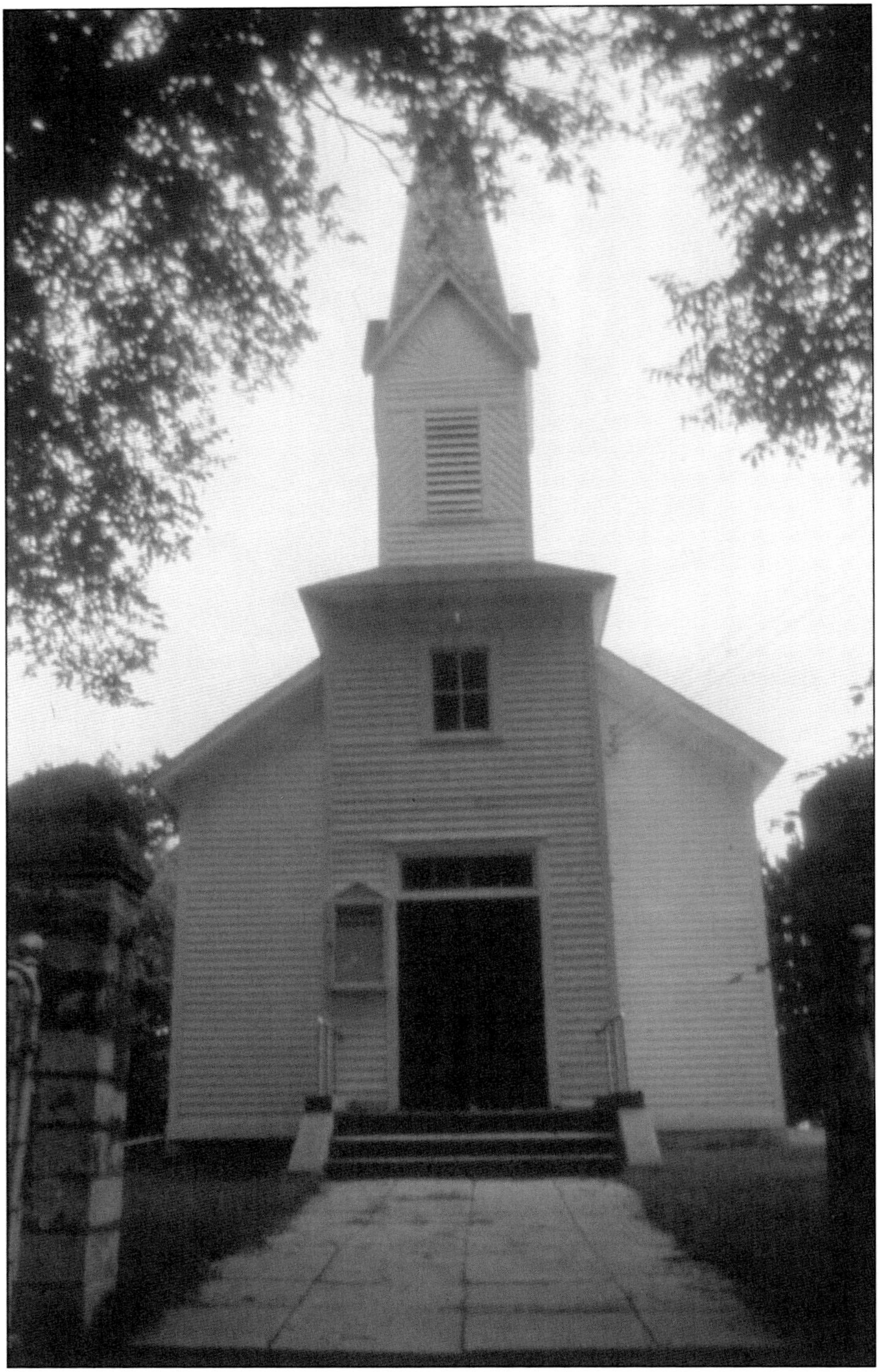

The Swedish Evangelical Lutheran Church, later named Our Saviour's Lutheran Church, was founded in 1872. It still stands and is the only building in Ham Lake in the National Register of Historic Places. Logs for the church were cut and hauled via oxen across Coon Lake. (Courtesy of the Anoka County Historical Society.)

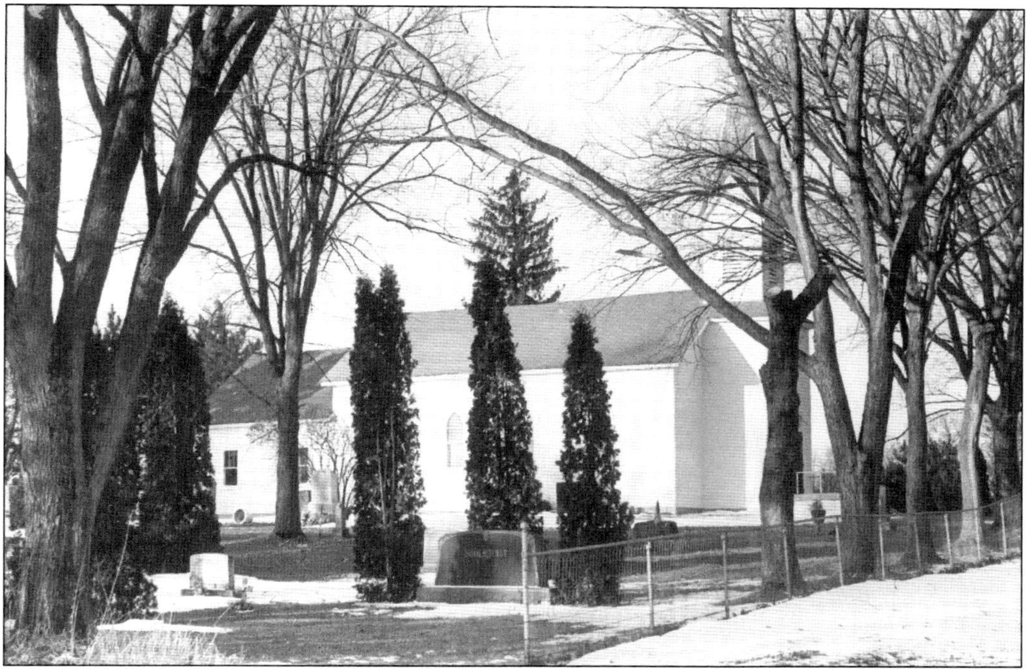

This is a view of the Swedish Evangelical Lutheran Church cemetery. The building was constructed on land donated by Johan and Fredericka Magnuson. (Courtesy of the Anoka County Historical Society.)

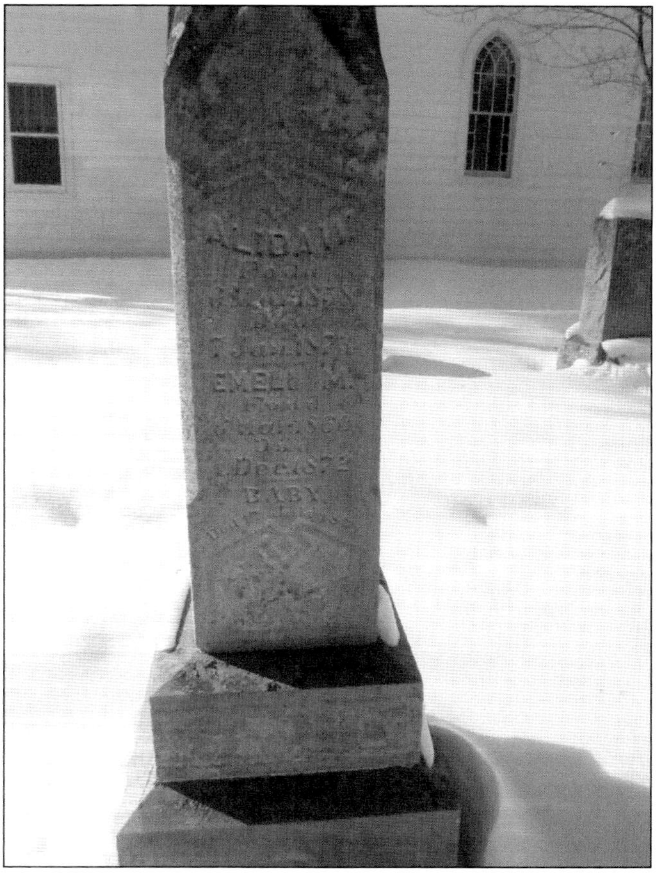

Alida and Emila Magnuson, daughters of Johan and Fredericka Magnuson, died of typhoid fever. They were buried in the front yard of their house, and these deaths drew attention to the need for a permanent cemetery. The two were reburied and the first to be interred in the cemetery at Swedish Evangelical Lutheran Church, which is still in use today. (Author's collection.)

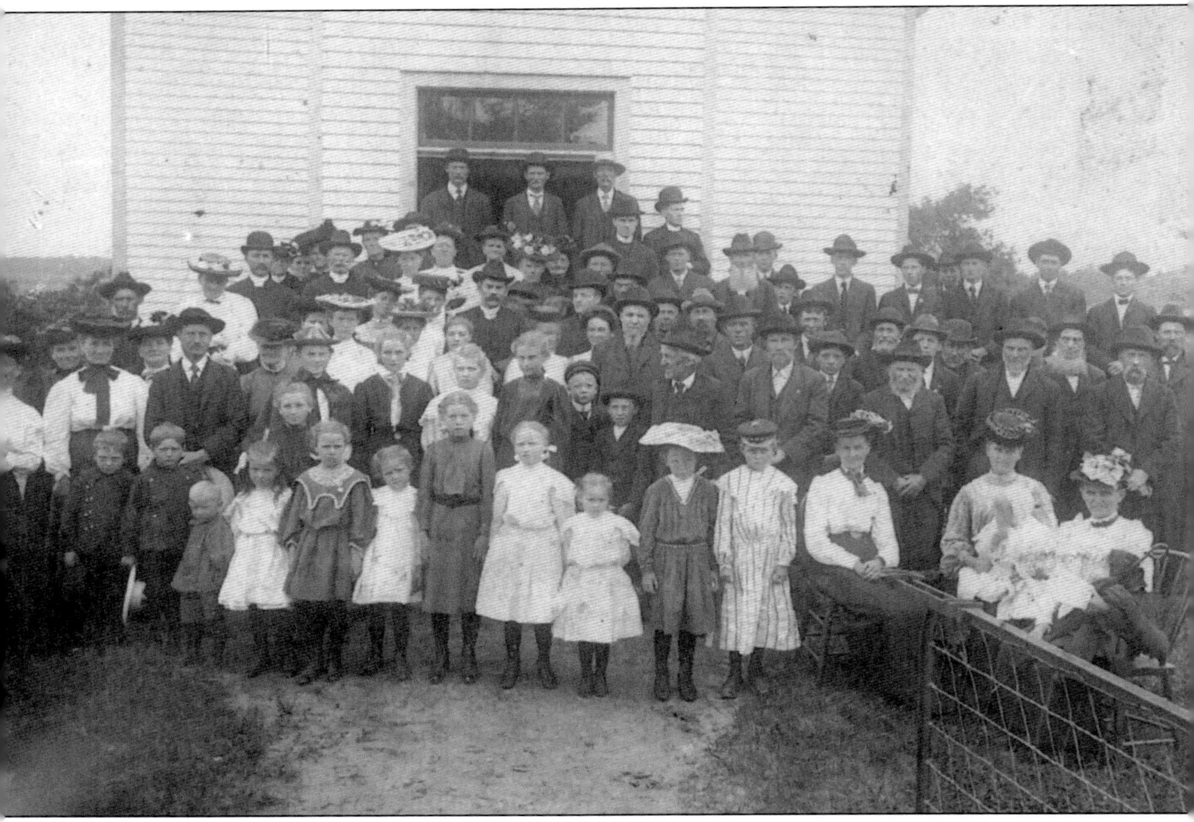

The two major Lutheran churches continued to grow. This is the Swedish Lutheran Church congregation in 1906. (Courtesy of the Anoka County Historical Society.)

Our Saviour's Luther Hall was built in 1917 not only as a place for Sunday school classes but also for such events as farewell parties of young men going into the military, banquets, wedding lunches, and church suppers. The building was sold after the new church was built and was used as a storage building. (Courtesy of the Anoka County Historical Society.)

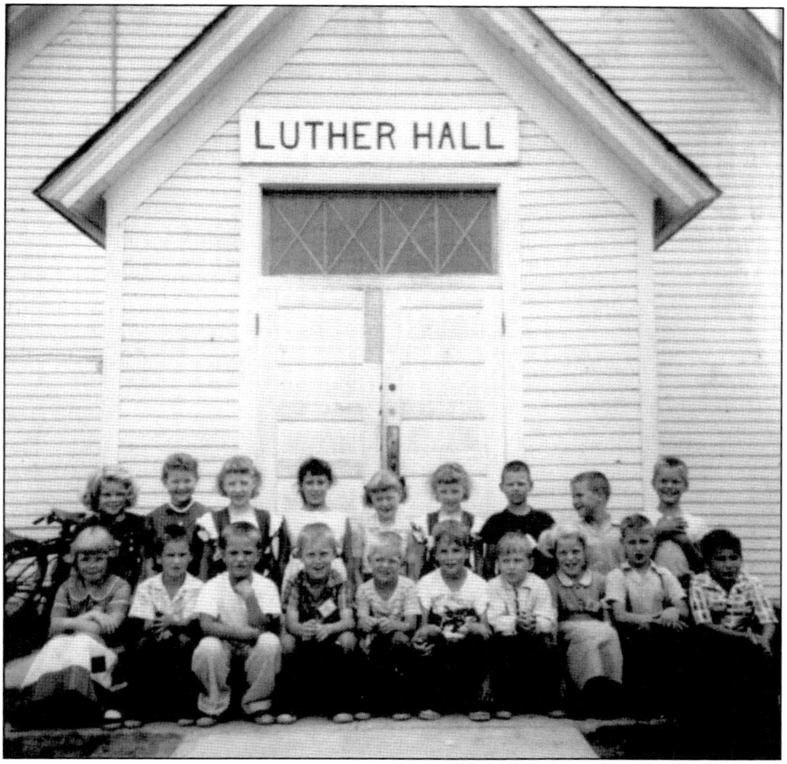

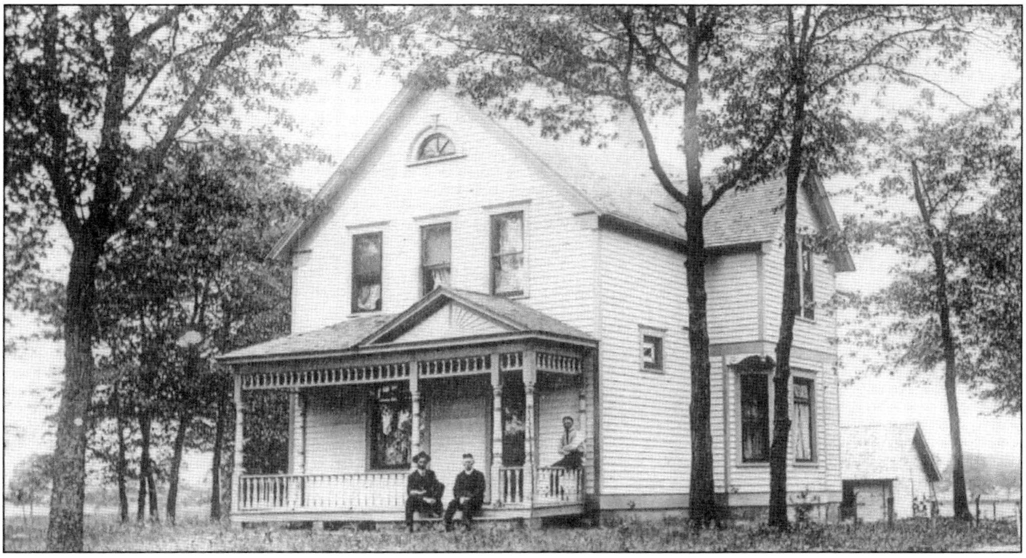

Our Saviour's Luther Hall stood across the road from the church parsonage. Pictured is the Swedish Lutheran Church parsonage in 1903. (Courtesy of Our Saviour's Lutheran Church.)

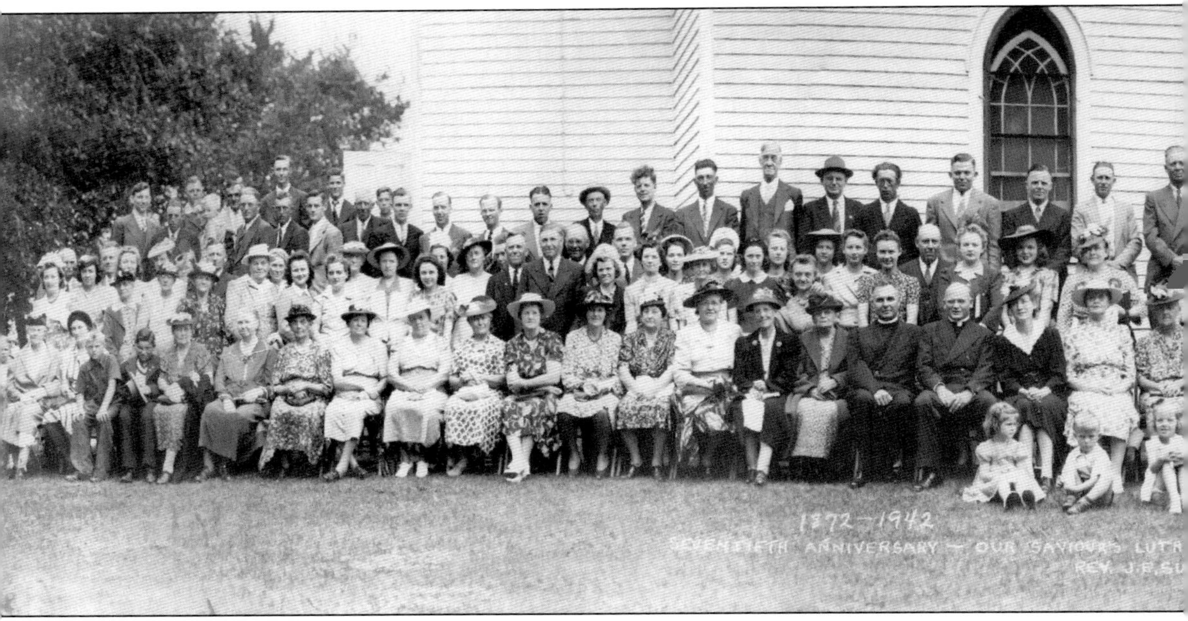

This photograph was taken of the congregation at the 70th anniversary of Our Saviour's Lutheran Church in June 1942. J.E. Sutherland was the pastor. (Courtesy of Our Saviour's

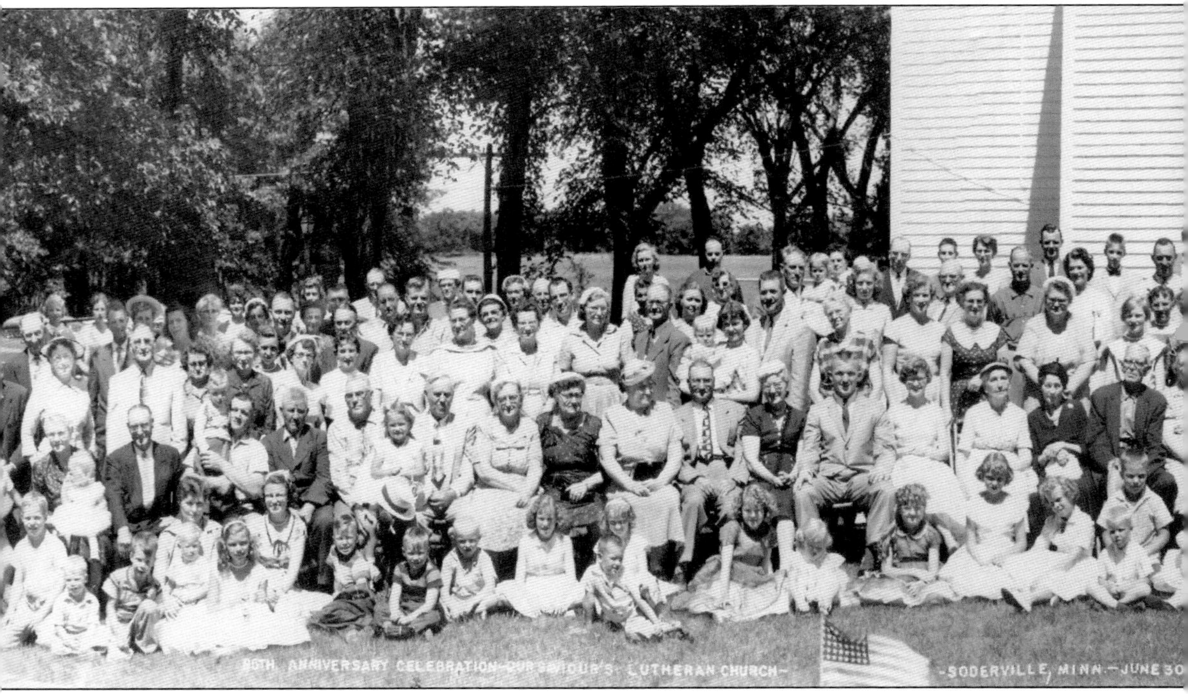

Pictured is Our Saviour's Lutheran Church's 85th anniversary in June 1957. R.R. Van Loon was

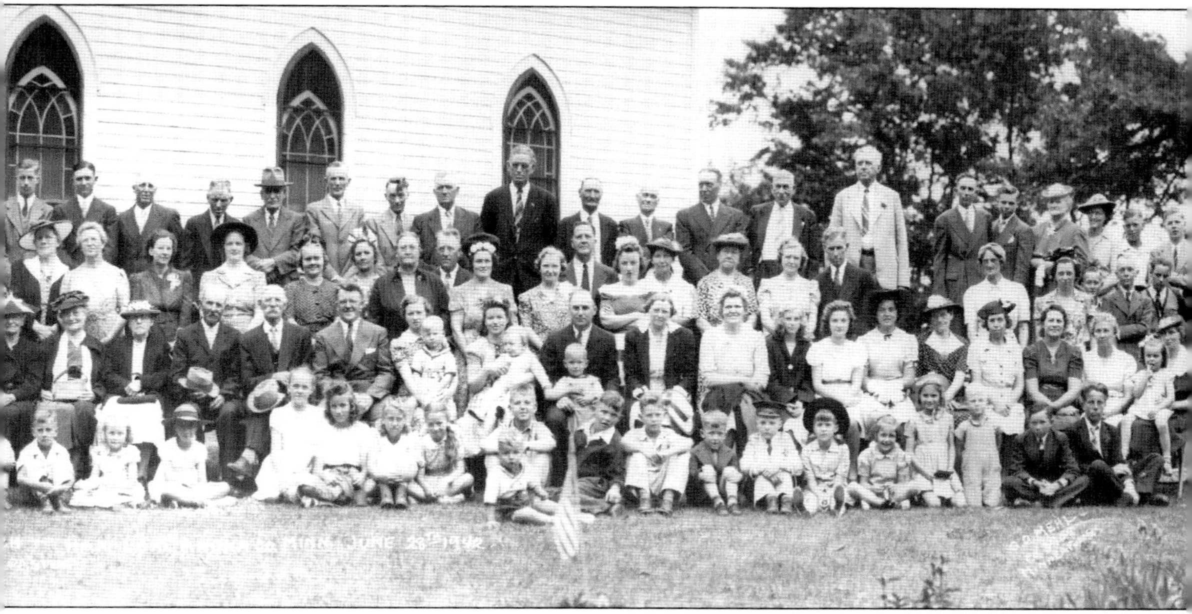

Lutheran Church.)

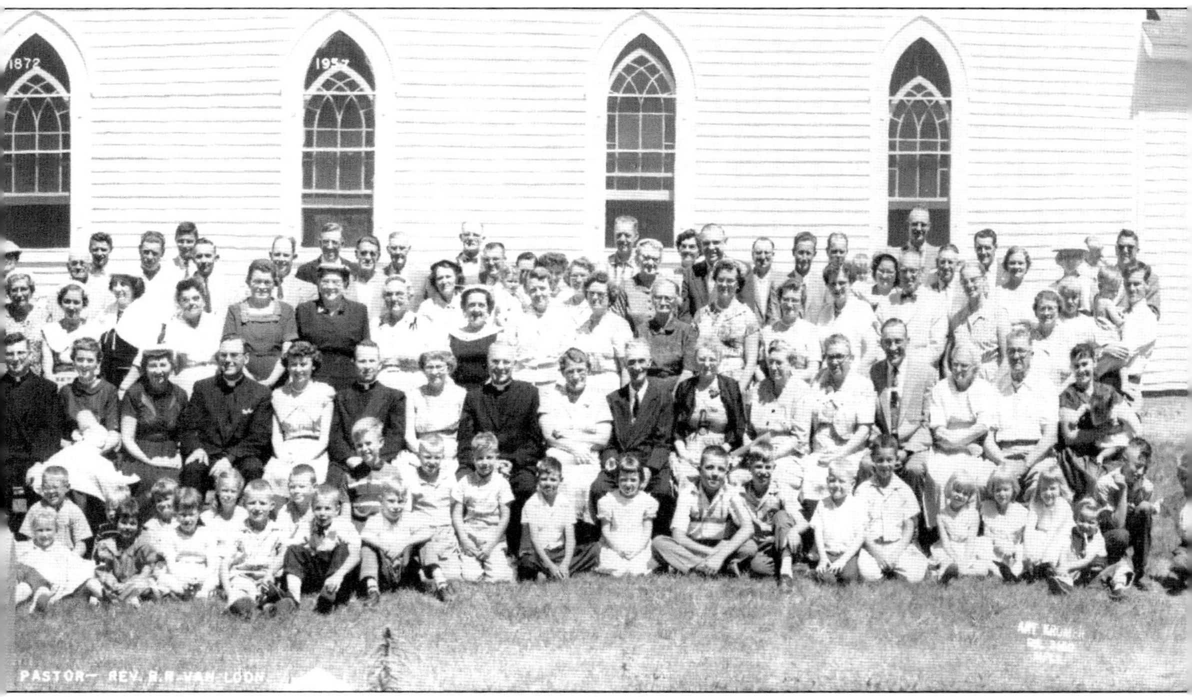

the pastor. (Courtesy of Our Saviour's Lutheran Church.)

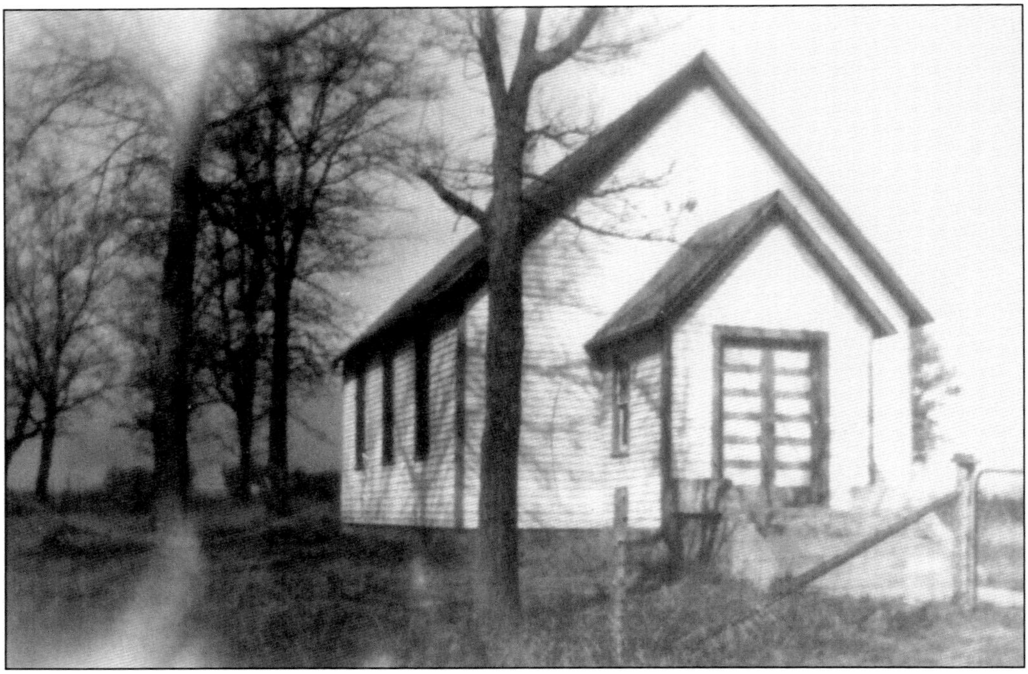

Central Avenue Mission Church began in 1899 at the southwest corner of Crosstown Boulevard and Highway 65 and disbanded in 1940. (Courtesy of the Anoka County Historical Society.)

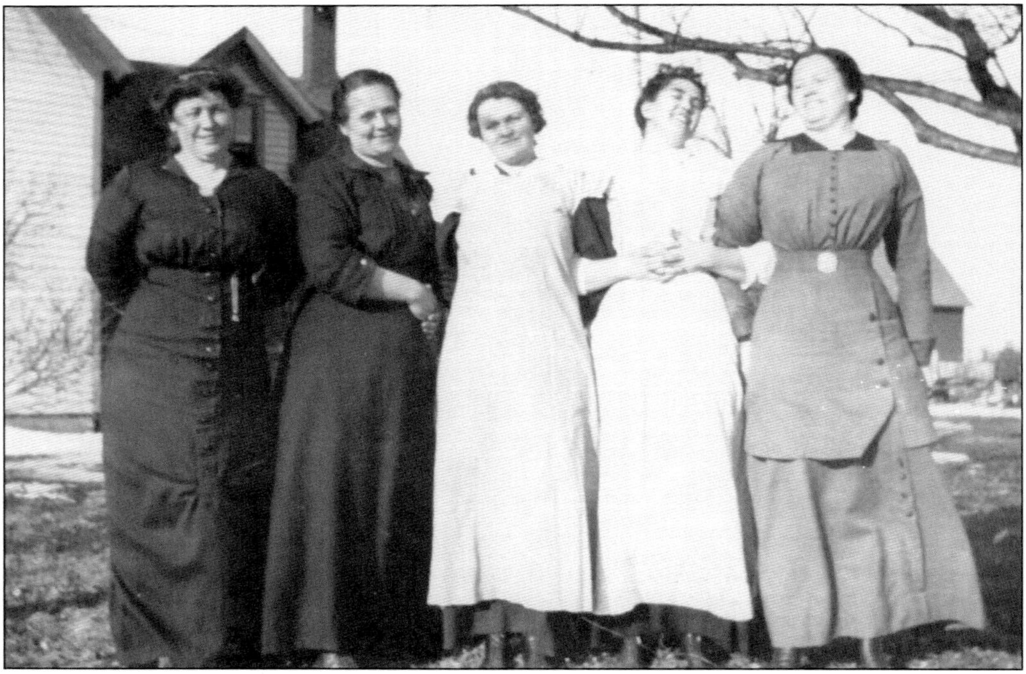

The Free Church of God, or Fair Oaks Church, was located in Lake Netta but had its Fair Oaks Cemetery at Crosstown Boulevard and Interlachen Drive. The church began approximately 1901 but moved to East Bethel in 1902. Seen here are members of the Fair Oaks Church Ladies Aid. They are, from left to right, Mrs. Amos DeWitt, Mrs. Robert Swanson, Mrs. Adolph Tilling, Mrs. Will Clarke, and Mrs. Berger Titterud. (Courtesy of the Anoka County Historical Society.)

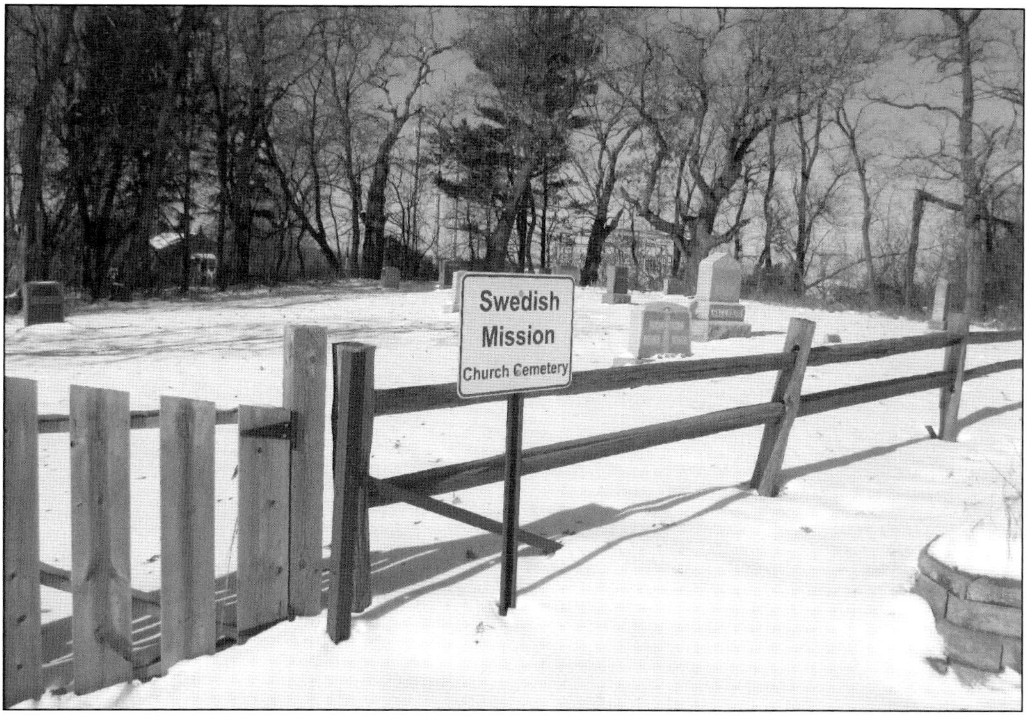

When Central Avenue Mission Church disbanded, it left a cemetery. It is now the responsibility of the City of Ham Lake. (Author's collection.)

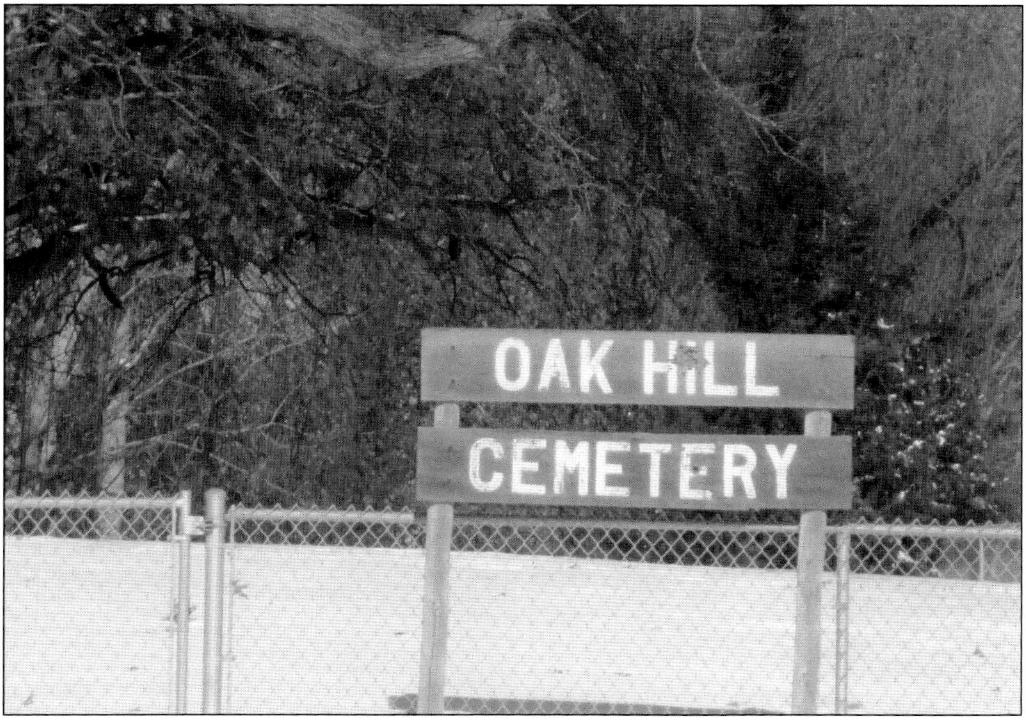

The same was true for Fair Oaks Church. It also left a cemetery that is now the responsibility of the City of Ham Lake. (Author's collection.)

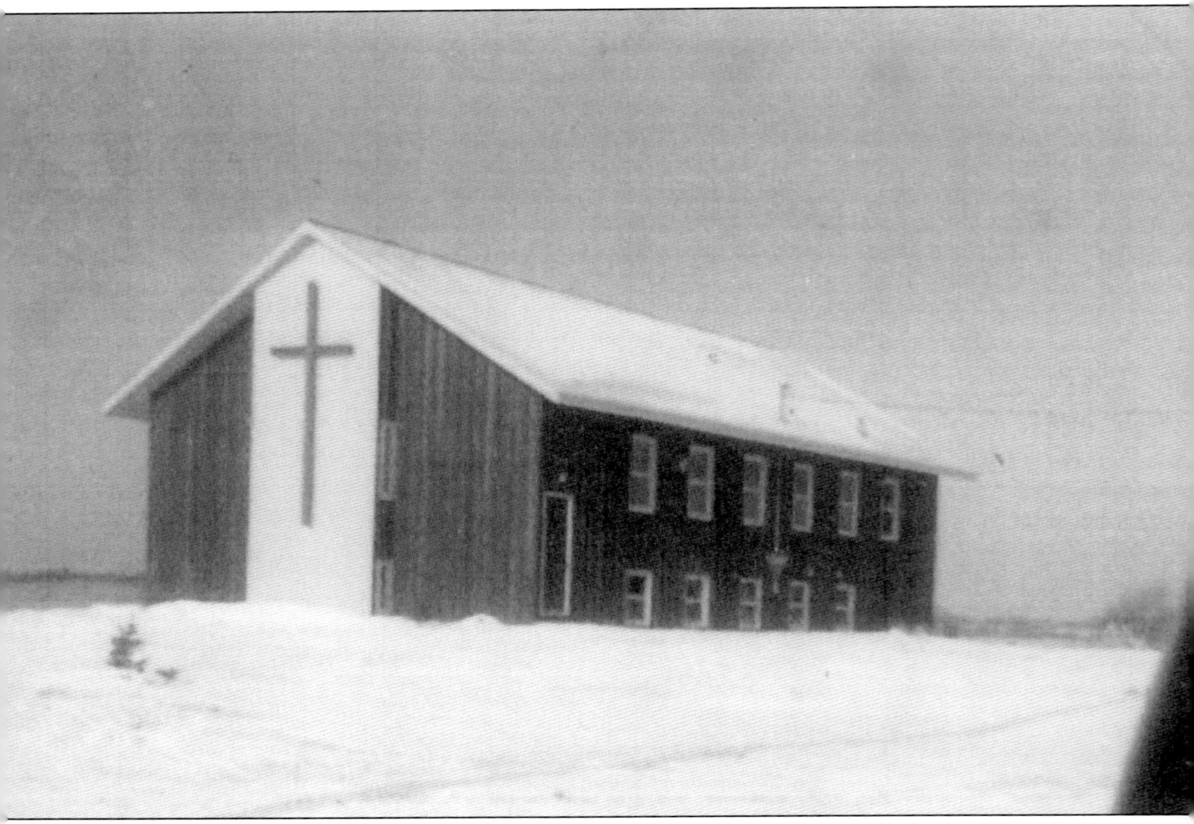

The following churches were also formed in Ham Lake: Cedar United Methodist Church, 1904; Oak Haven Church, 1965; Church of St. Paul Catholic Church, 1981; Spirit of Christ Lutheran Church, 1982; Radisson Road Baptist Church, 1987; Family of Christ Lutheran Church, 2004; Horizon Community Church, 2008; and Kingdom Hall of Jehovah Witnesses. Pictured here is Ham Lake Baptist Church, which was established in 1965 and then renamed Oak Haven Church. (Courtesy of Cindy Birkeland.)

Four

Schools

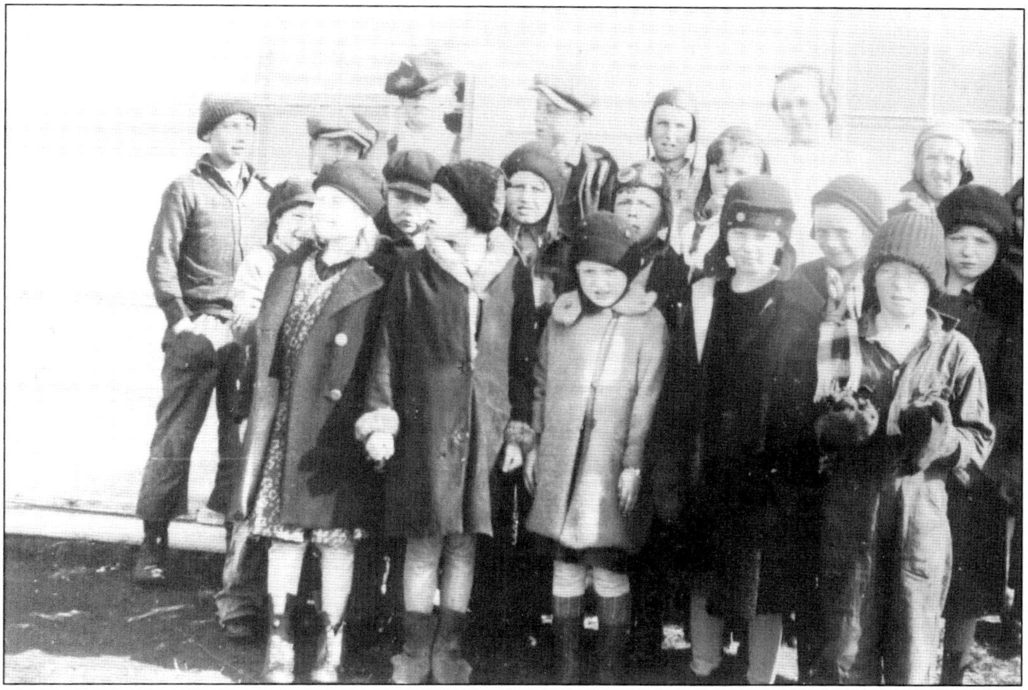

The Northwest Territories law provided the first national support for public schools. One section in each township was automatically set aside for public schools either as a location and/or to finance those schools. Ham Lake Township had five one-room schools. This high number may have been because early leaders saw education as an important aspect of the human condition or because the settlement in Ham Lake was scattered and they wanted schools closers to their homes. The oldest of those schools was Lake Netta School. The original Lake Netta School District No. 24 was organized in 1871, and classes were held in farmers' homes. The first school was built in 1877, three miles south of Lake Netta, but was moved across the lake in 1889 with the aid of horses. In 1935, that school was replaced. The new Lake Netta School was eventually purchased and converted into a private home. (Courtesy of the Anoka County Historical Society.)

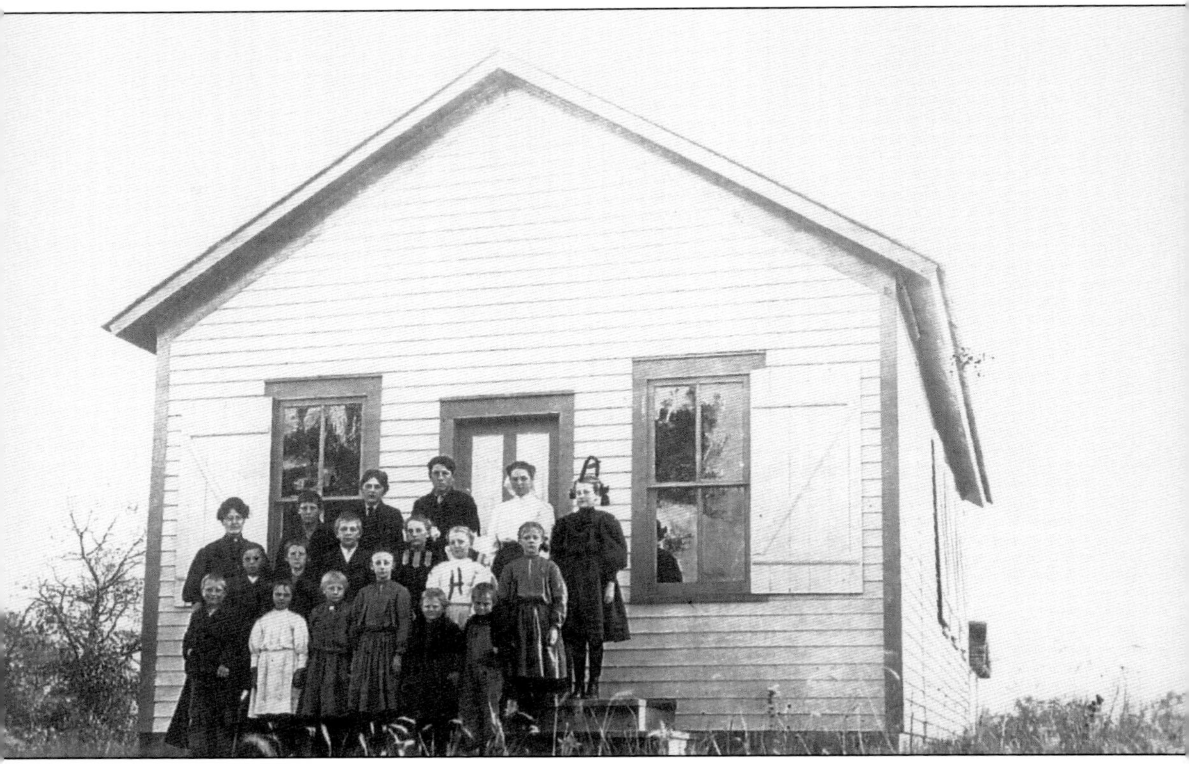

Here is Lake Netta School in 1905. The students shown include Arthur Solem, Melvin Peterson, Emil Solem, Mabel Walberg, Alpha Nordstrom Rasmussen, Geoffrey Nelson, Roy Walberg, Adrian Matson, Florence Welberg, Helen Nordquist Benson, Sophie Erikson Osborne, Oscar Solem, Edith Nelson McKay, Ada Erickson, Mabel Erickson, Clarence Solem, and Wilhelm Nelson. (Courtesy of the Anoka County Historical Society.)

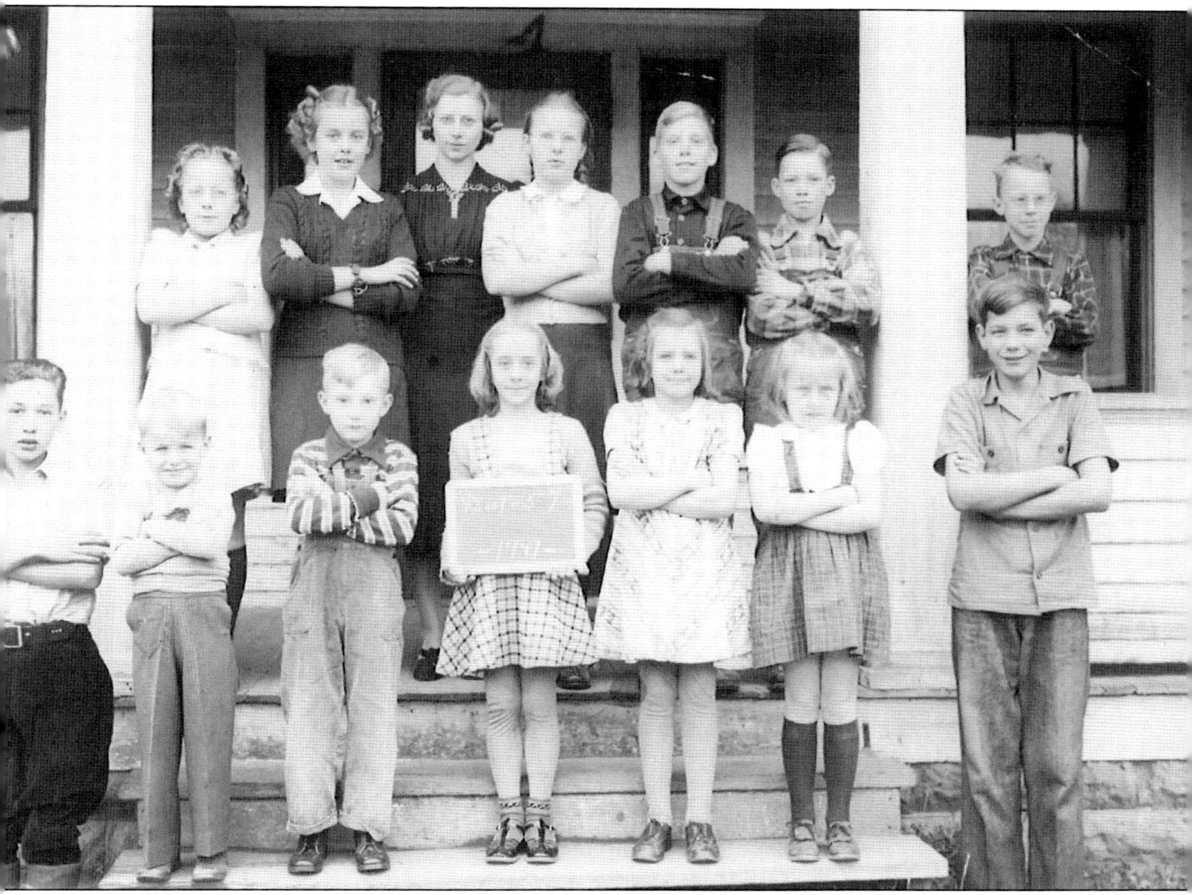

At Glen Cary School District No. 37, classes were taught in Norwegian when it was built in 1889. The building became Ham Lake City Hall in 1961 and was extensively remodeled in 1976. It was demolished in 1990 when a new city hall was constructed. The class of 1941 includes, from left to right, (first row) Arthur Lawrence, Gary Titterud, Glenn Gustafson, Doris Sauter, Ada Baumgardner, Delaine Titterud, and Dickey Baumgardner; (second row) Joanne Titterud, Elaine Peterson, teacher Miss Coretta Rick, Betty Moe, Marvin Olson, Ellwood Gustafson, and Leroy Lindberg. Betty Moe (Sannerud) was a student at Glen Cary School and returned to teach there after going to college. (Courtesy of Betty Moe Sannerud.)

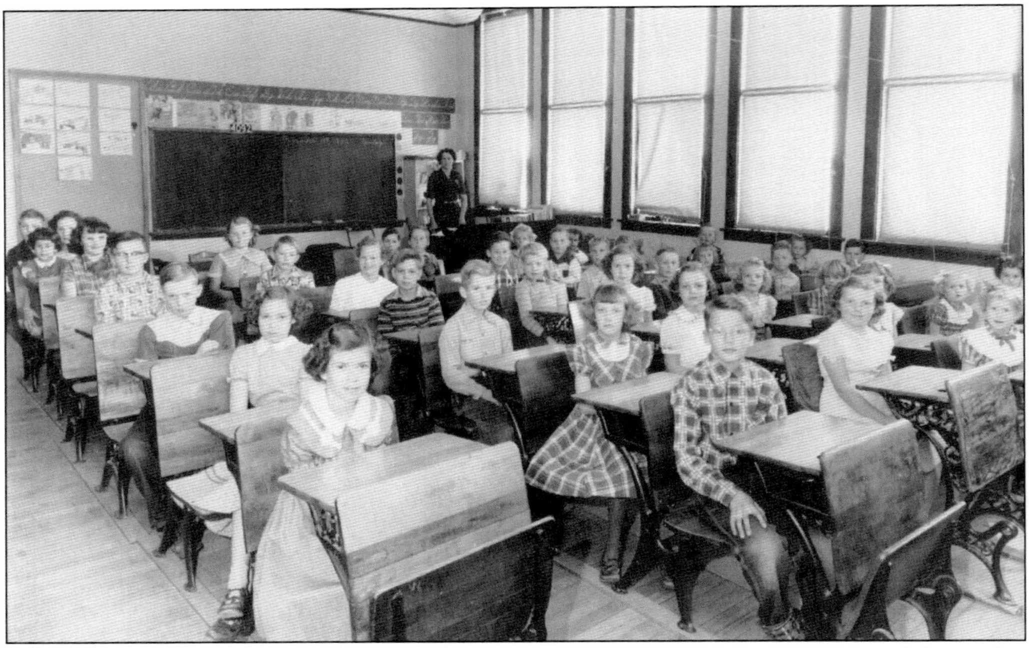

Pictured is a Glen Cary School class in 1952. Students posing for the camera are, from left to right, (first row) Mary Paulson, Patty Nichols, Bill Anderson, David Livgard, Melva Butler, unidentified, Mary Ann Woiz, and Rollie Erickson; (second row) Ron Butler, Loretta Hanson, Craig Erickson, unidentified, Judy Anderson, Neil Matson, and Marilyn Titterud; (third row) Shirley Titterud, Karen Livgard, Sharon Titterud, unidentified, Clyde Chase, unidentified, and David Turner; (fourth row) Suzy Titterud, two unidentified students, Tom Crandel, and the rest unidentified; (fifth row) Peggy Crandel and the rest unidentified; (sixth row) Kathy Titterud, Richard Anderson, and the rest unidentified. (Courtesy of the Anoka County Historical Society.)

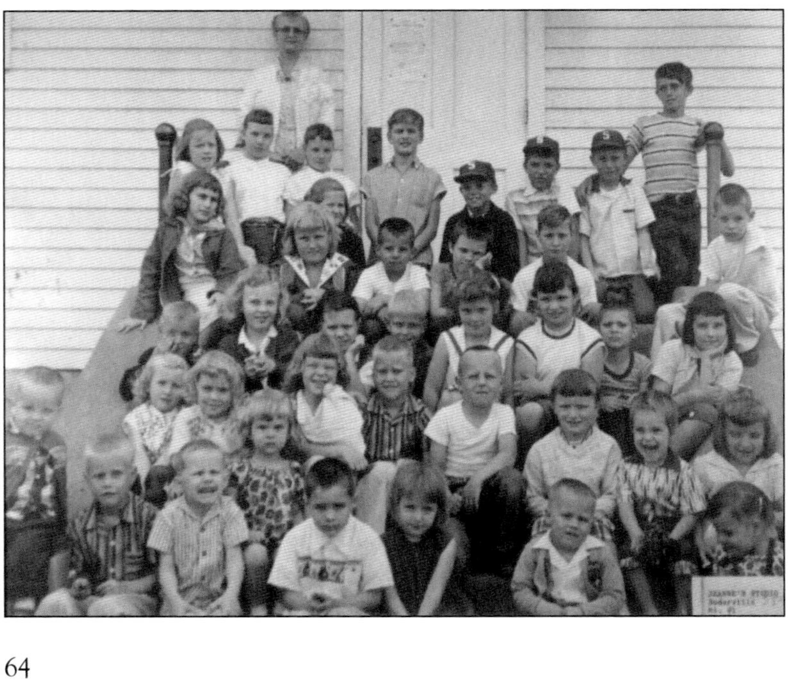

This is how the one-room Glen Cary School looked in 1958. Pictured is Mrs. Bergshin's class. (Courtesy of the Anoka County Historical Society.)

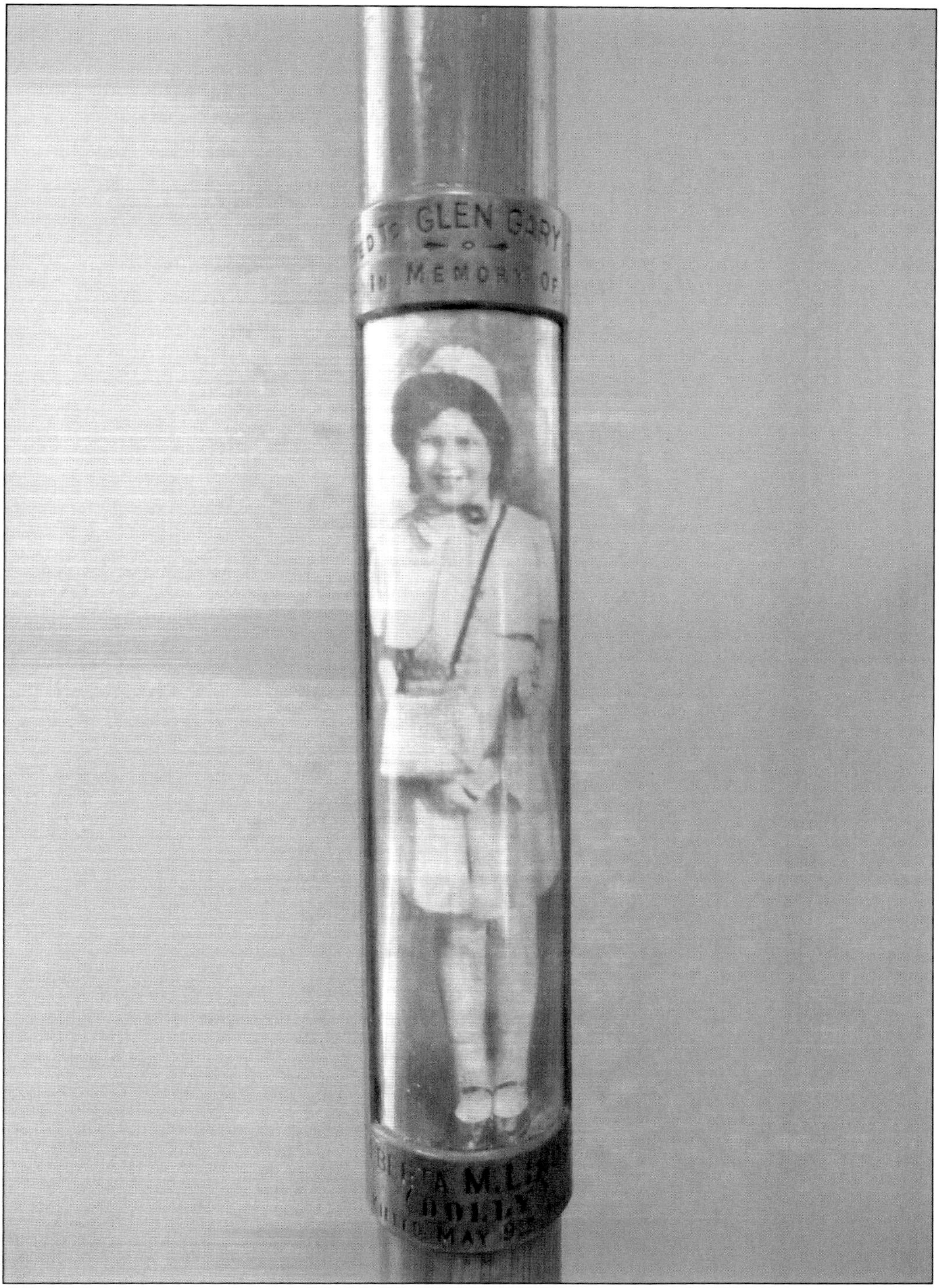

In all of the unconsolidated one-room schools in Ham Lake, only one student died while going to, leaving, or attending classes: Elberta Lindsey. She was struck by an automobile on Highway 65. The Glen Cary schoolroom's flagstaff had a picture of her from 1948 until the school closed in 1965. (Author's collection.)

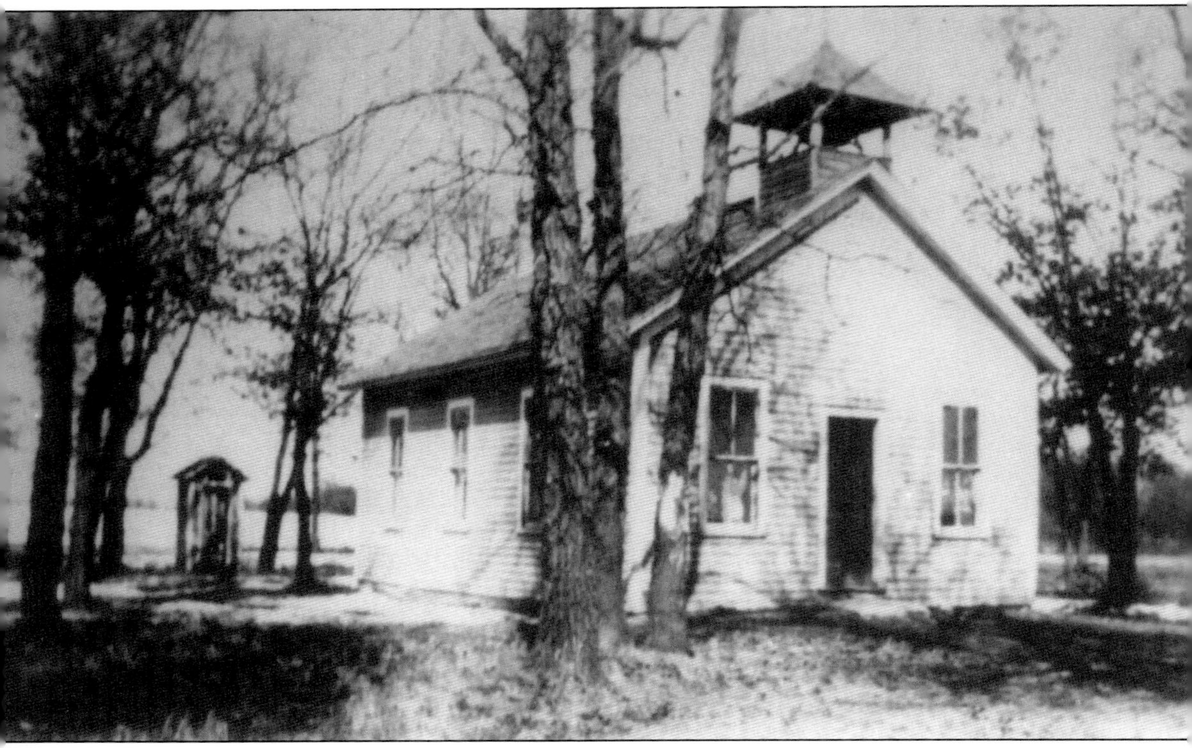

The original one-room Soderville School District No. 42 was built in 1890 on the Ado Olson property southwest of Soderville. (Courtesy of the Anoka County Historical Society.)

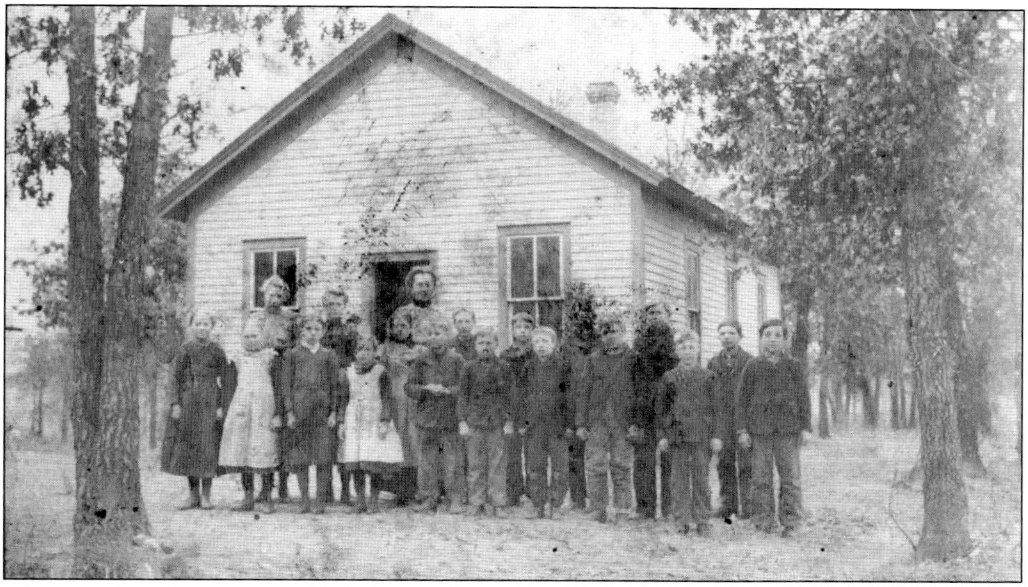

This is Soderville School in 1900. Pictured is the class of teacher Nellie Hilton. (Courtesy of the Anoka County Historical Society.)

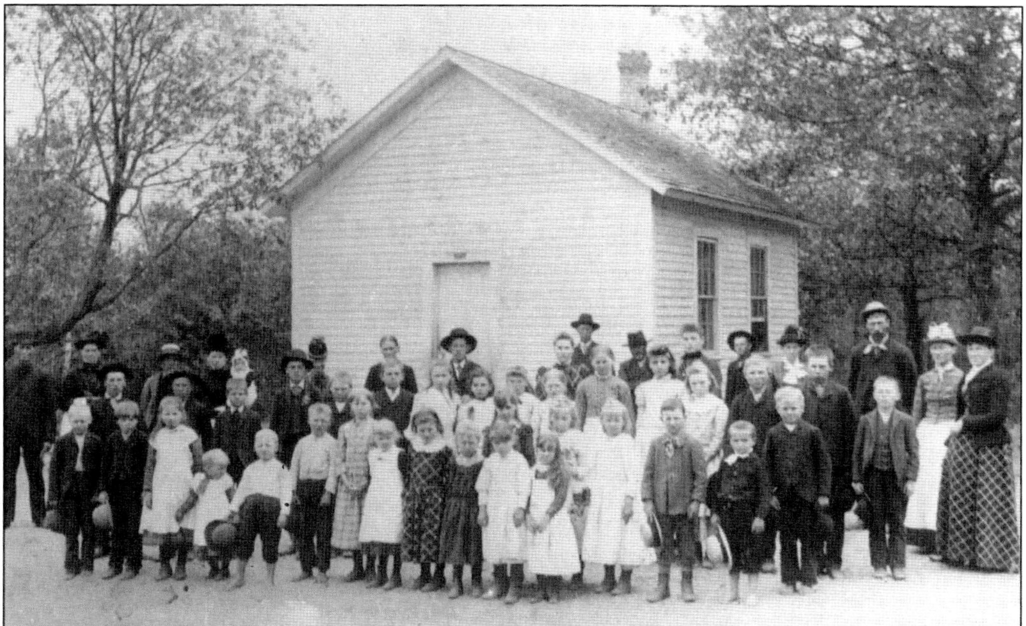

Family and students posed for a photograph at Soderville School District No. 42 in 1809. Shown among the group are Mr. and Mrs. Ole Peterson, Mr. and Mrs. Freeborn and baby daughter, Mrs. Gust Erickson, Mrs. Ole Japerson, Mrs. Matt Marty, Charles Peterson, Mathilda Titterud (teacher), Jonas Peterson, John Wold, Mrs. Anton Smith, Anton Smith, Ole Wold, Mrs. John Olson, Mrs. Frank Hart, Charles Hoglund, Tom Olson, Oscar Peterson, Edward Peterson, Helen Olson, Katy Marty, Ida Jasperson, Tillie Johnson, Christine Johnson, Francis Marty, Emma Smith, Annie Olson, Emma Olson, Adolph Olson, Alvin Olson, Bessie Hoglund, Hanna Freeman, Emma Severson, Una Hart, Annie Vanstrom, Amanda Peterson, Selma Peterson, Irving Hart, Martin Olson, and August Johnson. (Courtesy of the Anoka County Historical Society.)

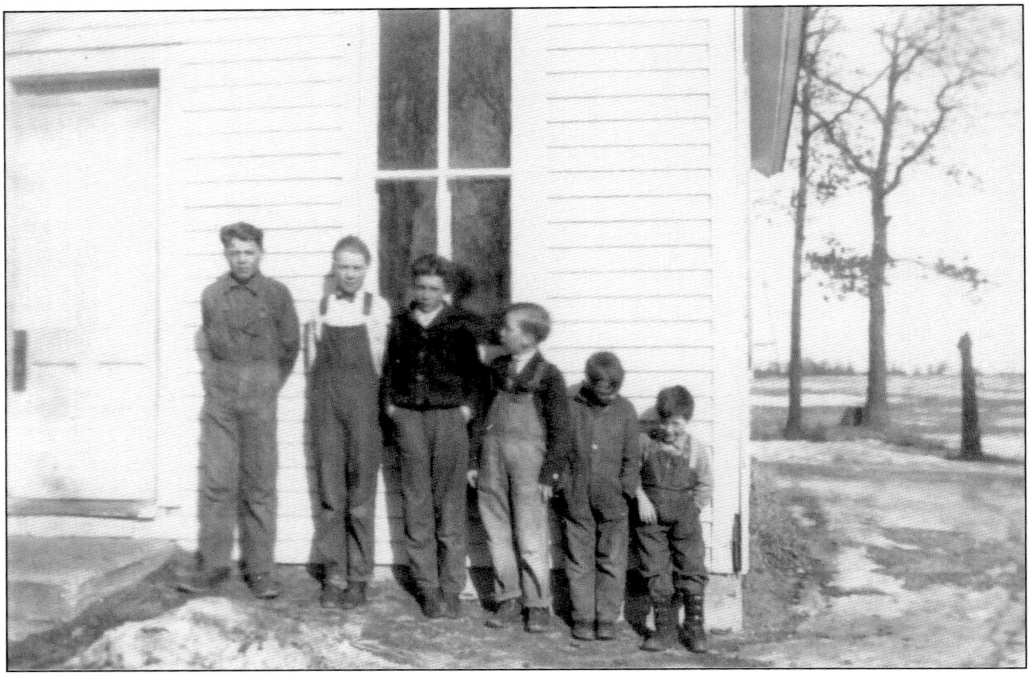

In addition to churches, schools were at the center of the community. Pictured are students of Soderville School. They are, from tallest to shortest, Ted Johnson, Clarence Livgard, Gust Stern, Walter Peterson, Clarence Vanstrom, and Stanley Olson. (Courtesy of the Anoka County Historical Society.)

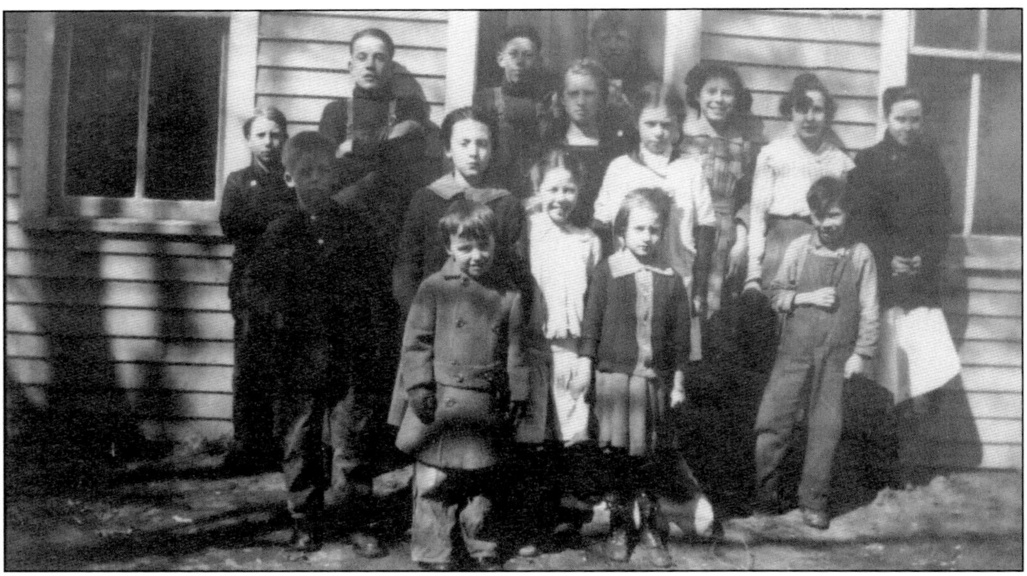

This is another Soderville School class. The students posing are, from left to right, (first row) Raymond White, Lucille Olson, and Mildred Johnson Buchholz; (second row) Walter Peterson, Clarence Lundberg, Curt Stern, Ted Johnson, Ester Olson Robinson, Alva Olson White, and Louise White; (third row) Clarence Vanstrum, Erella White, Edith Johnson Peterson, Ada Vanstrom Carlson, and Stanley Olson. (Courtesy of the Anoka County Historical Society.)

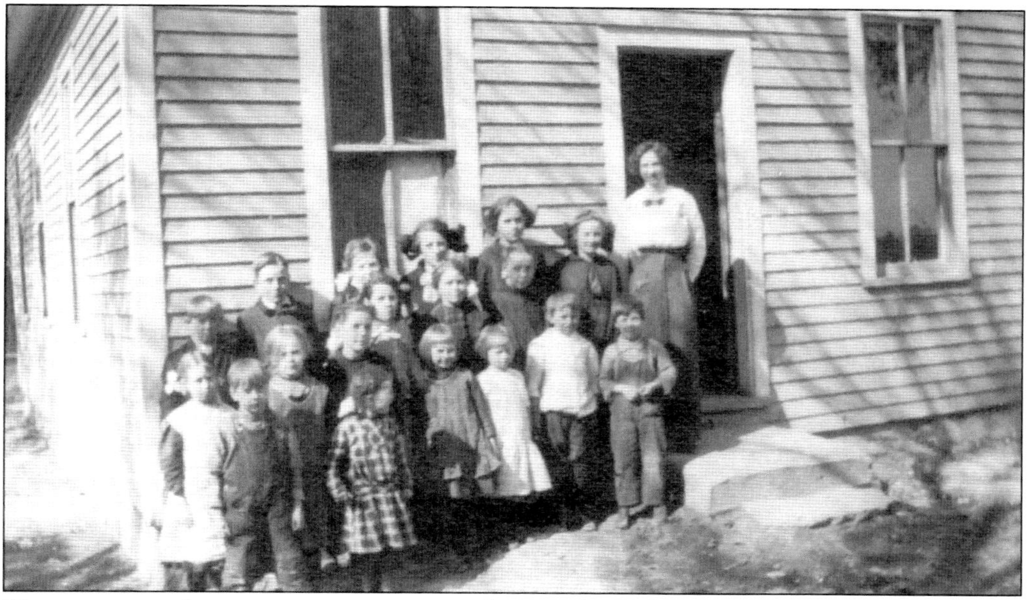

The community becomes stronger as its youths are educated. Here is a Soderville School class in 1910. (Courtesy of the Anoka County Historical Society.)

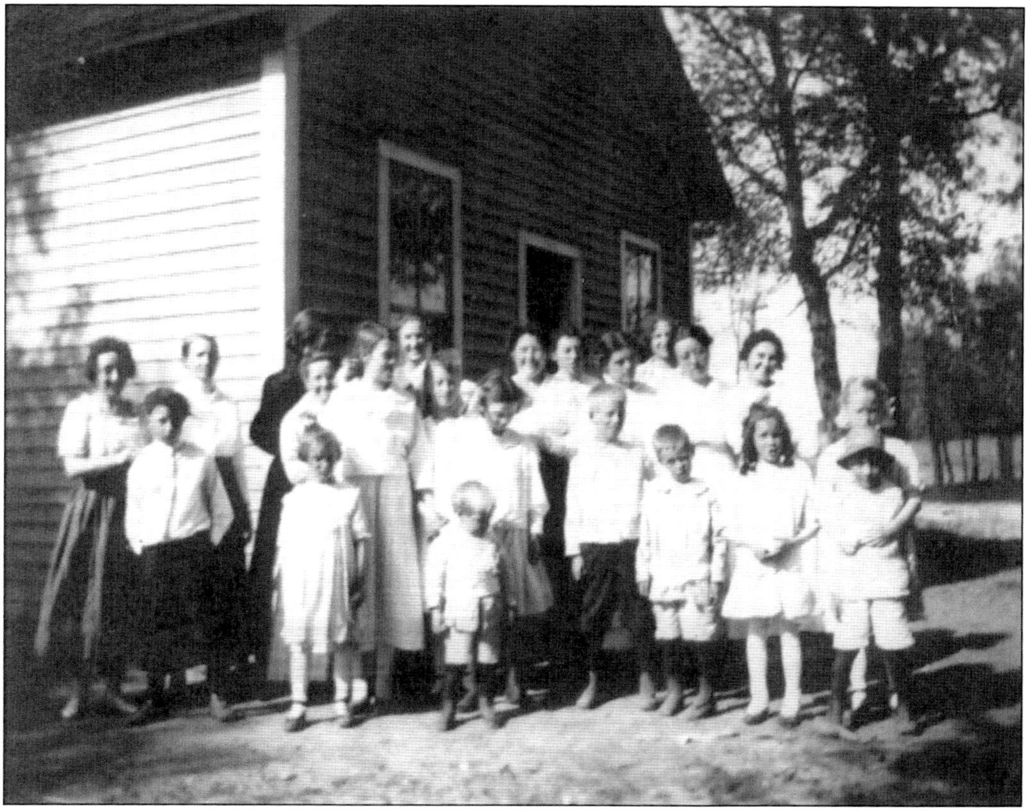

Pictured is the Soderville School class of 1918. (Courtesy of the Anoka County Historical Society.)

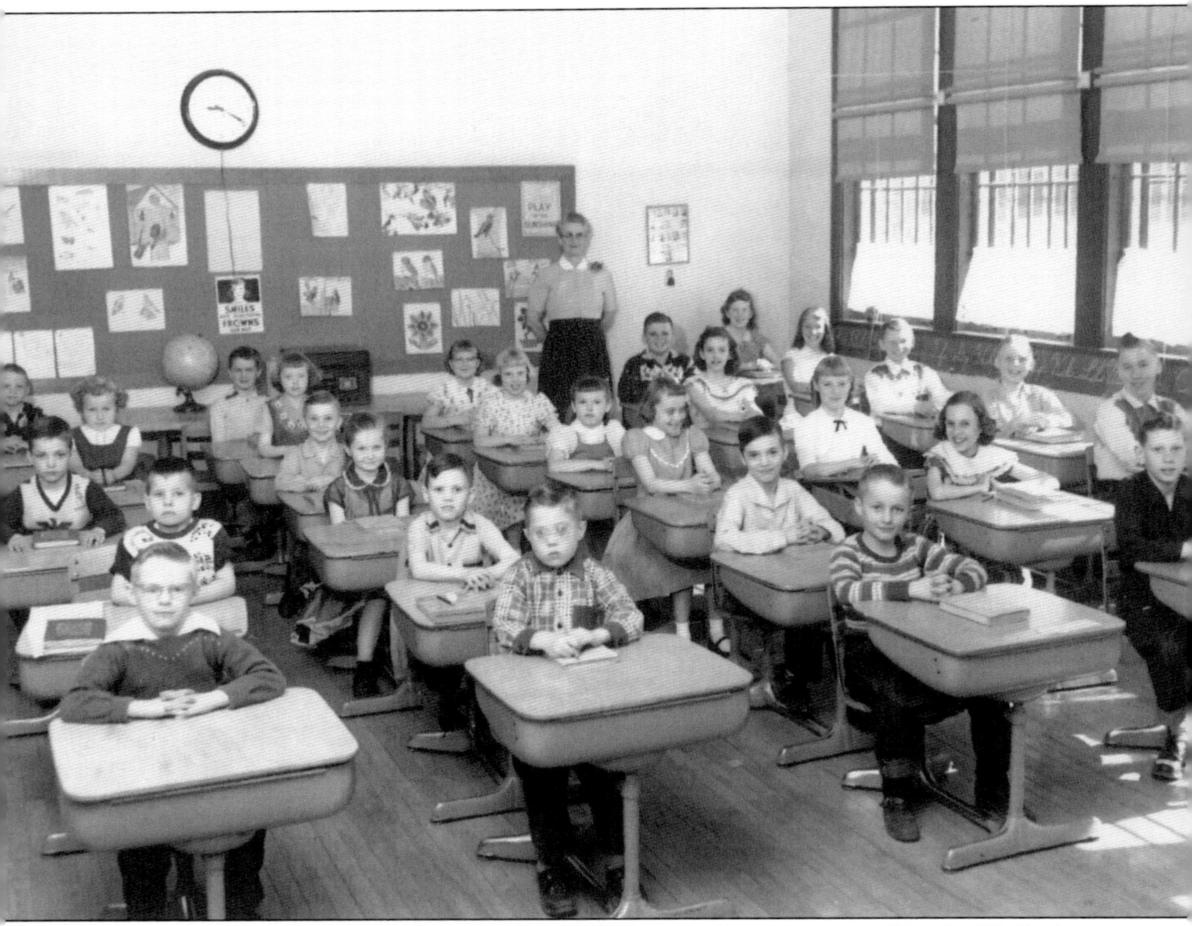

The old Soderville School was replaced in 1942 with a building constructed by the Works Progress Administration (WPA). A classroom is seen here in 1956. It had a library, and students were served hot lunches as long as every parent took their turn in providing them. Later, the school was moved and served as a storage building for many years. (Courtesy of Lorraine Soderquist.)

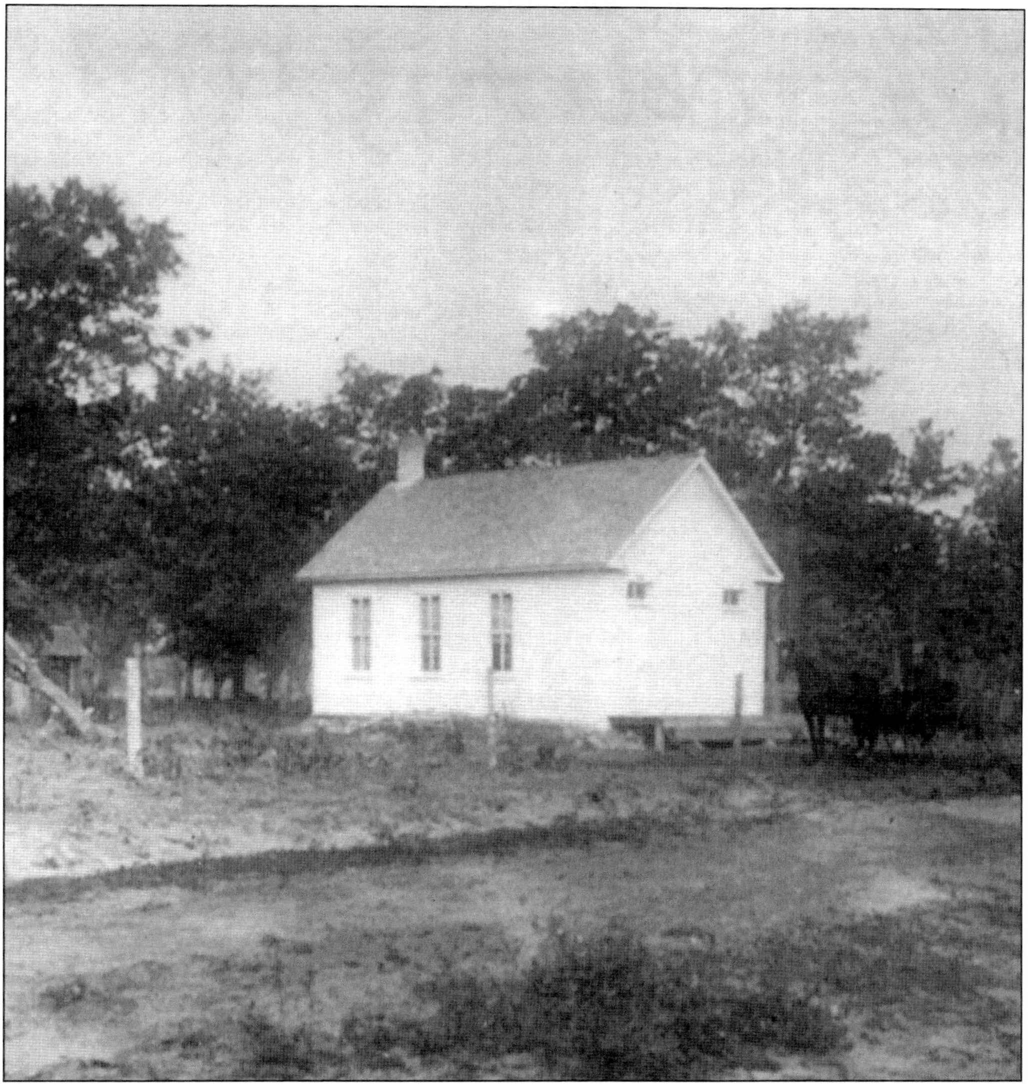

James T. Elwell built School District No. 48 in 1892, but it was decommissioned in 1914 when the Redbrick School was constructed. The original building was demolished. (Courtesy of the Minnesota Historical Society.)

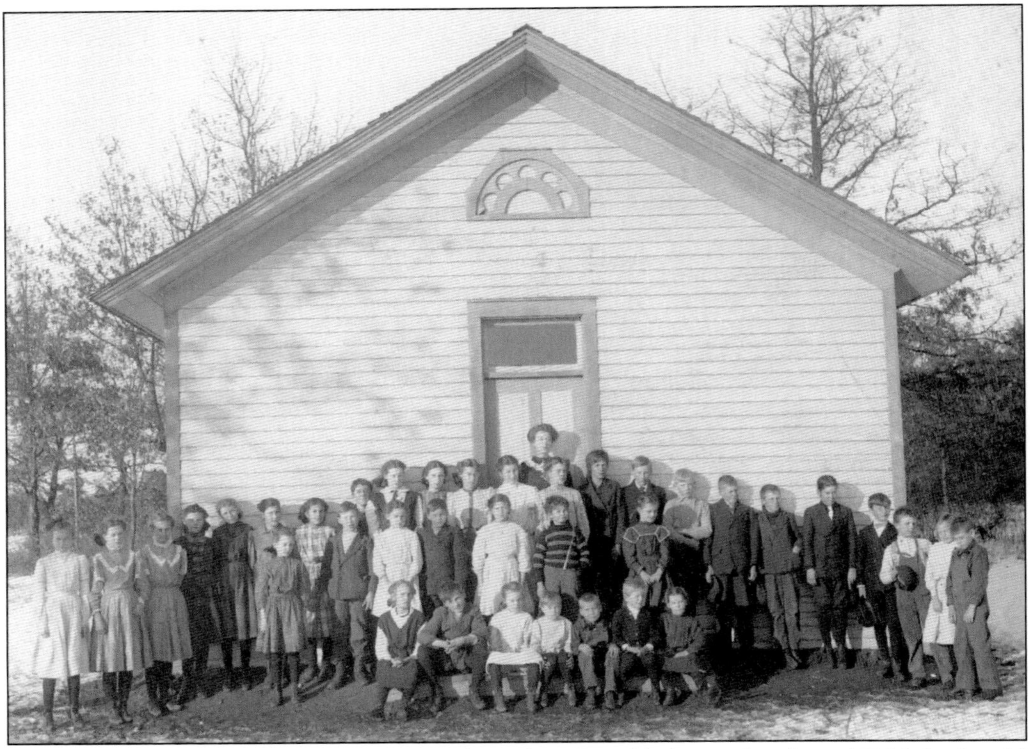

Pictured above is School District No. 48's class of 1905, and below is the class of 1906. In the old township, the location of a school depended on the neighborhood. District No. 48 served students in the south and southeast portion of the township. (Both, courtesy of Glen Cary Church.)

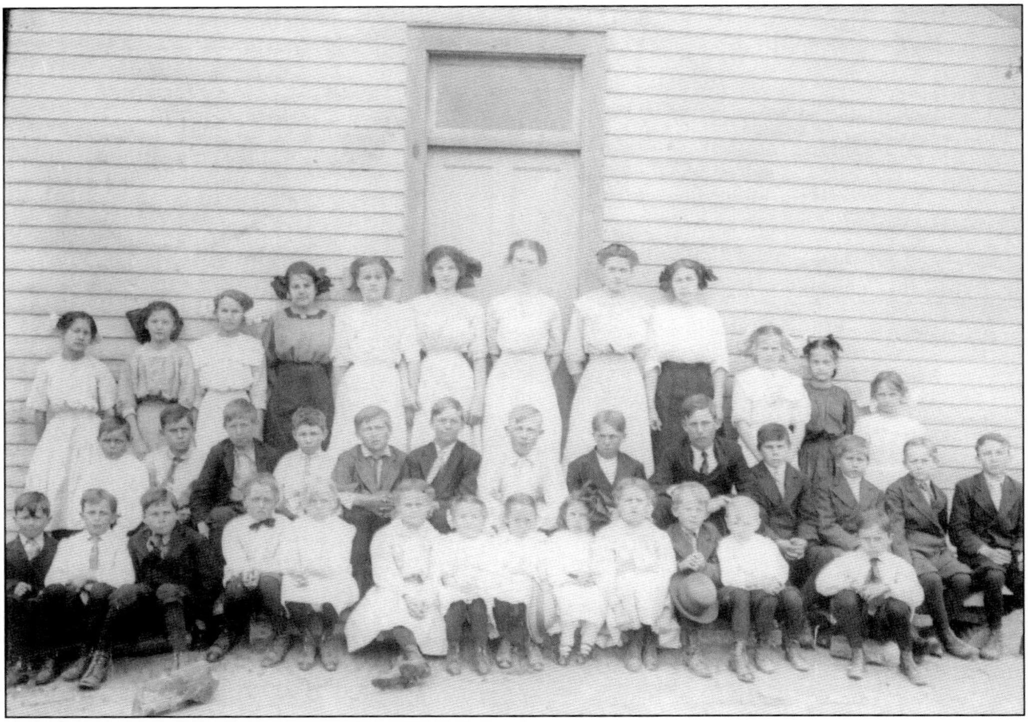

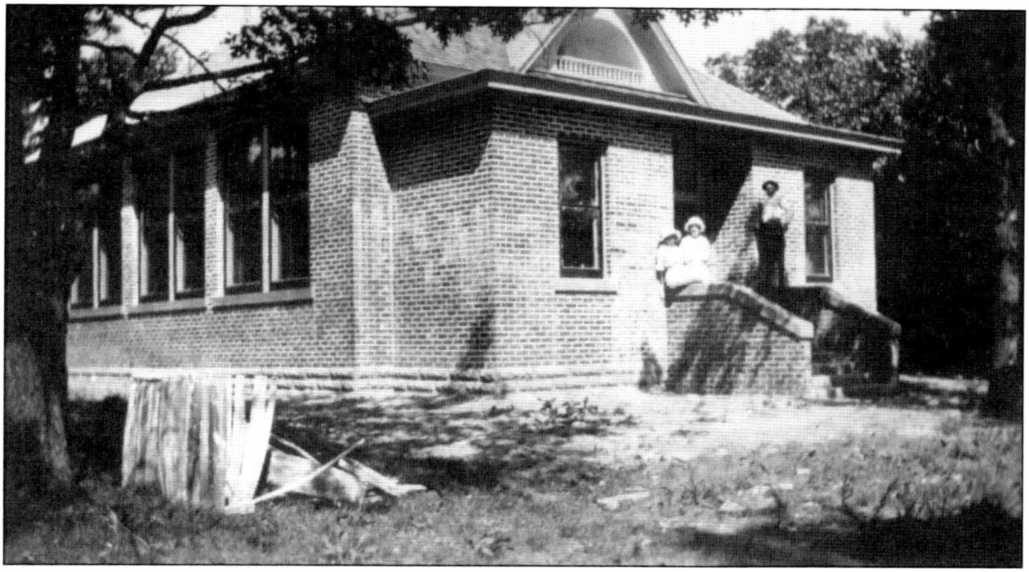

Redbrick School District No. 54 was one of the four one-room schools in Ham Lake and was located at Bunker Boulevard and Radisson Road. It served the students in the southeastern section of the township. Redbrick School was built in 1914 with bricks hauled by parents from the city of Andover. Pictured below is Redbrick School in the winter of 1914. (Both, courtesy of the Anoka County Historical Society.)

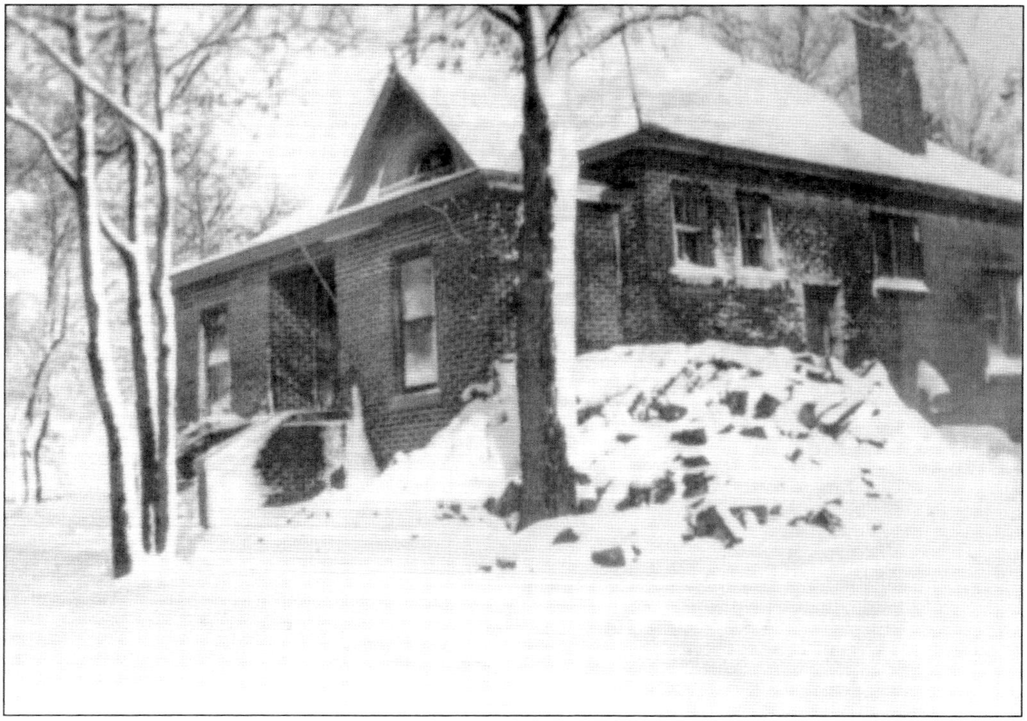

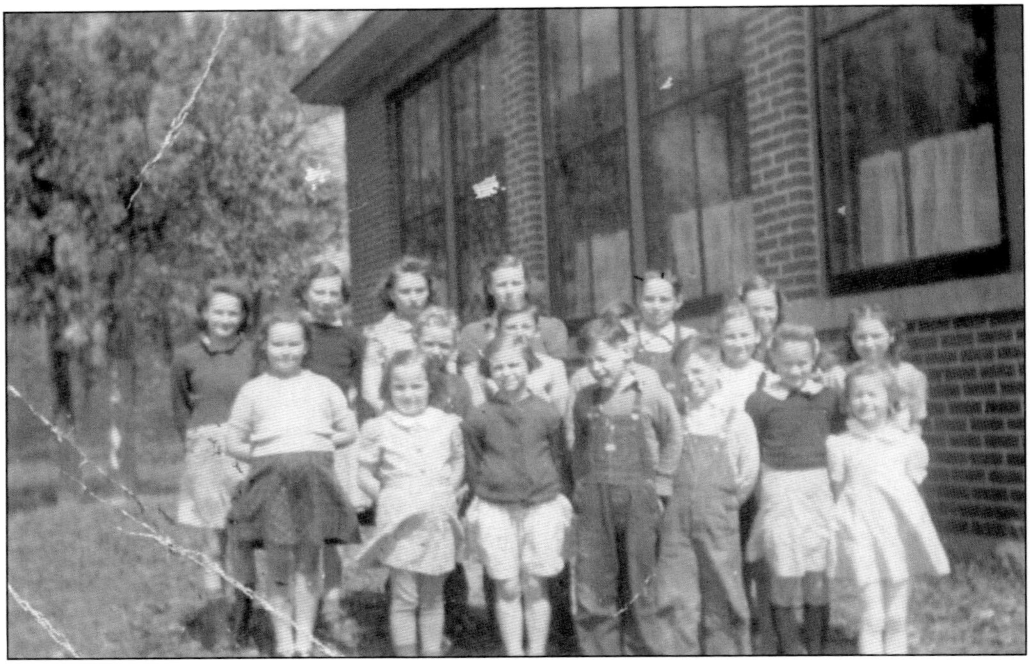

This is another Redbrick School class. Shown among the group are Margaret Moore, Oris Erickson, Elaine Christianson, Loraine Dickman, Norman Dyck, Doris Dyck, Audrea Clark, Lawrence Dirkman, Donald Moore, Dwight Hanson, Jean Herboldt, Lila Christianson, Ruby Erickson, Ann Brethold, Ronald Moore, Daryl Hamm, Ruth Moore, and Charlotte Buchholz. (Courtesy of Ronnie and Marylou Moore.)

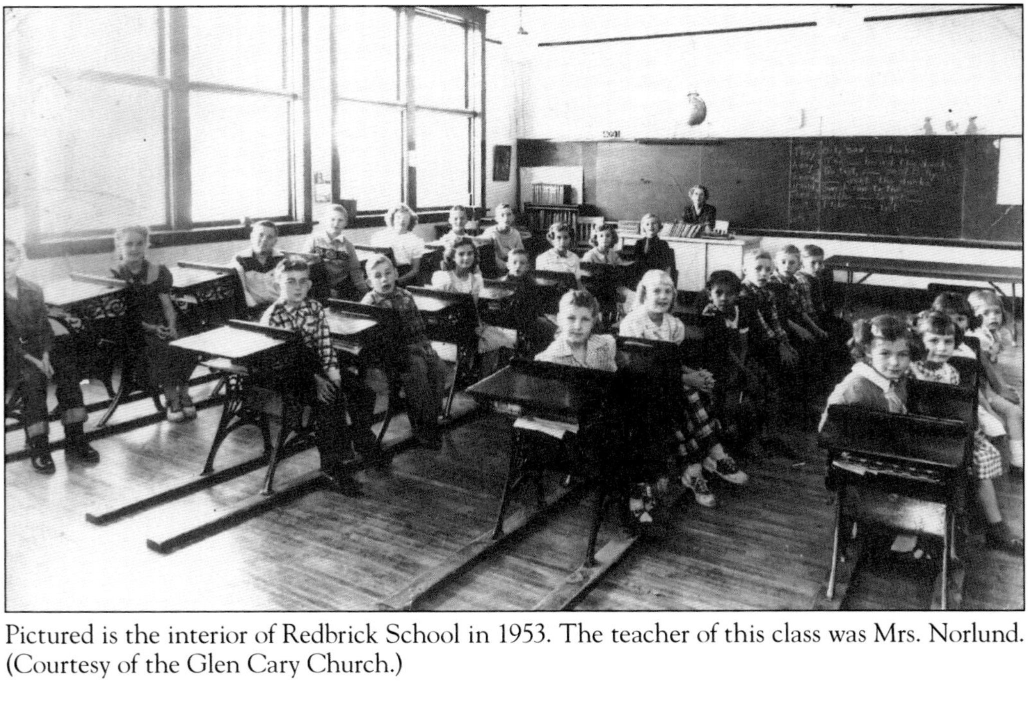

Pictured is the interior of Redbrick School in 1953. The teacher of this class was Mrs. Norlund. (Courtesy of the Glen Cary Church.)

All the schools became the center of their individual communities. Redbrick School hosted many events for the parents of students. Seen just outside of Redbrick School are, from left to right, Doris Dyck, Margaret Moore, Bonnie Robinson, and Loraine Dykman. (Courtesy of Ronnie and Marylou Moore.)

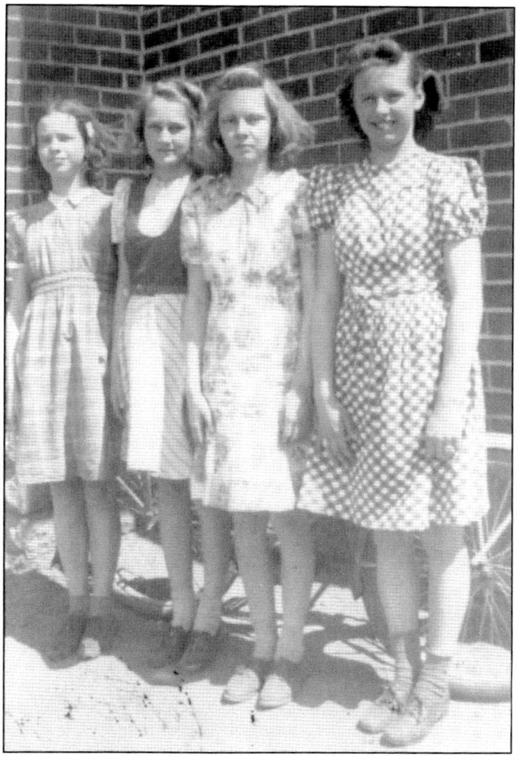

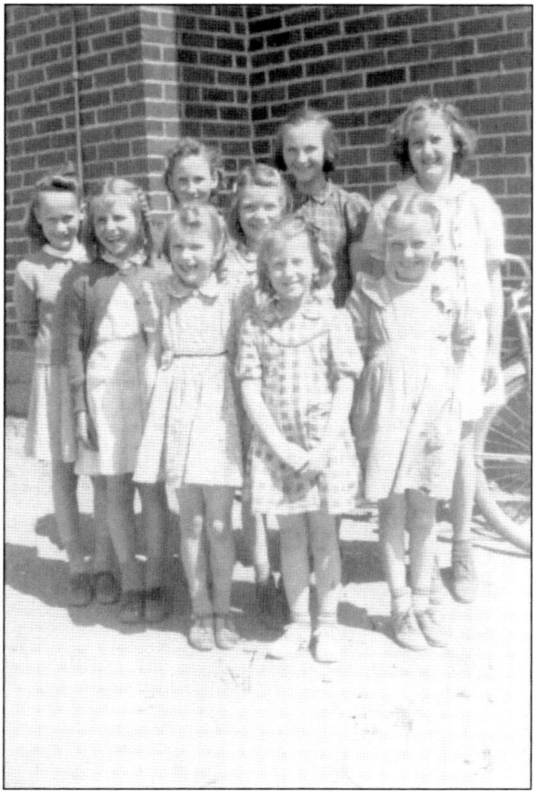

Seen in almost the same spot are, from left to right, Ruth Moore, Jean Herboldt, Wanda Robinson, unidentified, Anna Barthold, Charlotte Buchholz, unidentified, Barbara Hamm, and Ruby Erickson. (Courtesy of Ronnie and Marylou Moore.)

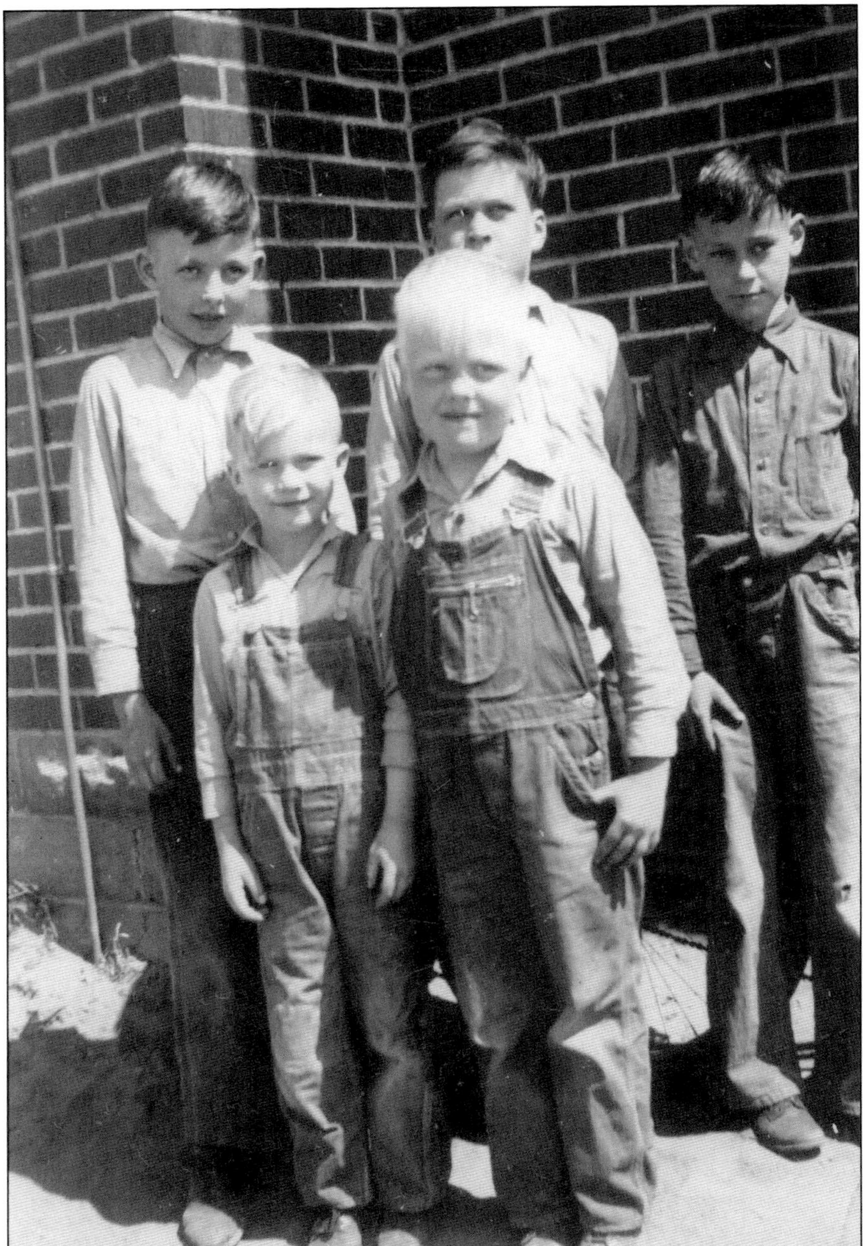

Pictured are a few male students at Redbrick School. They are, from left to right, Donald Moore, Dwight Hamm, Ron Moore, Darrell Robinson, and Bill Nelson. Some students who lived in Ham Lake went to Constance School District No. 41, built in 1890, and Andover School District No. 8, both in the neighboring city of Andover. Those students and others from Lake Netta, Glen Cary, Soderville and Redbrick all were consolidated into Anoka-Hennepin Independent School District No. 11. The one-room schoolhouses were closed and either sold or demolished. They were replaced by one large, modern elementary school that was built along Constance Boulevard, just east of Highway 65, on 14 acres of property donated by the Burton and Chester Livgard families. Its dedication was held on March 30, 1965, for the new school named McKinley Elementary. (Courtesy of Ronnie and Marylou Moore.)

Five

COMMERCE

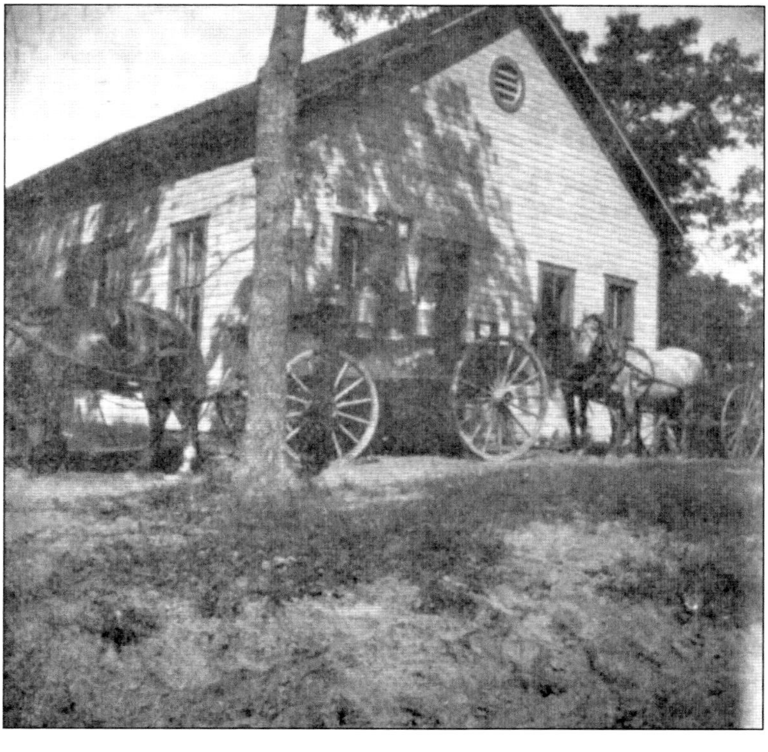

The first industries in Ham Lake were farming and lumbering, which led to the first commercial business, a creamery. Farmers built it as a cooperative in 1894. Pictured is the creamery in 1899. (Courtesy of Lorraine Soderquist.)

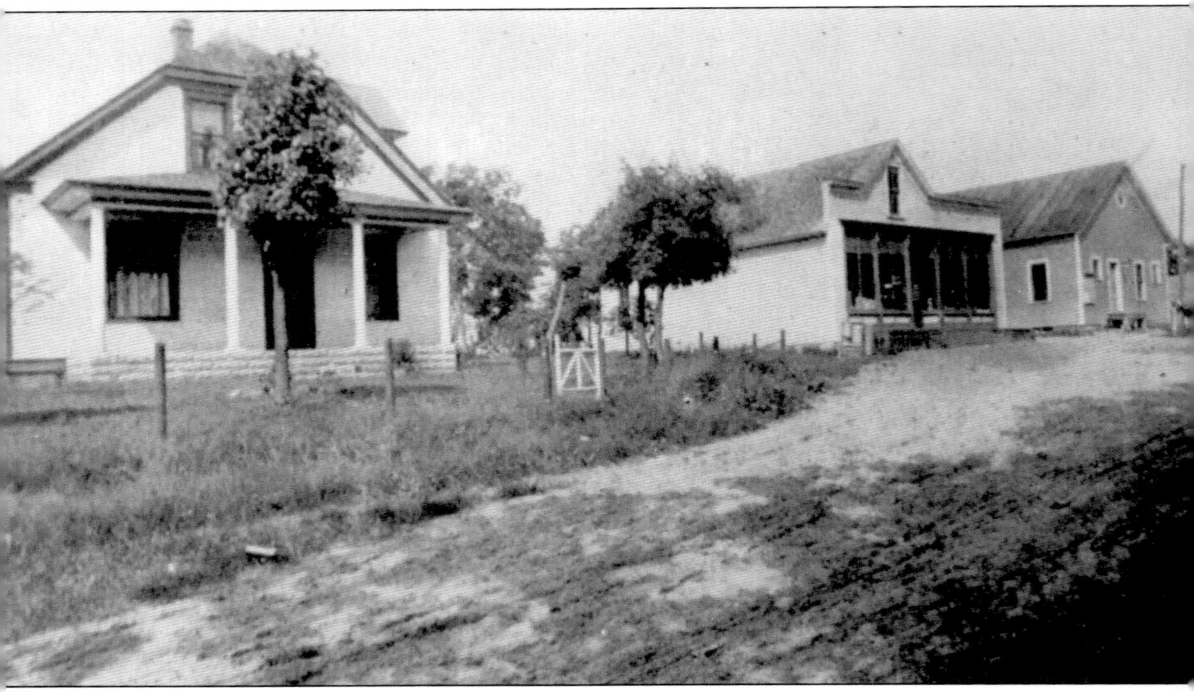

C.M. Nordquist and a Mr. Ryberg built the first store in 1900. Pictured are the residence and store of Nordquist. Ryberg sold his portion in 1902, and Nordquist ran the store until he sold it to Clarence and Harry Peterson in 1924. (Courtesy of the Anoka County Historical Society.)

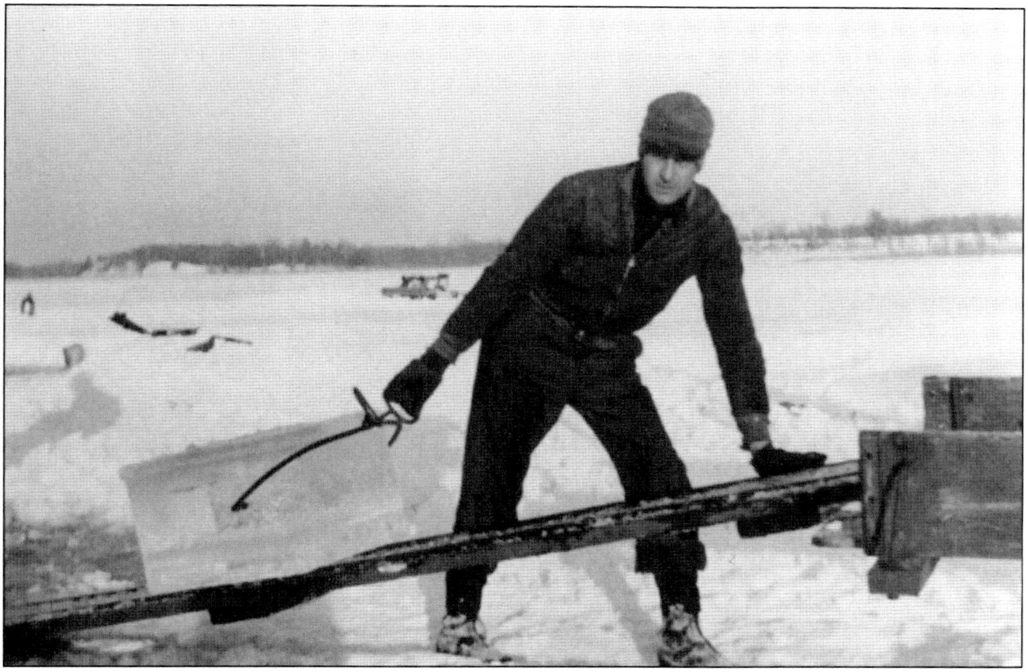

The ice business followed the creamery. Lakes often froze 20 inches thick, and ice chunks would be cut out, sawed by hand, and loaded onto horse-drawn sleds. The first ice was cut for the creamery, but soon it was a business with ice going to grocery stores and meat markets or often sold directly to local farmers. (Courtesy of the Anoka County Historical Society.)

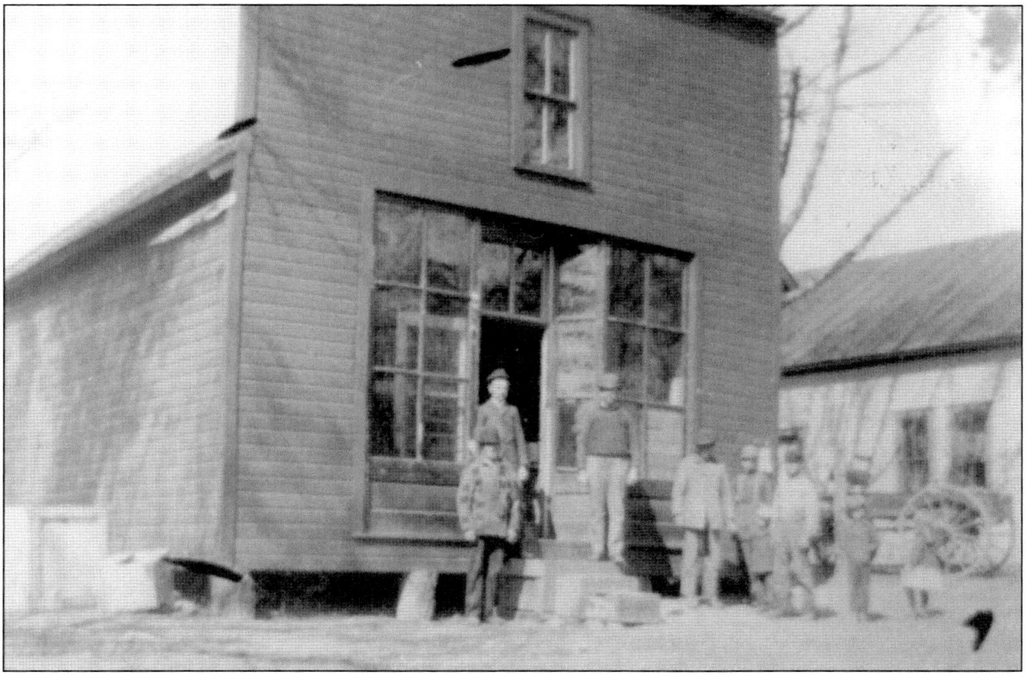

Pictured is the Lake Netta Store. The adults congregated in front of the store are, from left to right, John Moe, Charles Nordquist, J.B. Ryberg, Nelson Solem, and Alpha Nordquist Rasmussen. (Courtesy of the Anoka County Historical Society.)

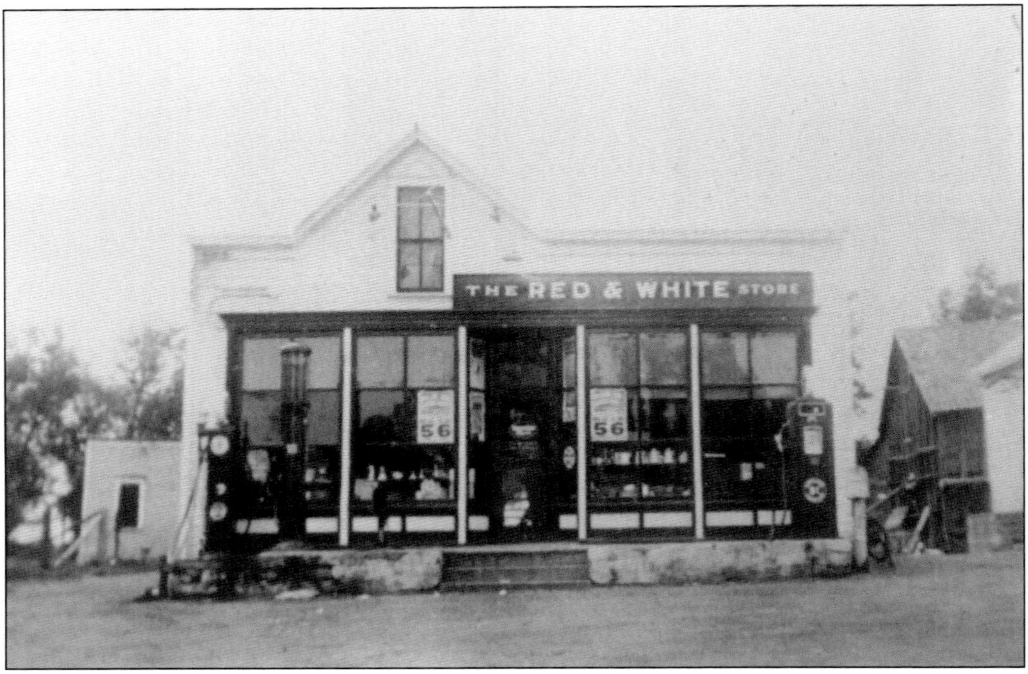

The Red and White Store at Lake Netta is seen here in 1940. The store was sold to Clifford Peterson, who then sold it to Ben Bauer. (Courtesy of the Anoka County Historical Society.)

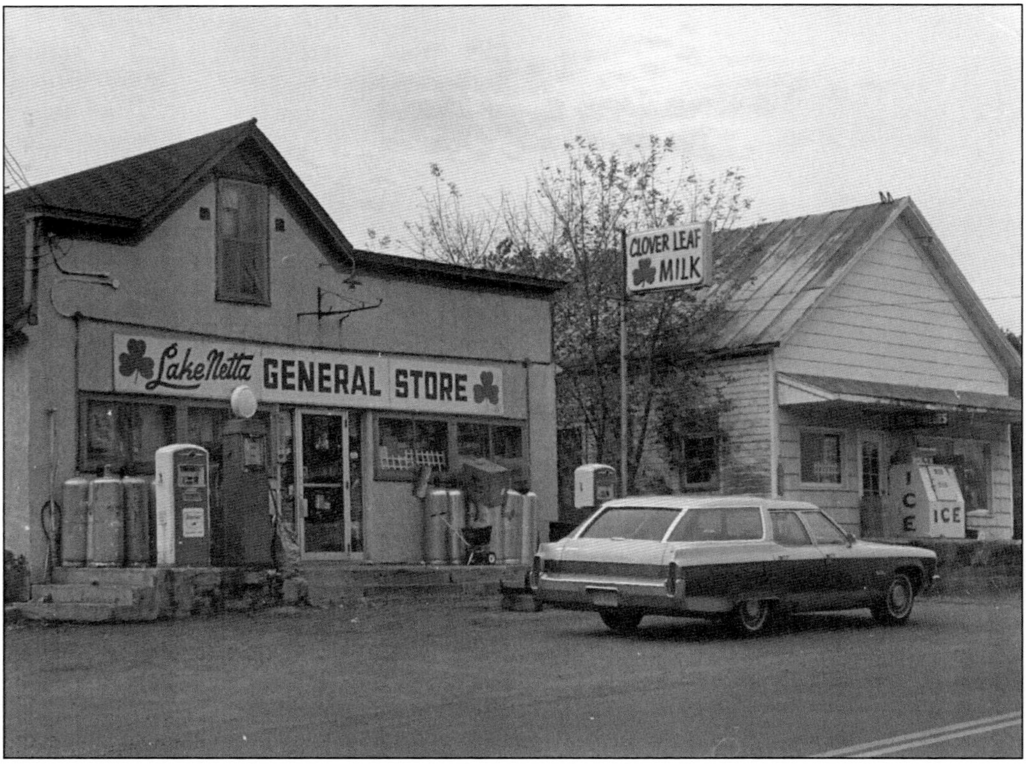

Major roads bypassed the community of Lake Netta, but the Lake Netta General Store was still operating in 1951. (Courtesy of Lisa Bauer.)

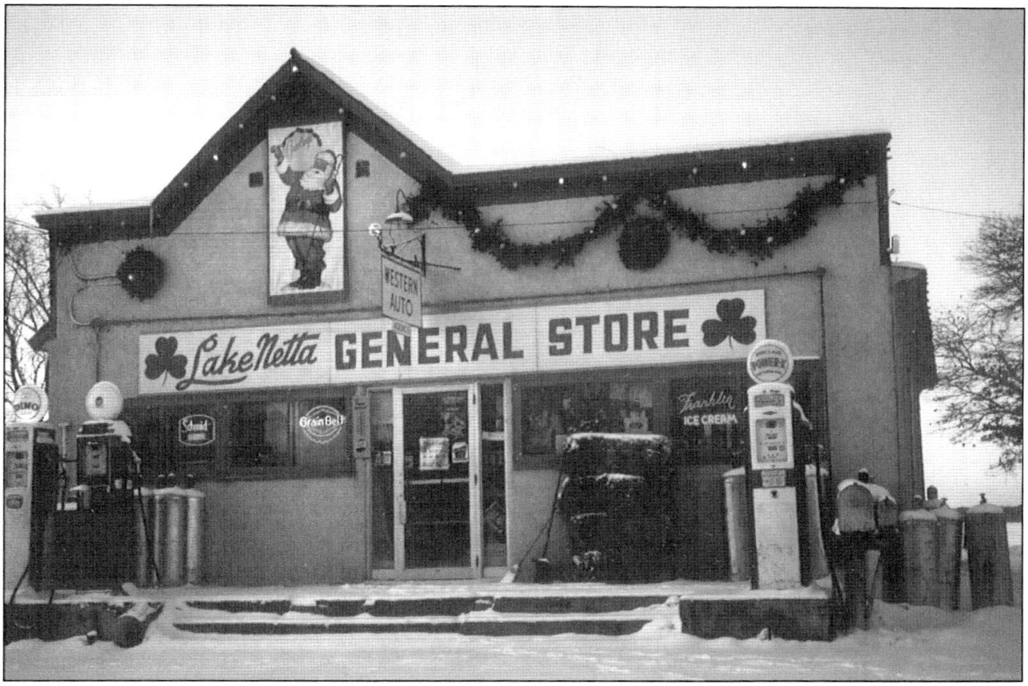

The Lake Netta General Store continued to serve people in the area until conditions forced it to close. The building now houses an antique store. (Courtesy of Lisa Bauer.)

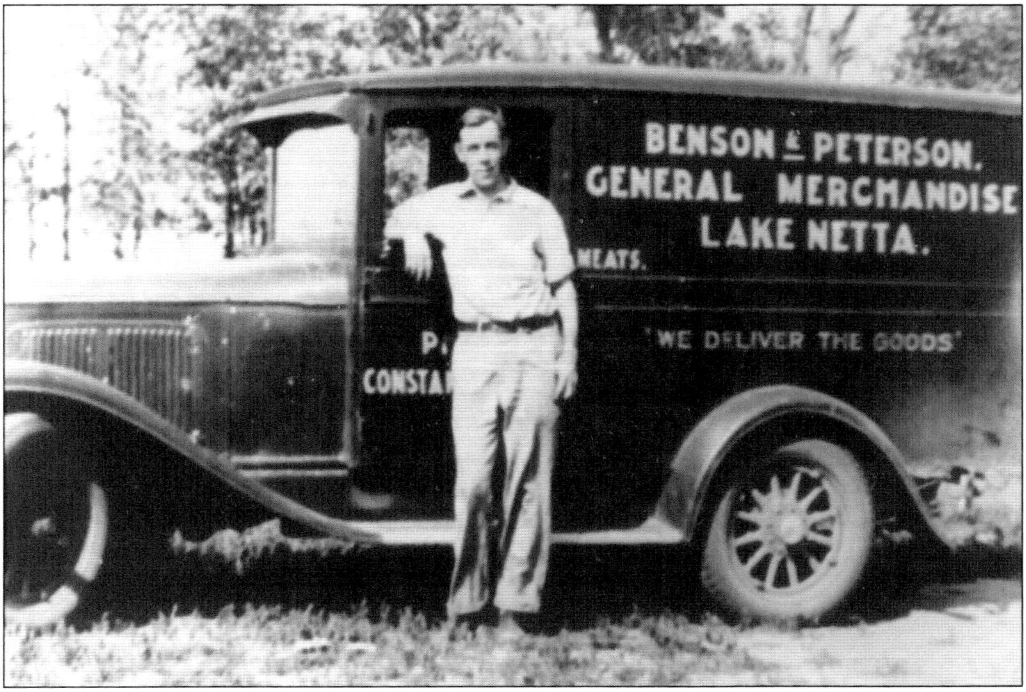

Like on the farm, commercial transportation changed with the times from horses to motorized vehicles. Pictured is Leonard Sanstrom with the Benson & Peterson delivery truck from Lake Netta. (Courtesy of the Anoka County Historical Society.)

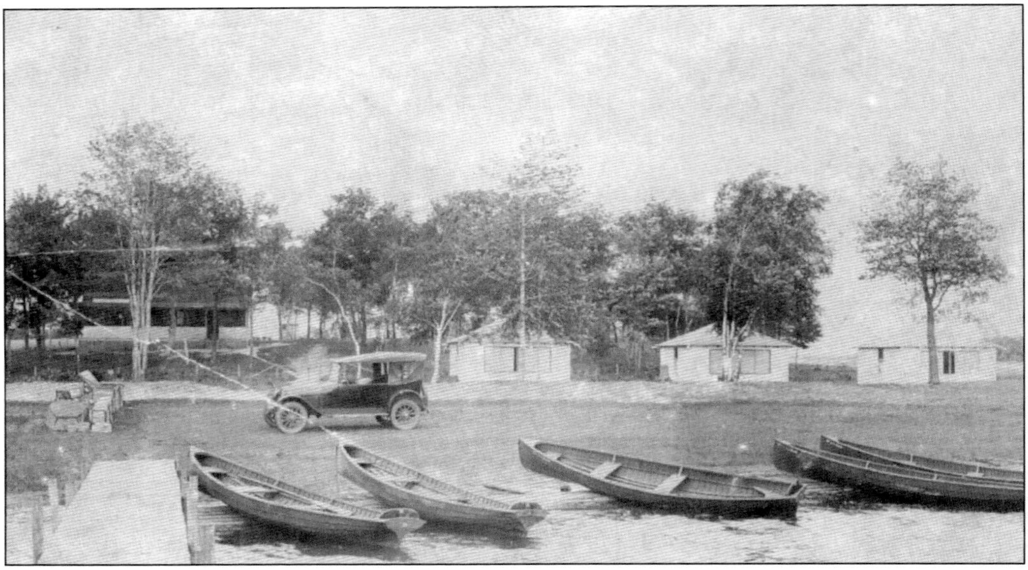

Coon Lake was "up north" for the people in the Twin Cities of Minneapolis and St. Paul in the early 1900s. Individual cabins and resorts were built where one could rent cabins and boats by the day, week, or month. This is Alex Olson's place on the Coon Lake Narrows. (Courtesy of the Anoka County Historical Society.)

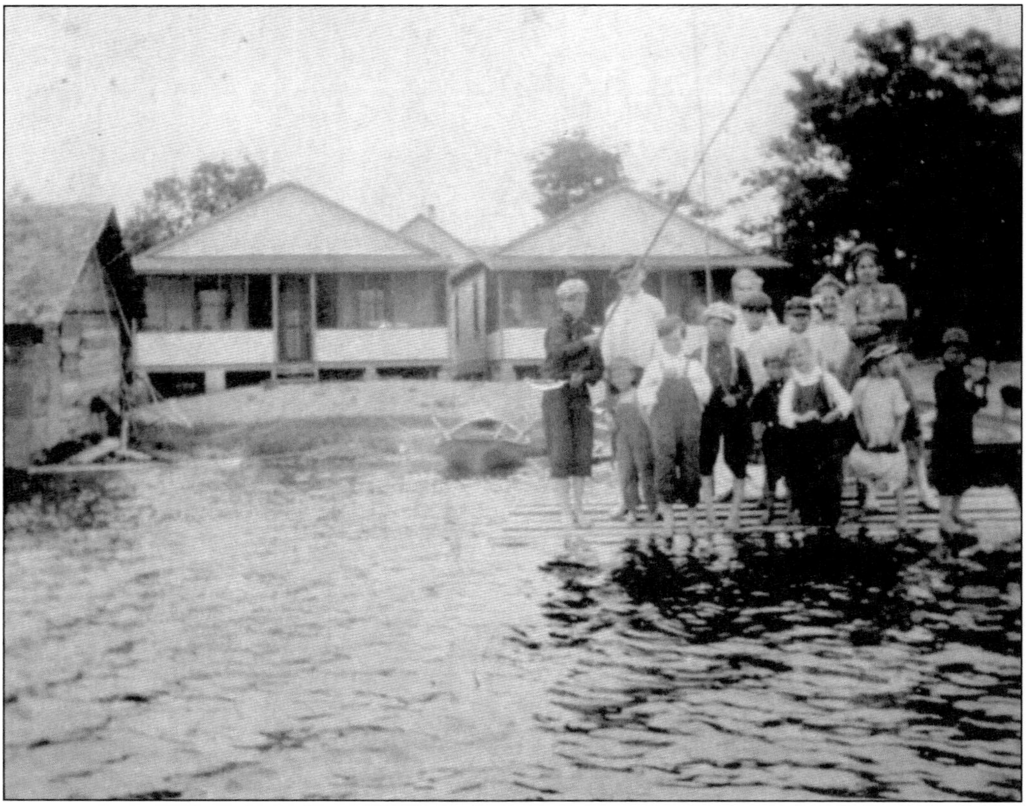

The area had a number of resorts. This is the Peter Johnson's resort on Coon Lake. (Courtesy of the Anoka County Historical Society.)

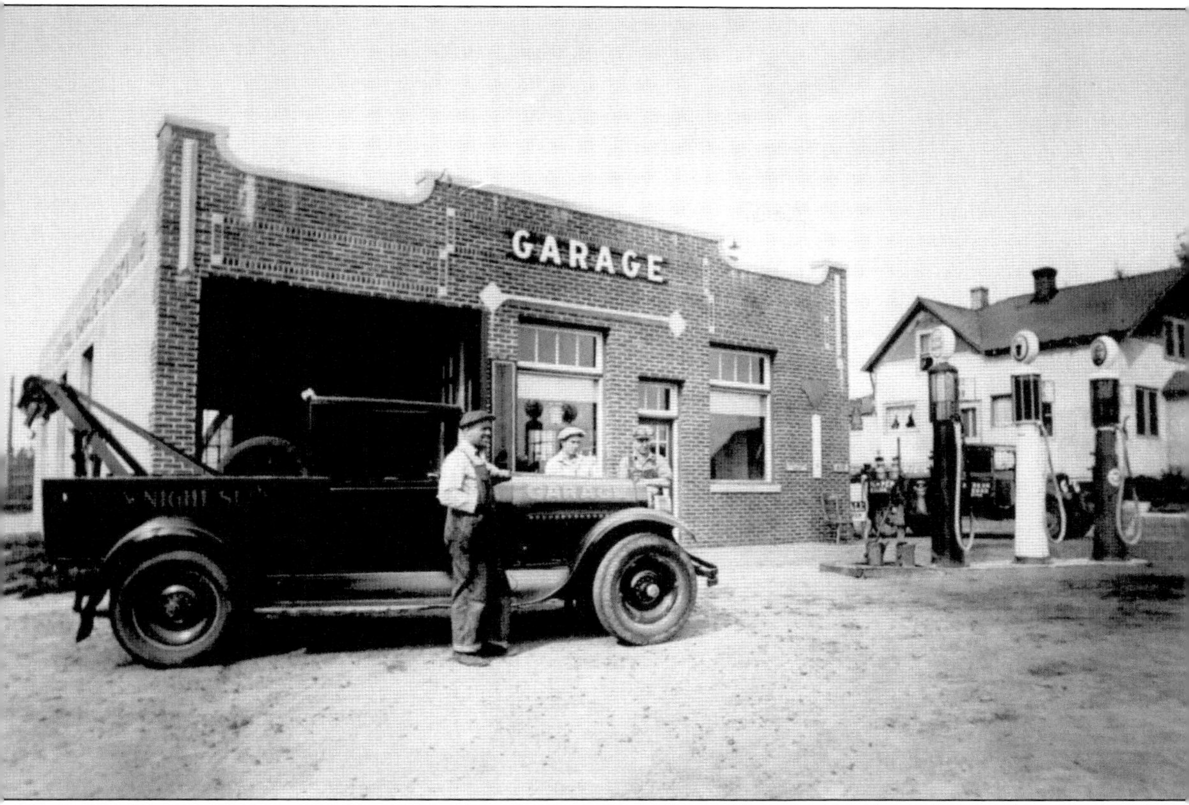

In 1921, Bill and Gunnar Soderquist began repairing farm equipment and welding for local farmers out of a shed. The shed was replaced by a garage in 1922 and was called the Tile City Garage because of the building materials, Swansen Tiles, which were made in Truman, Minnesota. Later, the name Central Garage was chosen because of the centralized location, the only garage located between Minneapolis and Cambridge. It had two gasoline pumps and a kerosene pump because people used kerosene lanterns. Central Avenue was a sand trail, then gravel, and finally the hard-surfaced Minnesota Highway 65. This photograph is from 1924, with Earl Anderson's 1915 pickup in front of the garage. (Courtesy of the Anoka County Historical Society.)

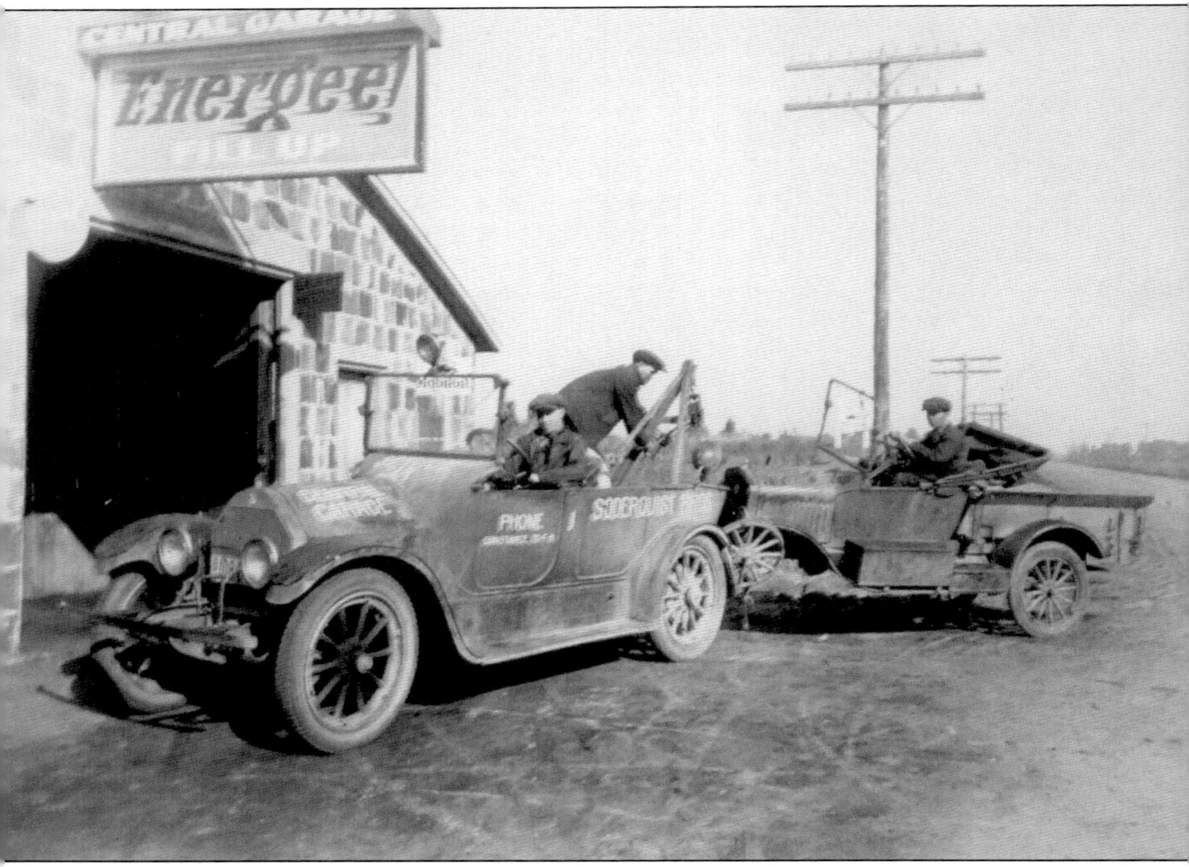

Pictured from left to right are Bill Soderquist, Elgie Ashey, and Gunnar Soderquist. In 1924, Soderquist and Ray Dahlman hand-built the first tow truck from a Cole touring car. Soderquist took first-aid training and was a first responder for the area, often driving people to the hospital in Anoka. Central Garage became the location for the volunteer fire department to get water from the water tank hung on the wall. It also became the Greyhound Bus stop. Central Garage sold tickets and put a flag on a pole to show bus drivers when there were passengers. Additionally, it became the first post office for Soderville. (Courtesy of the Anoka County Historical Society.)

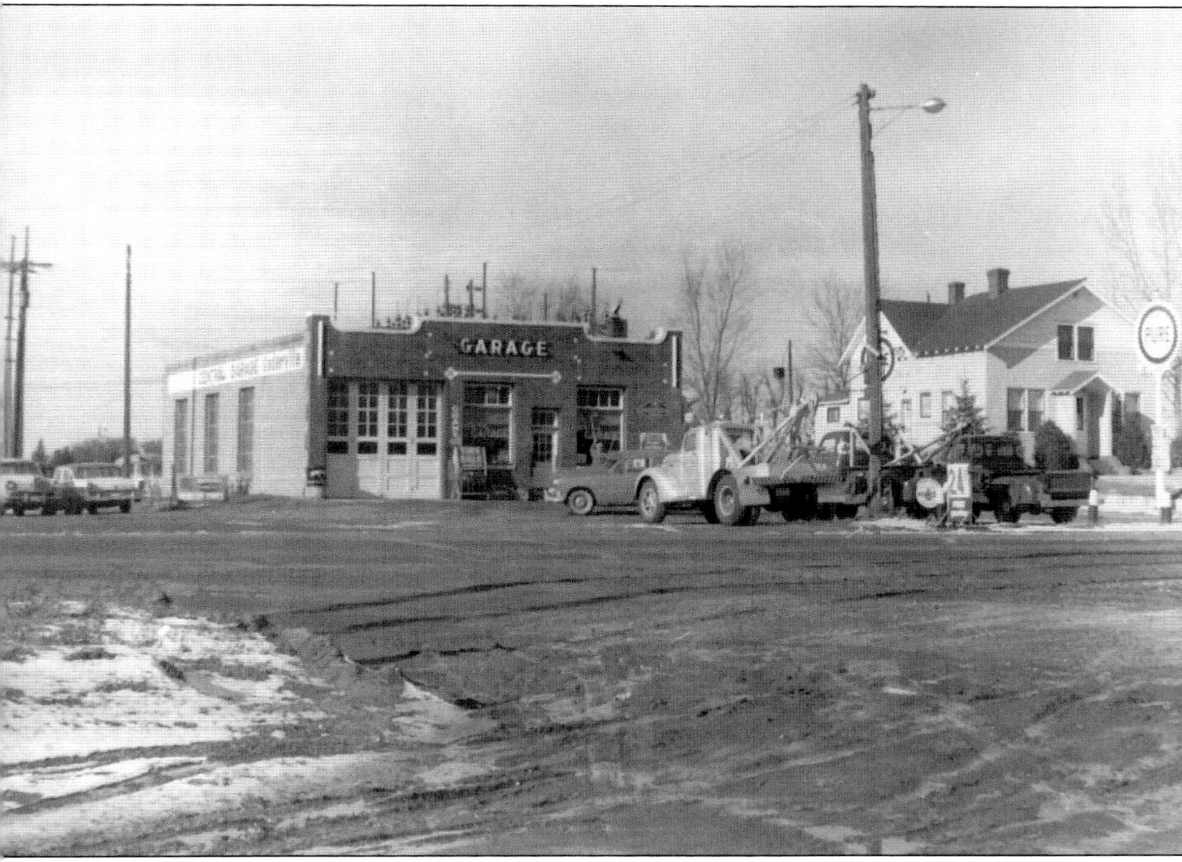

Old Soderquist Garage stood where Highway 65 crossed County Road 18, which became Crosstown Boulevard. Anoka County constructed Crosstown Boulevard to connect this growing commercial center, called Soderville, to the city of Anoka. In 1932, when Highway 65 was widened, the original garage was torn down, and a new one was built 100 yards to the west. The old tiles were reused to make an addition to the new garage. If vehicles needed extended repair, customers were often put up for the night at the Soderquist home. When Bill Soderquist died, Charles Livgard became the partner of Gunnar Soderquist. (Courtesy of Lorraine Soderquist.)

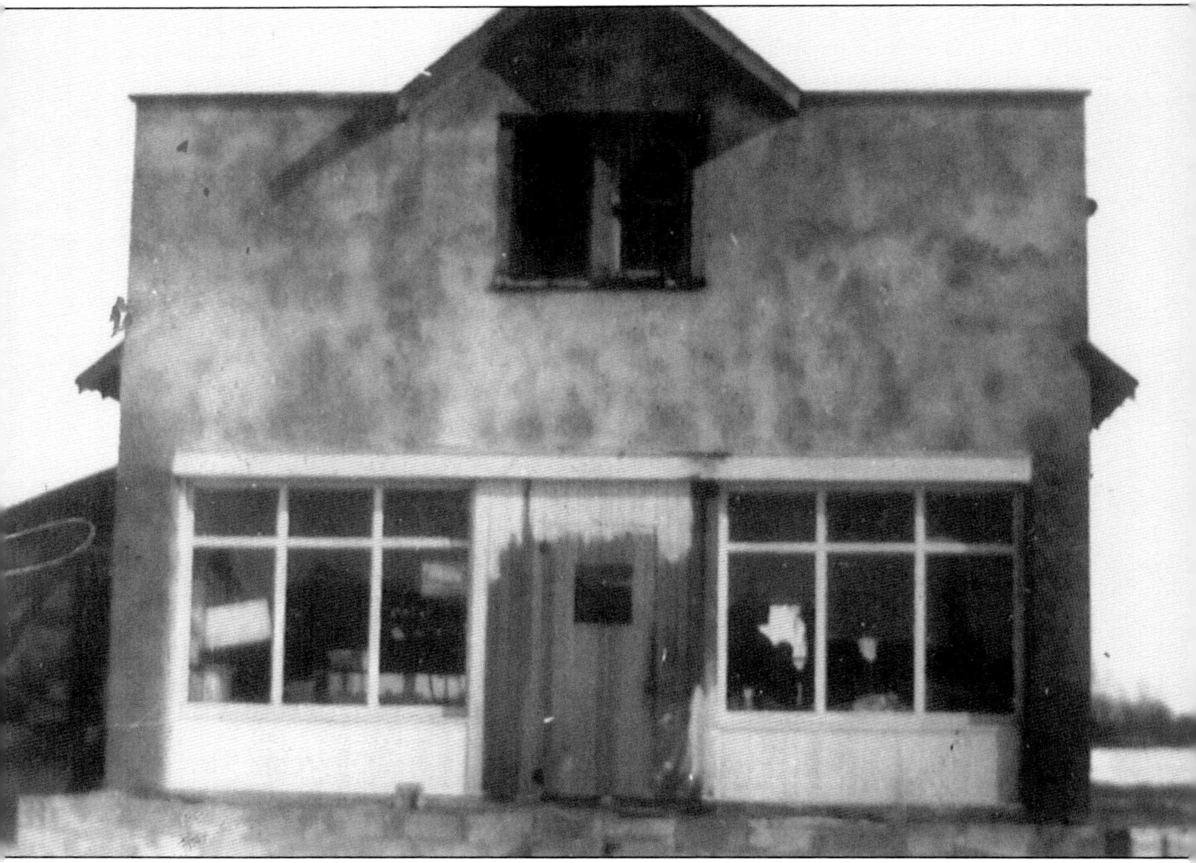

Iver Soderquist began the Soderville General Store in 1925, but the first building was taken by a cyclone before it even opened for business. The Soderquist boys built a dwelling for their parents, Johannes and Anna Soderquist. Other houses on the avenue belonged to Gunnar Soderquist, Albert Soderquist, Ray Dahlman, and Donald Stienke. (Courtesy of Lorraine Soderquist.)

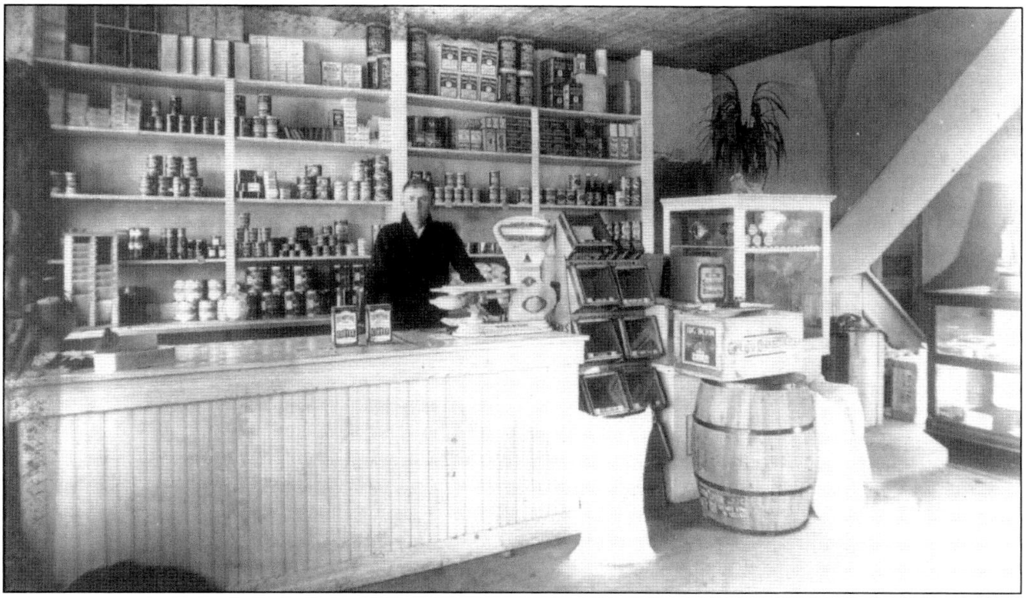

Iver Soderquist is seen in the old general store. By 1926, brothers Albert and Iver had rebuilt following the cyclone and opened for business. Patrons gave them a shopping list, and the lists were filled. Credit was given in a ledger, knowing that local farmers would pay when they could. Iver lived over the Soderville General Store until he built a home on the west side of Highway 65. (Courtesy of Lorraine Soderquist.)

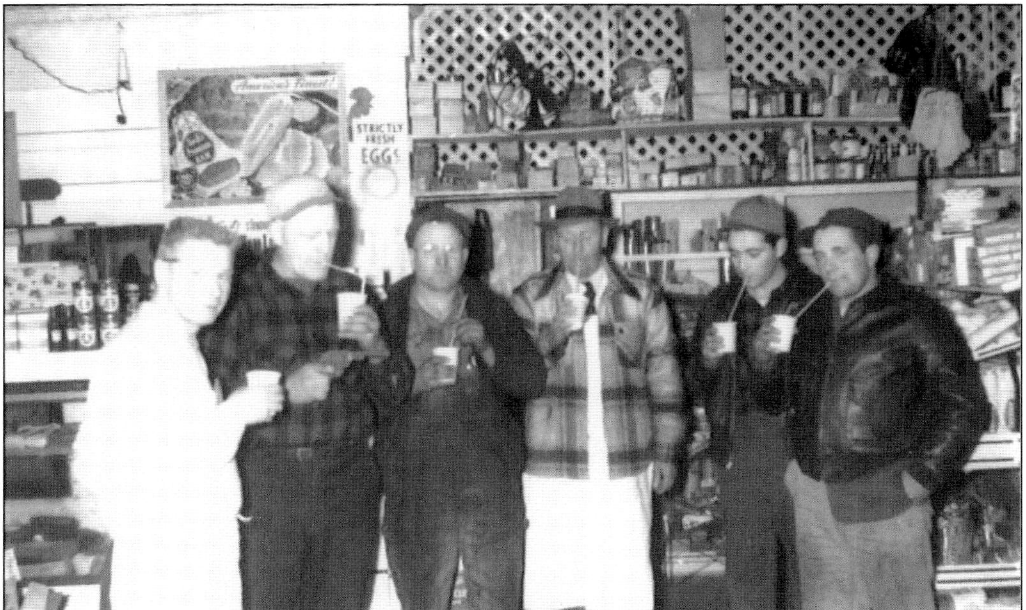

At the old Soderquist General Store are, from left to right Virgil Soderquist, Charlie Livgard, Ray Dahlman, Iver Soderquist, Dan Waldoch, and Bud Sauter. The store carried a large line of groceries and livestock feed. They purchased and/or bartered for milk, cream, eggs, meat, fresh vegetables, and fruit from local farmers. They soon added farm machinery, appliances, dry goods, and hardware. Ice was harvested from local lakes to keep the perishables fresh. (Courtesy of the Anoka County Historical Society.)

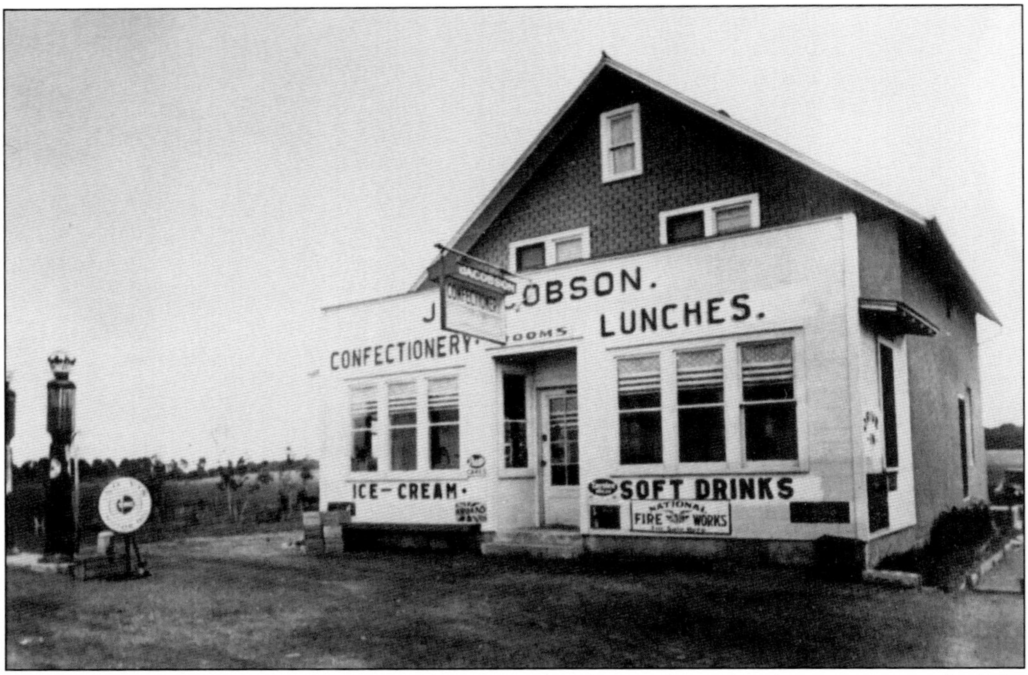

There were other businesses in Soderville. Pictured is the Jacobson Confectionery store, built by Julius Jacobson. (Courtesy of the Anoka County Historical Society.)

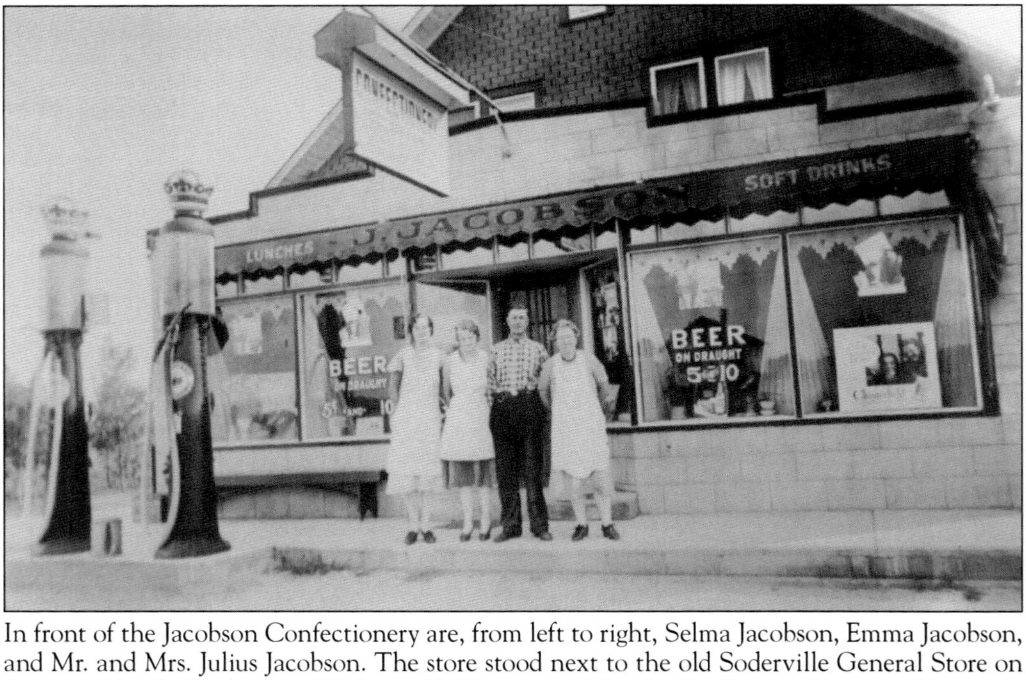

In front of the Jacobson Confectionery are, from left to right, Selma Jacobson, Emma Jacobson, and Mr. and Mrs. Julius Jacobson. The store stood next to the old Soderville General Store on the east side of what became Highway 65. (Courtesy of the Anoka County Historical Society.)

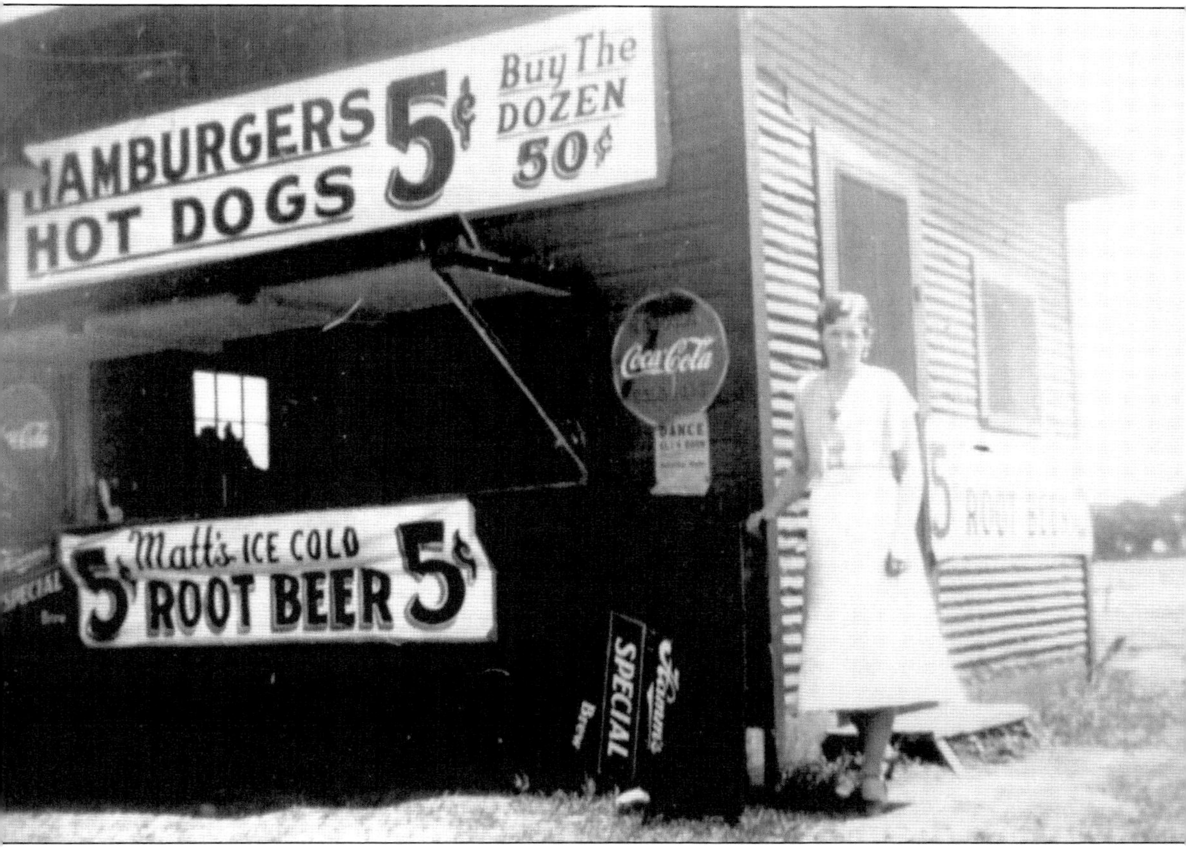

Before there was A&W, Ham Lake had a root beer and hamburger stand, owned by Mr. Matthews of Anoka. Margaret Soderquist, daughter of Bill and Minnie Soderquist, is seen at the root beer stand in 1932. Note that hamburgers were 50¢ a dozen. Ado Olson built a tavern; it eventually became the Wiggle Inn and then the Veterans of Foreign Wars (VFW) club of Ham Lake. (Courtesy of the Anoka County Historical Society.)

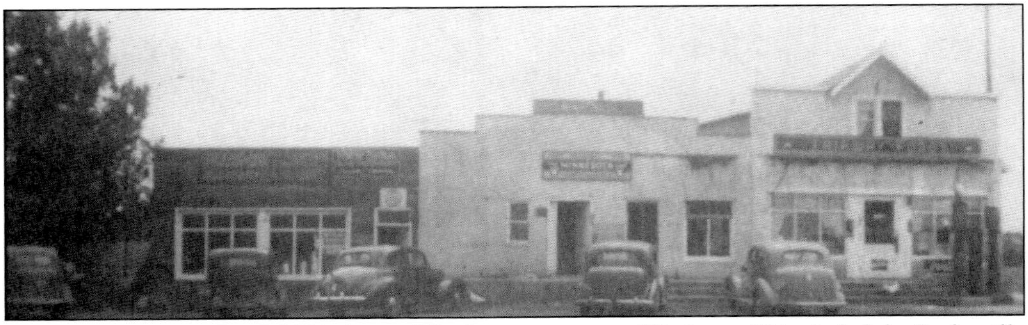

Stores on the east side of old Highway 65 before expansion of Highway 65 included the Soderville Café, Albert Soderquist home, barbershop, and Soderville General Store. People remember the outdoor movies that were shown on the wall of the café. (Courtesy of Lorraine Soderquist.)

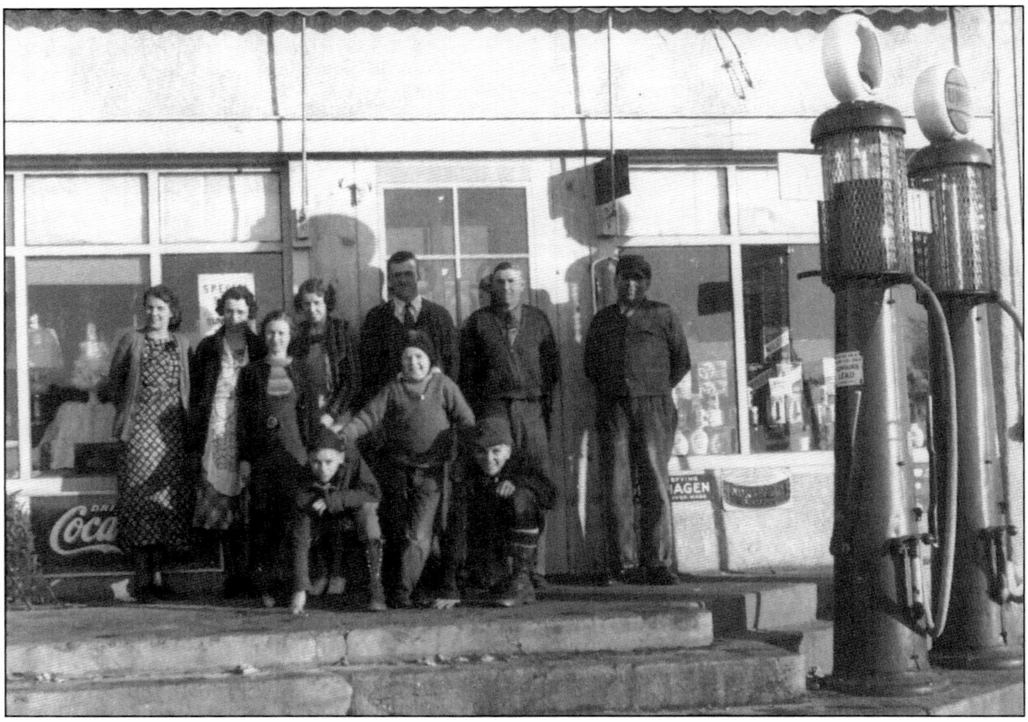

The Soderville General Store was the commercial center for much of Ham Lake. It often carried barrels of lutefisk and locally made potato sausage to meet the needs of the Scandinavian community. The potato sausage is still sold in major markets. (Courtesy of the Glen Cary Church.)

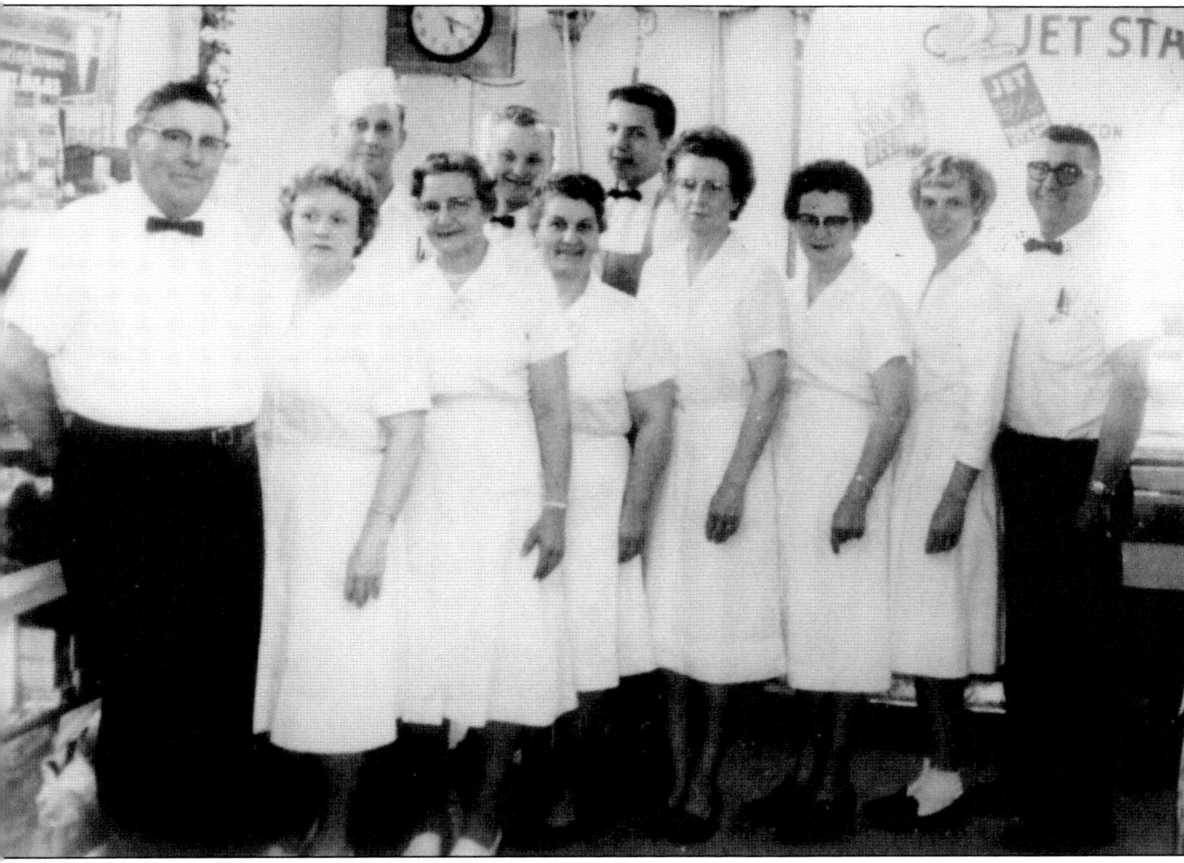

These are employees of Soderquist Super Fair grocery store, which was relocated on the west side of Highway 65 in 1962. Included in the image are Albert Soderquist, Viola Fiddyment, Florence Ekvall, Vic Landborg, Margaret Livgard, Ada Carlson, and Lorraine and Don Soderquist. (Courtesy of the Anoka County Historical Society.)

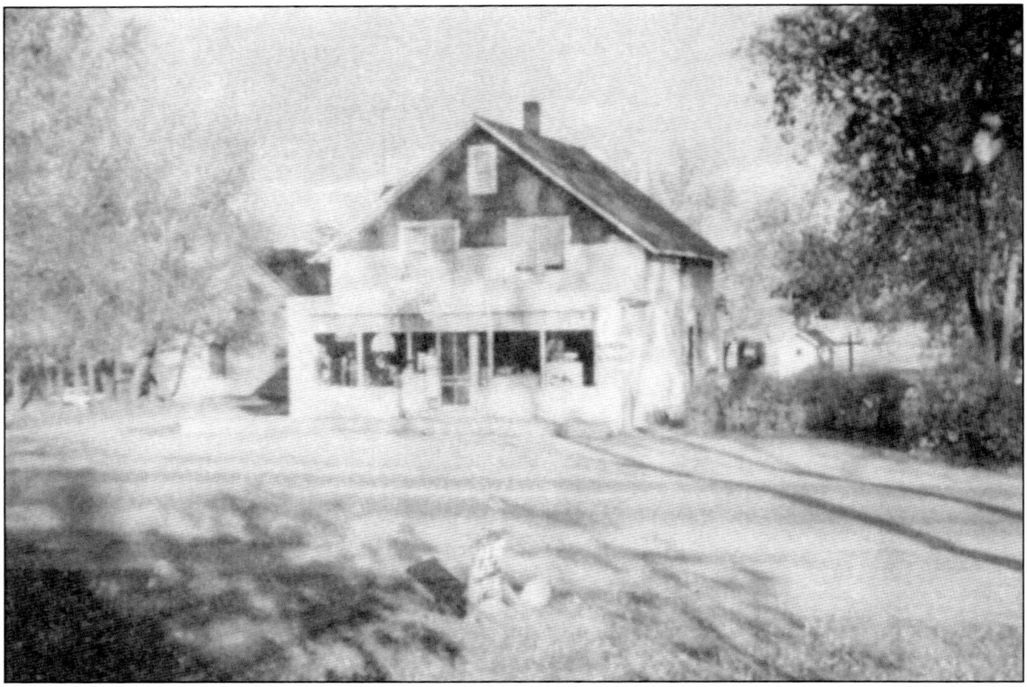

The Soderville Café for many years was the only eating establishment between the Twin Cities of Minneapolis–St. Paul and Cambridge. It also helped make Soderville a major commercial center. (Courtesy of the Anoka County Historical Society.)

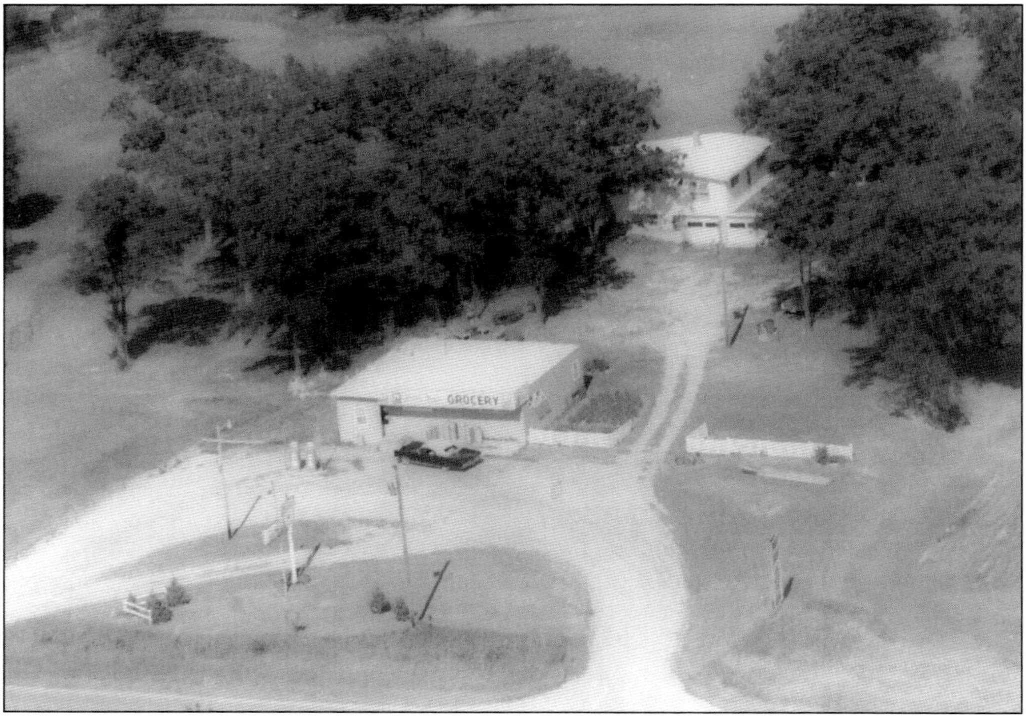

There were other businesses that served specific areas of the township. On Lexington Avenue, there was Matheson's Store; it is pictured here in 1967. (Courtesy of Betty Moe Sannerud.)

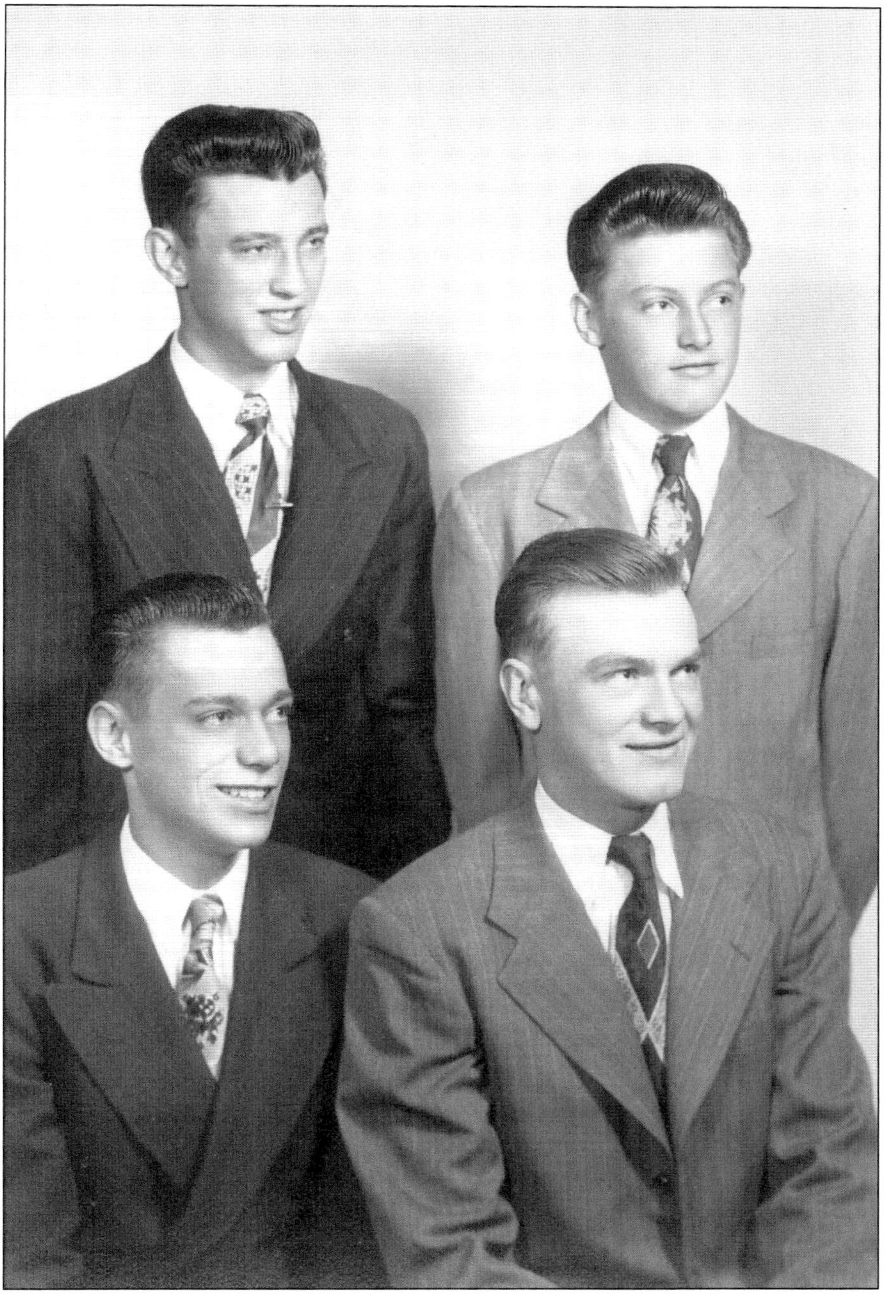

Arriving in Anoka County in 1948, the Braastad brothers established themselves in Ham Lake in the 1950s. They shared an entrepreneurial spirit. Kenny (top right) was a barber for many years until in 1983, when he started Braastad Nursery on the corner of 153rd Avenue and Highway 65. He also served on the city council from the establishment of the city in 1974 until his death in 2001. Ronald (top left) began the Braastad Plumbing and Heating Business, and when the Soderquists moved their store back to the east side of Highway 65, they purchased the buildings and established Soderville Hardware. Harold (bottom right) began Braastad Electric, which is still run by the family. Howard (bottom left) ran a gasoline station on the corner of 149th Avenue and Highway 65. (Courtesy of Janette Brastaad.)

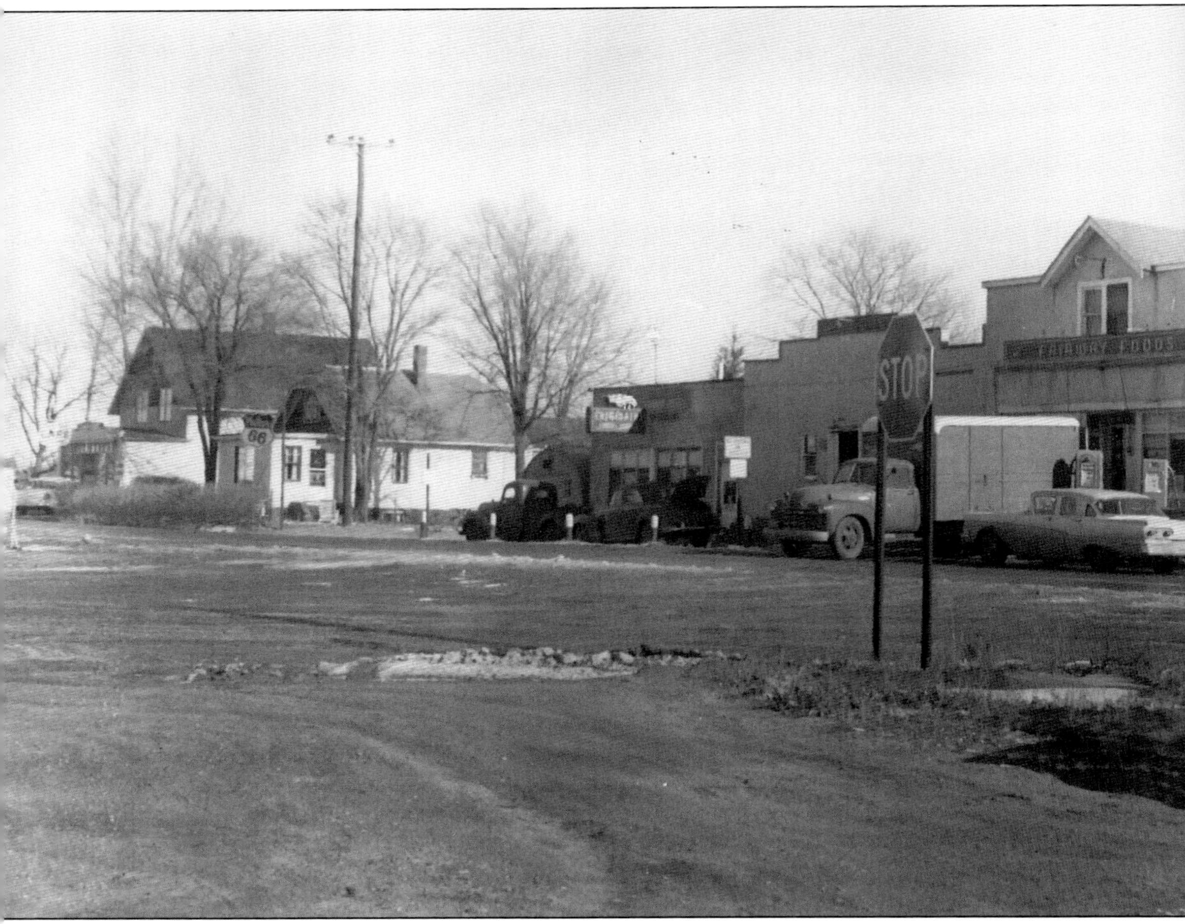

In 1957, plans were made for the much-needed expansion of Highway 65 to handle the amount of traffic, and it was promoted to help businesses along the highway; however, there were ramifications. The highway had to be moved west of the Glen Cary Cemetery because there was not room to widen it in its original location. More importantly, as it came through Soderville, the expansion took out the whole east side of the growing downtown. This photograph was taken looking north at the intersection of Highway 65 and Crosstown Boulevard before the highway expansion. (Courtesy of Lorraine Soderquist.)

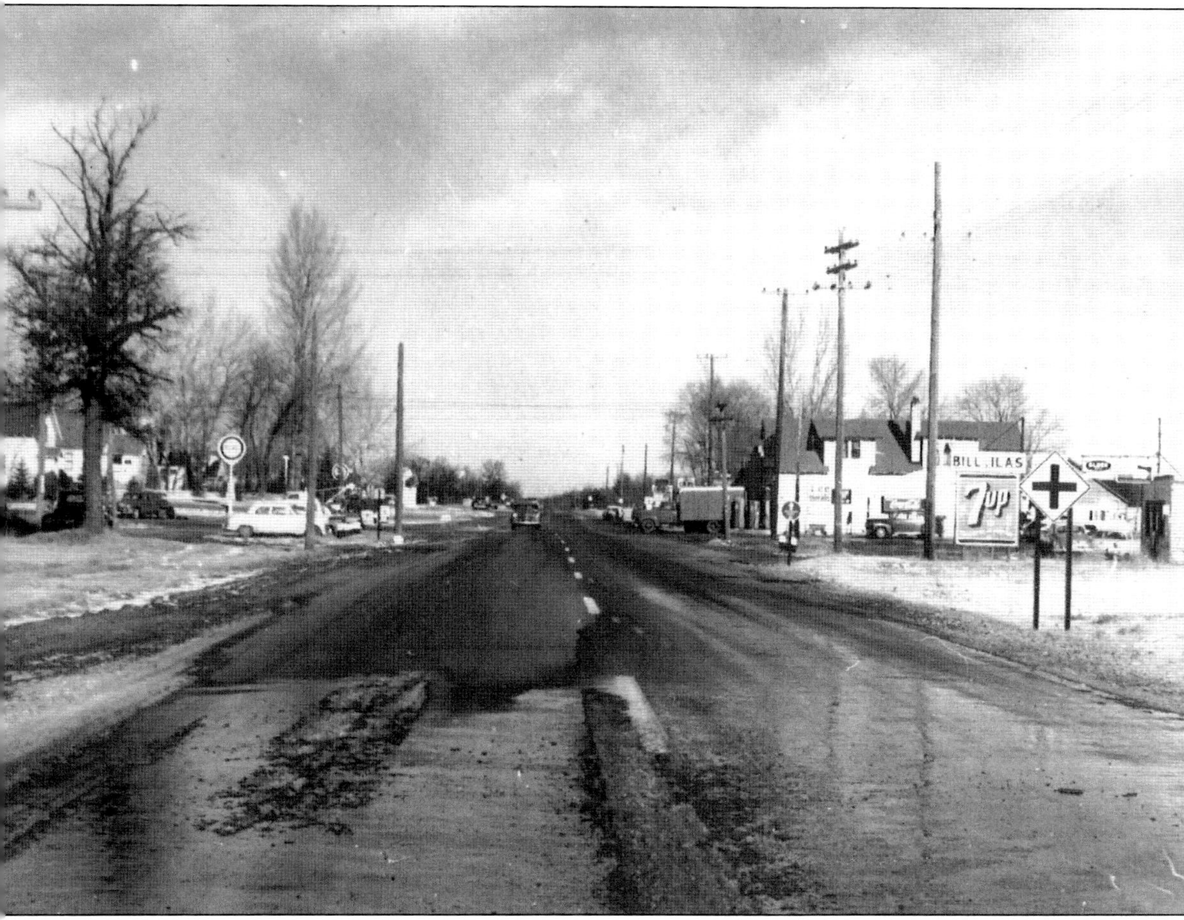

Soderville was beginning to look like a real downtown in a small town in 1958. The highway expansion was necessary for traffic and commerce, but it did take up the whole east side of what was becoming Soderville. (Courtesy of Lorraine Soderquist.)

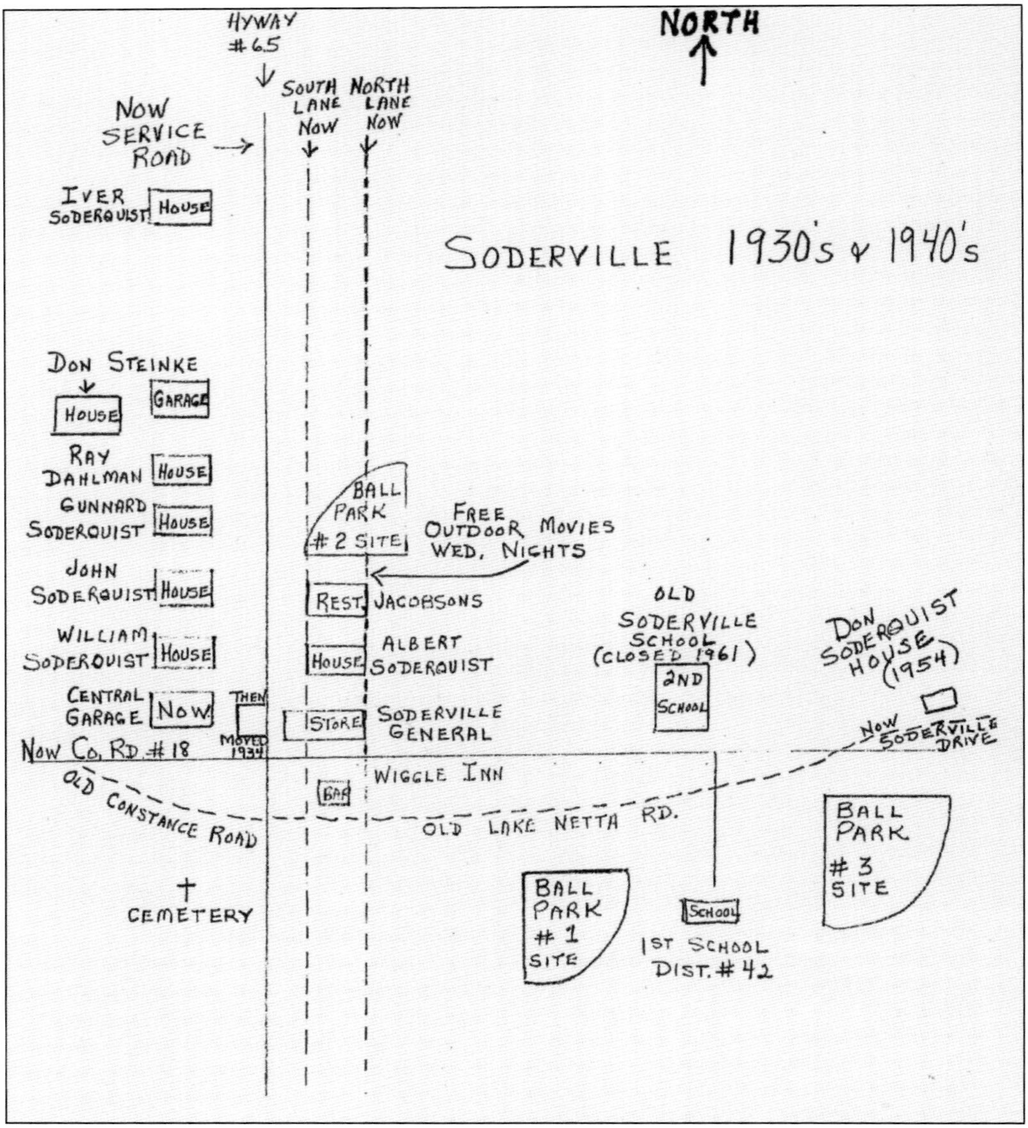

Here is a diagram of Soderville showing where buildings were and what was lost to the highway expansion. (Courtesy of Lorraine Soderquist.)

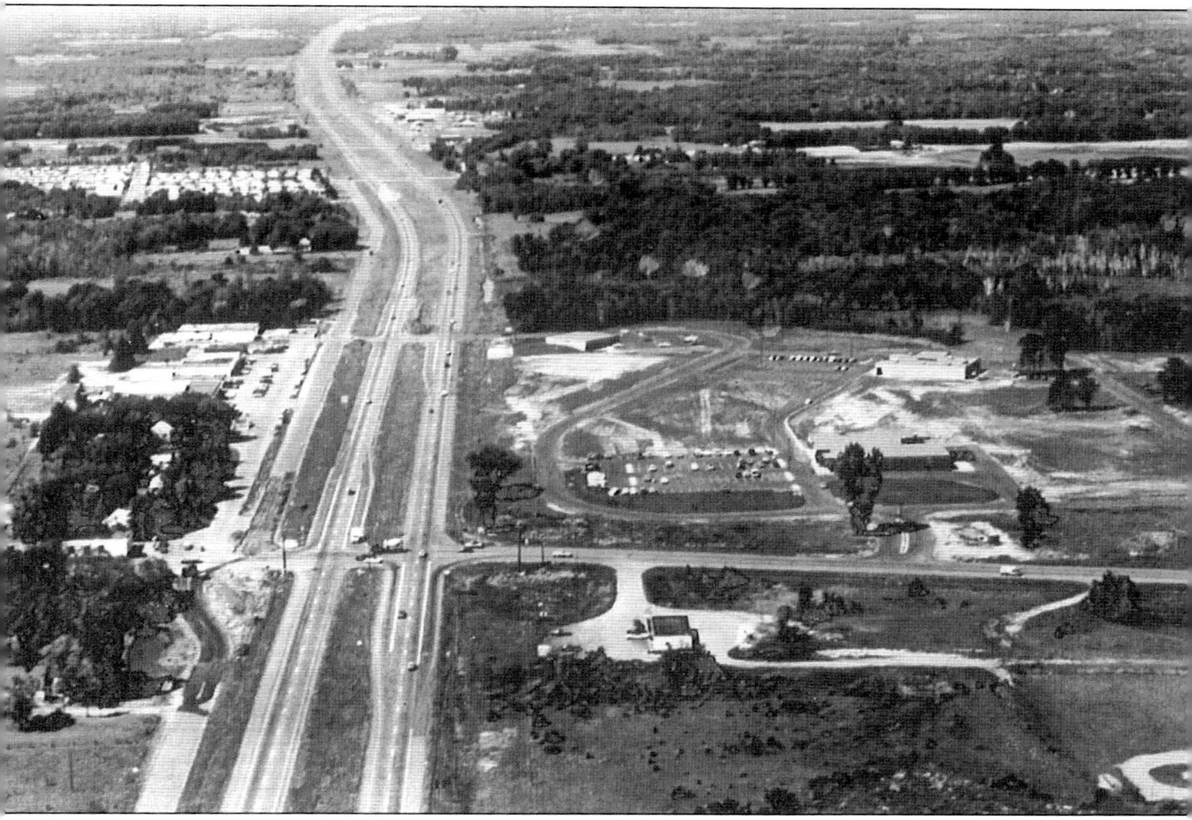

This is Soderville after the highway expansion. The commercial building on the east side of the highway is gone. (Courtesy of Lorraine Soderquist.)

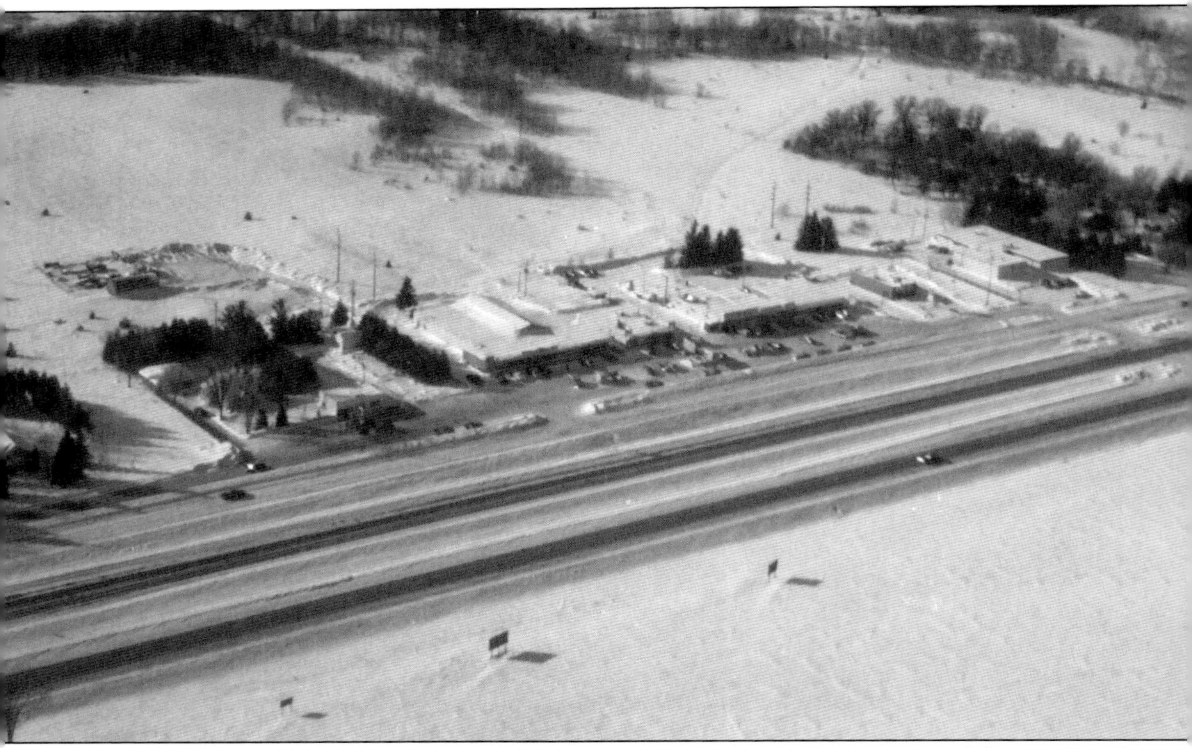

The Soderquists' businesses moved to the west side of the new highway. Iver, with his son Virgil, took charge of the hardware and appliances and became Soderquist Hardware and Appliance. Albert and his son Donald took charge of the grocery, dry goods, and feed business and became Soderquist General Store, which eventually became Soderquists' Super Fair. Donald and his wife, Lorraine, eventually purchased the grocery store. (Courtesy of Lorraine Soderquist.)

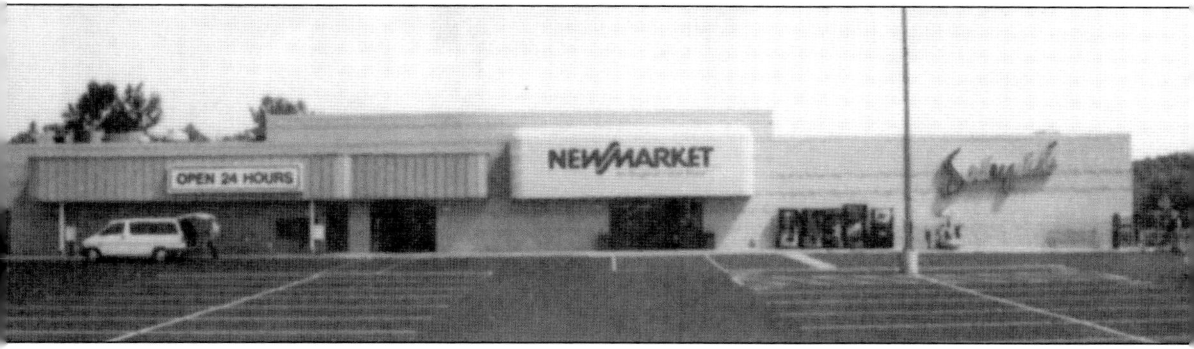

Donald and Lorranie Soderquists eventually opened a larger grocery store again on the west side of Highway 65. This was part of a new shopping center that was built. (Courtesy of Lorraine Soderquist.)

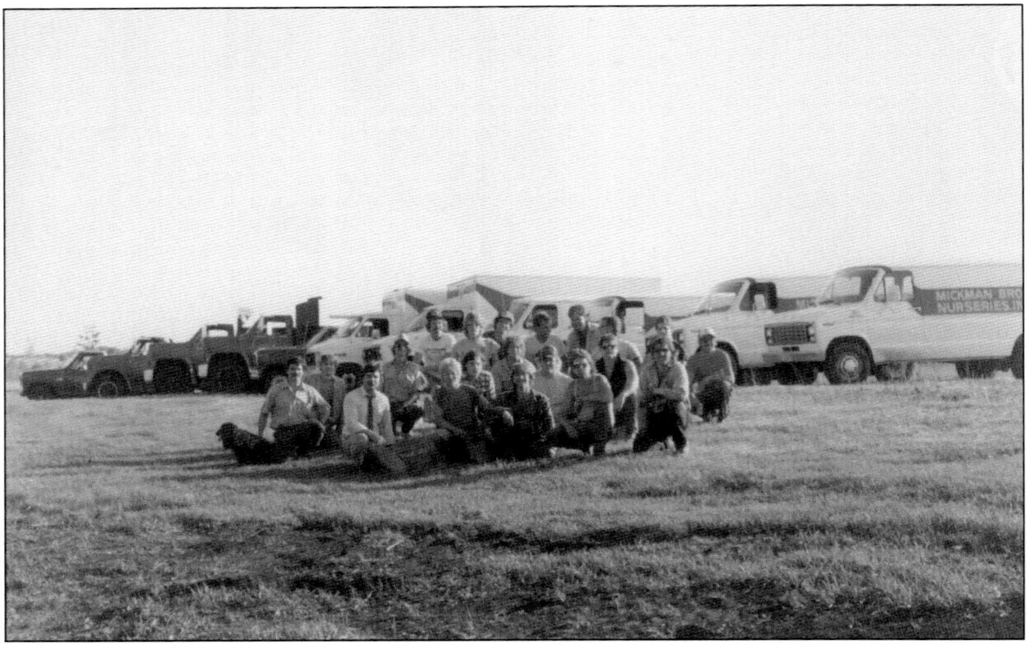

The US Small Business Administration has awarded small businesses statewide each year for over 30 years. Two Ham Lake businesses have received one of these awards after being nominated by the Ham Lake Chamber of Commerce. John Mickman Sr., when he was a boy of 12 in 1934, took a Christmas wreath that his mother had made from the door of their home and sold it. His mother was not angry, and instead she made more wreaths—and he sold those, too. John became an engineer but also ran a wreath-making operation as a side business, and his sons worked at that operation. (Courtesy of the Mickman family.)

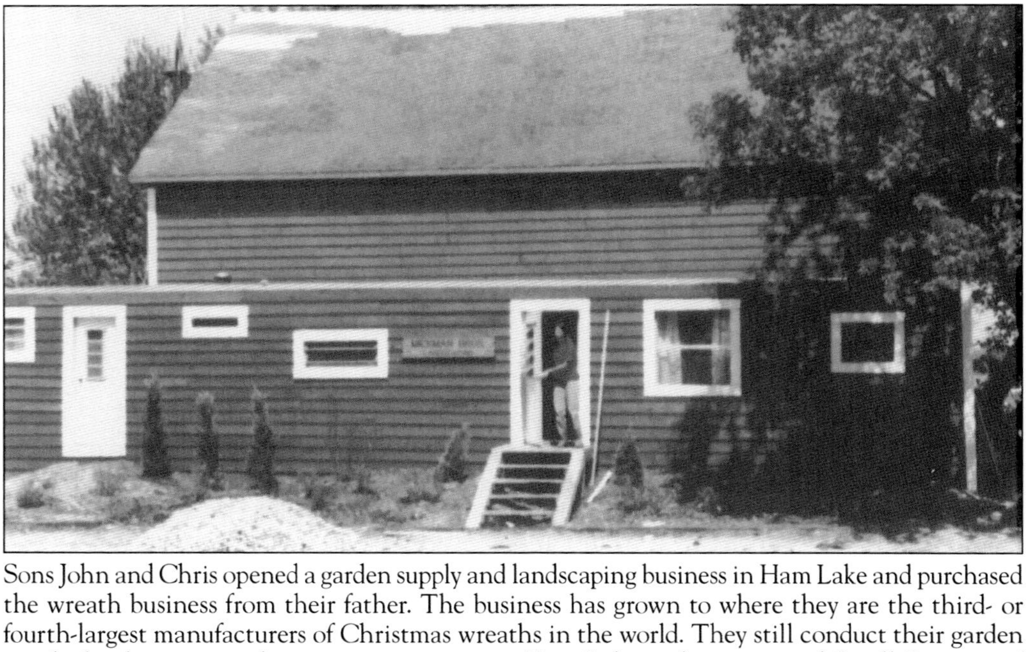

Sons John and Chris opened a garden supply and landscaping business in Ham Lake and purchased the wreath business from their father. The business has grown to where they are the third- or fourth-largest manufacturers of Christmas wreaths in the world. They still conduct their garden supply, landscaping, and irrigation operation in Ham Lake and were named Small Business of Year for Minnesota in 2003. (Courtesy of Mickman brothers.)

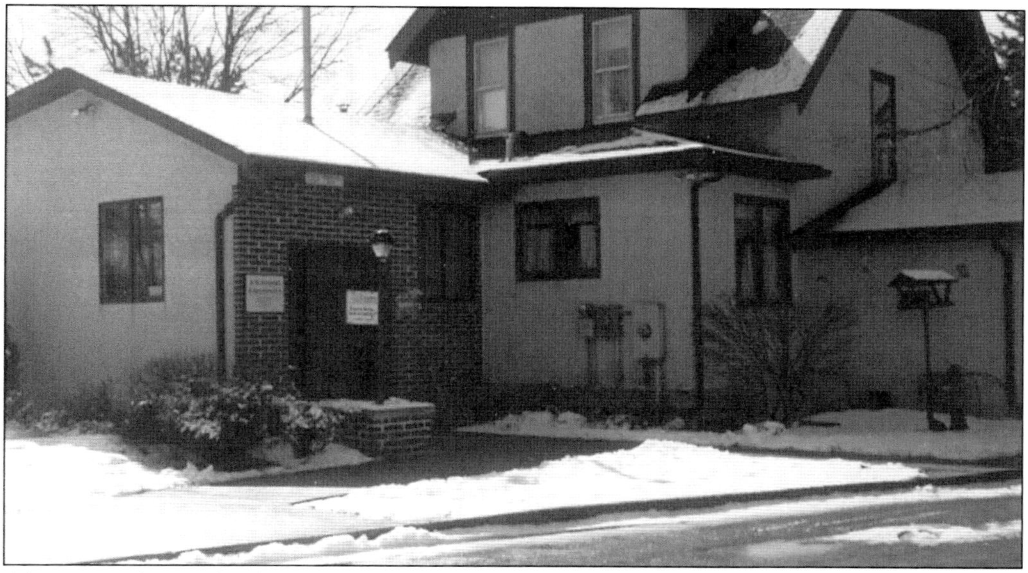

Al Sannerud started Lake Accounting and Management Services, Inc., with his wife, Margaret "Betty," in 1951 after years of working in the public sector. The first office was located in the basement of the farmhouse of Betty's family, the Peterson/Moe farm. As the practice grew, they needed more space. In 1983, they built an addition on the original farmhouse, which allowed for a separate office entrance and a conference room. Daughter Susan joined the firm in 1983 and became the managing partner in 1988. The name was changed to Sannerud, Savarese and Associates P.A. in 2002. (Courtesy of Susan Savarese.)

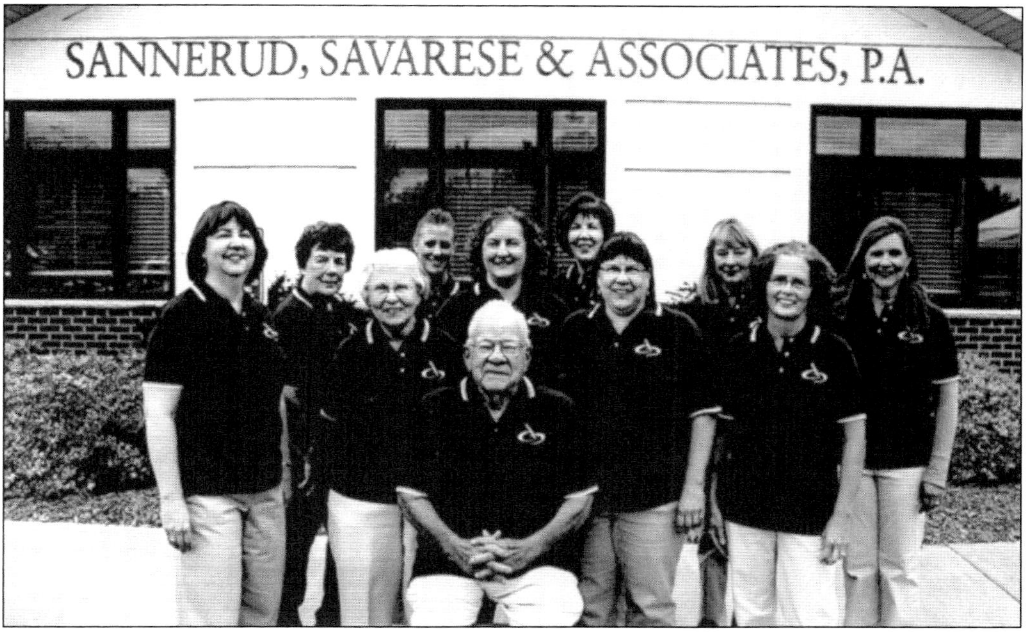

The new office building was constructed in 2005 at the corner of Constance Boulevard and Buchanan Street on approximately five acres of the original farmstead. Al and his family have been active in starting the local bank, served on various city commissions, and helped start a program that gives used cars and bikes to the needy in Anoka County. This business was selected as the state's Financial Service Business of the Year in 2012. (Courtesy of Susan Savarese.)

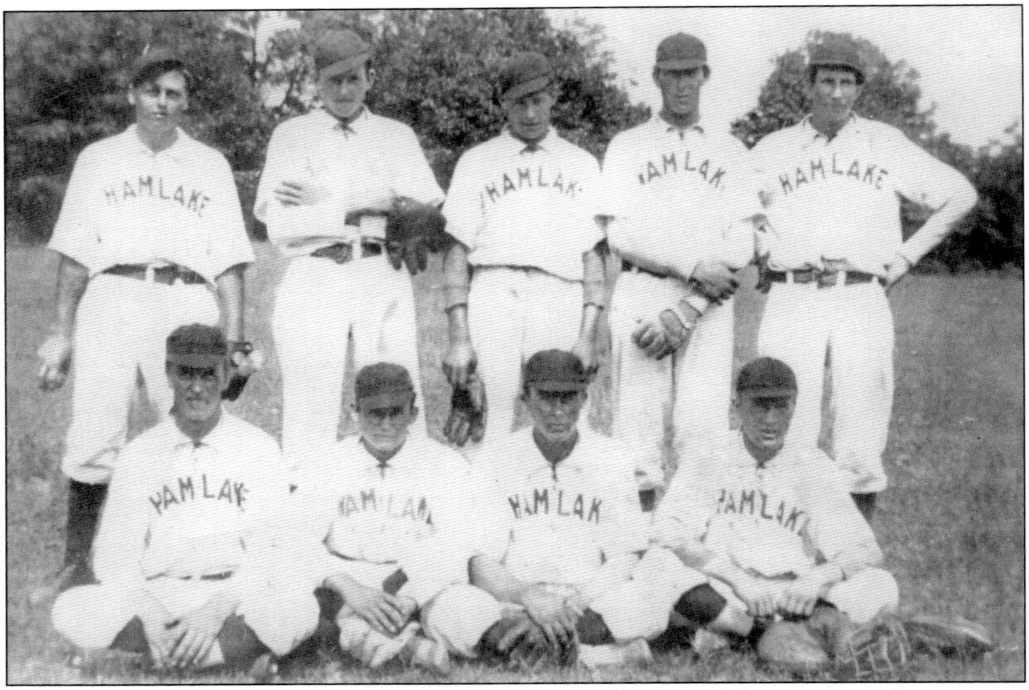

Sports, especially baseball, became important to the city. This is an adult team originally sponsored by Johnville Packing Company, but by the time of this image the sponsor was the Soderville Athletic Association. Pictured here sometime before 1994 are, from left to right, (first row) Oliver Livgard, Sidney Moore, Sam Moore, and Charlie Moore; (second row) Bill Peterson, Willie Anderson, Alfred Livgard, Osborn Moore, and Elmer Soderberg. (Courtesy Ronnie and Marylou Moore.)

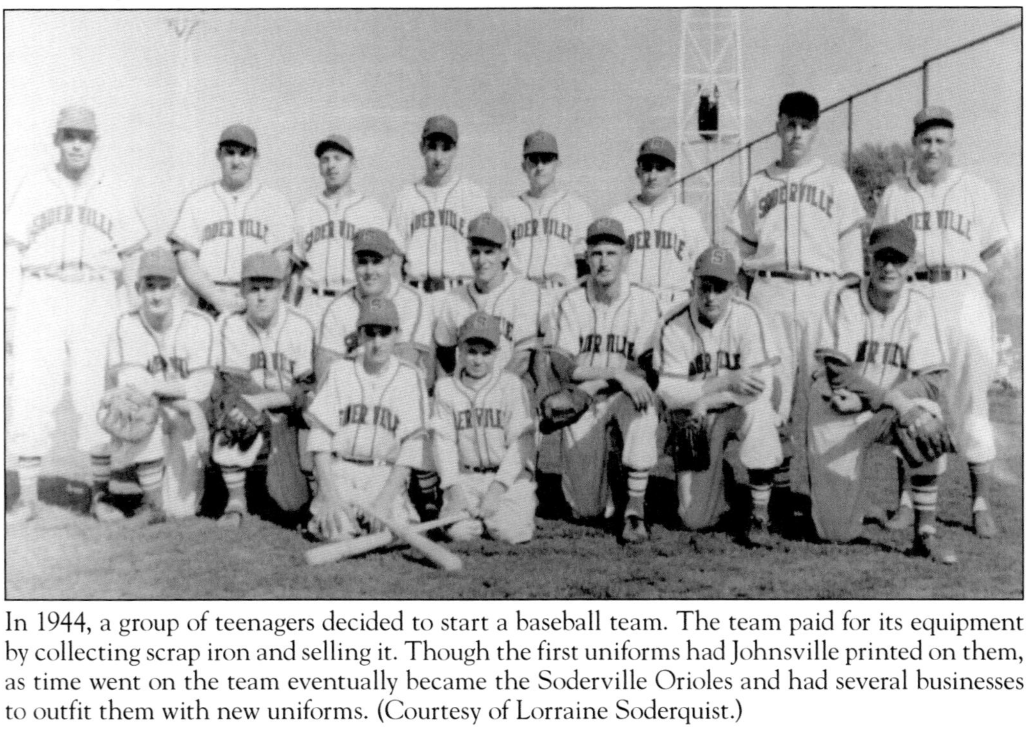

In 1944, a group of teenagers decided to start a baseball team. The team paid for its equipment by collecting scrap iron and selling it. Though the first uniforms had Johnsville printed on them, as time went on the team eventually became the Soderville Orioles and had several businesses to outfit them with new uniforms. (Courtesy of Lorraine Soderquist.)

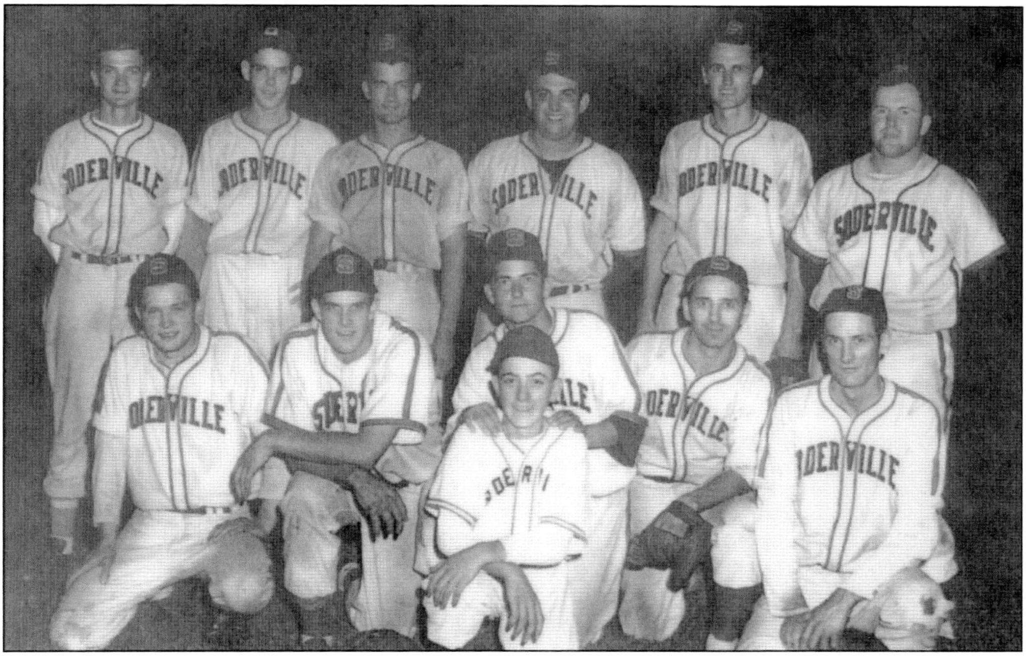

Pictured is the 1949 Soderville baseball team. Members are, from left to right, (first row) Jerry Meyers, Arnie Ott, George Masko, Larry Winkler, and John Norton; (second row) Don Johnson, Milt Gregorie, Dick Johnson, Bill Marchiniak, Quinton Peterson, and Dave Spencer; in front is batboy David Williams. (Courtesy Soderville Athletic Association.)

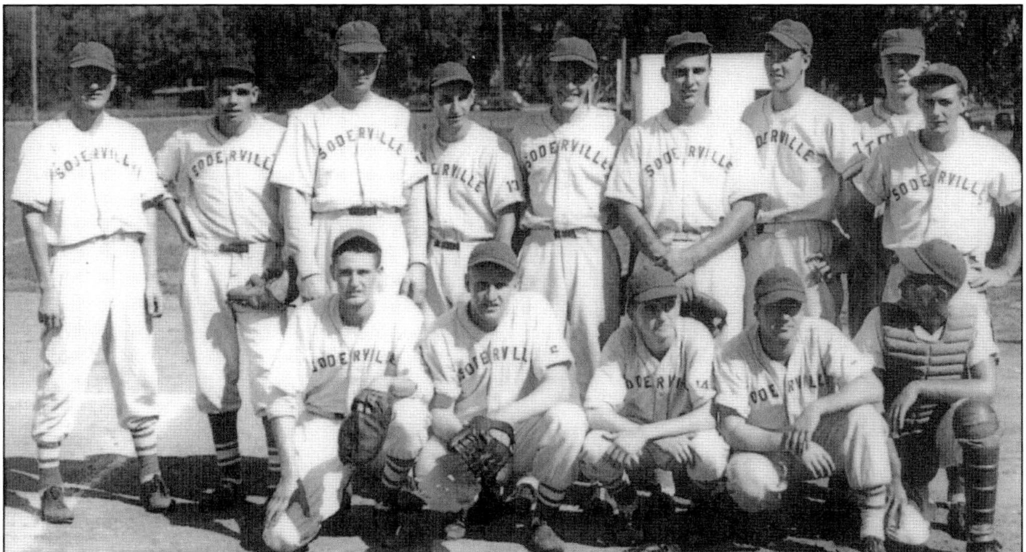

Pictured is the 1950 Soderville baseball team. Members are, from left to right, (first row) Quinton Peterson, Don Schwartz, George Masko, Boots McCarty, and Dick Johnson; (second row) Howard Letrane, Forrest Hendrickson, Charlie Peterson, Larry Winkler, George Peterson, Bernie Julkowski, Bob Paquin, Don Nelson, and Bill Ekmark. On January 1, 1951, the Community Athletic Association of Soderville, Minnesota, was organized and shares sold at $10 per share. This money was used to prepare a new Soderville ball field located on Crosstown Boulevard, east of Highway 65, on land donated by the Soderquist family. (Courtesy Soderville Athletic Association.)

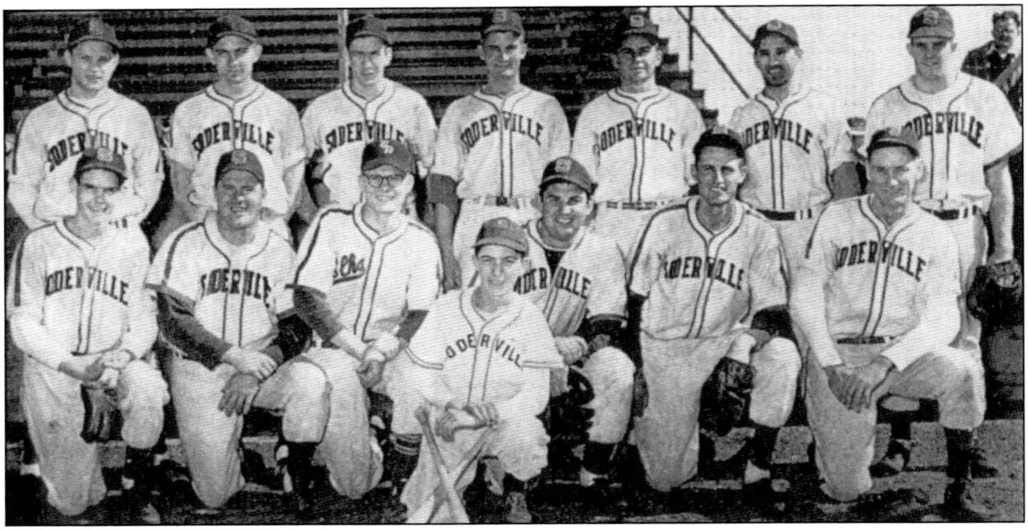

The headline on the sports page of the September 16, 1951, *St. Paul Sunday Pioneer Press* read, "Soderville Wins State B Title." Pictured is the 1951 champion team. The players are, from left to right, (first row) Milt Gregoire, David Spencer, Dan Anderson, Bill Marchiniak, Quinton Peterson, and John Norton; (second row) Jerry Meyer, Jim Faust, Leo Schleisman, Dick Johnson, George Masko, Larry Winkler, and Arnie Oss; the batboy in front is David William. (Courtesy Soderville Athletic Association.)

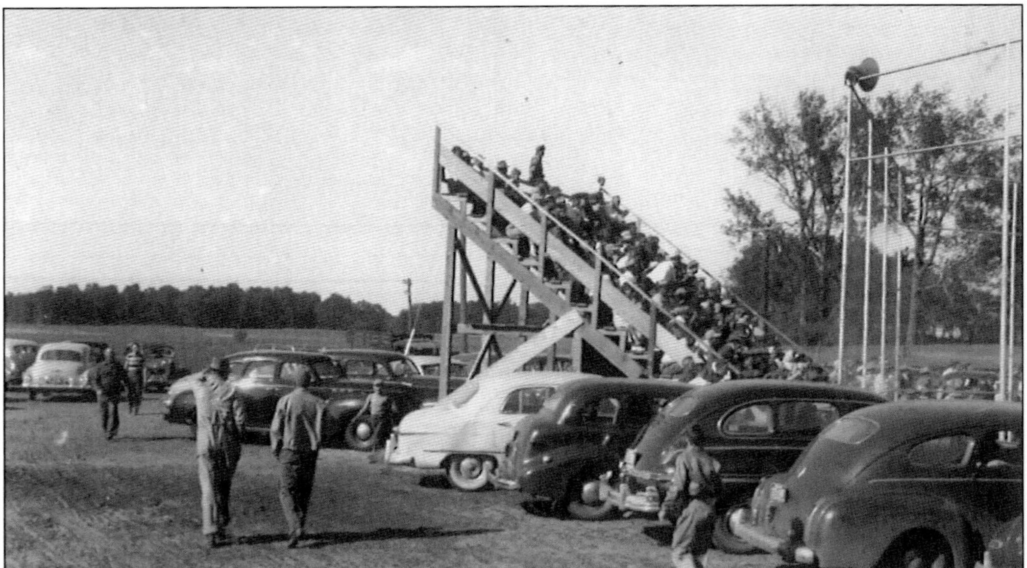

The Soderville Athletic Association (SAA) grew to provide in-house recreational-level youth baseball and fast-pitch softball, traveling competitive-level fast-pitch softball, and traveling baseball opportunities to children in many communities. SAA provides this youth sports experience to kids residing in or attending schools in the communities of Ham Lake, Blaine, East Bethel, Oak Grove, St. Francis, Burns Township, Bethel, and portions of the surrounding communities of Andover, Coon Rapids, and Isanti. In the 1940s and 1950s, the Sunday morning games were the social event of the week. The early refreshment stand was food prepared and taken to the game by the Soderquist grocery. Pictured is the Soderville baseball field during the 1950s. (Courtesy of Lorraine Soderquist.)

Six

Interesting Residents

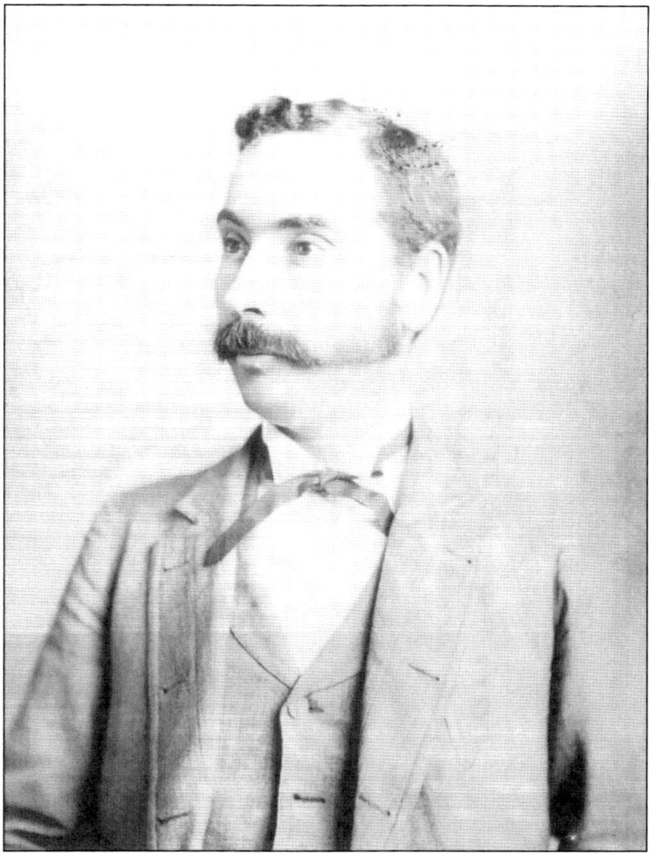

Everyone is sure that his or her ancestors were the most interesting people, but the author selected a few that he believed deserved some special consideration. They are his selections and certainly could be disputed. James Elwell attended Carleton College and in 1871 at the age of 17 patented an innerspring mattress, which evolved into the Minneapolis Bedding Company. He also started the Minnesota Furniture Company, which he sold to his brother Charles. James took that money to develop 750 acres in southeast Minneapolis and built and sold 55 homes. The land had been considered wasteland because it was so wet, but he invented a system of box drains and drain tiles, which he later used for his properties in Anoka County. (Courtesy of the Minnesota Historical Society.)

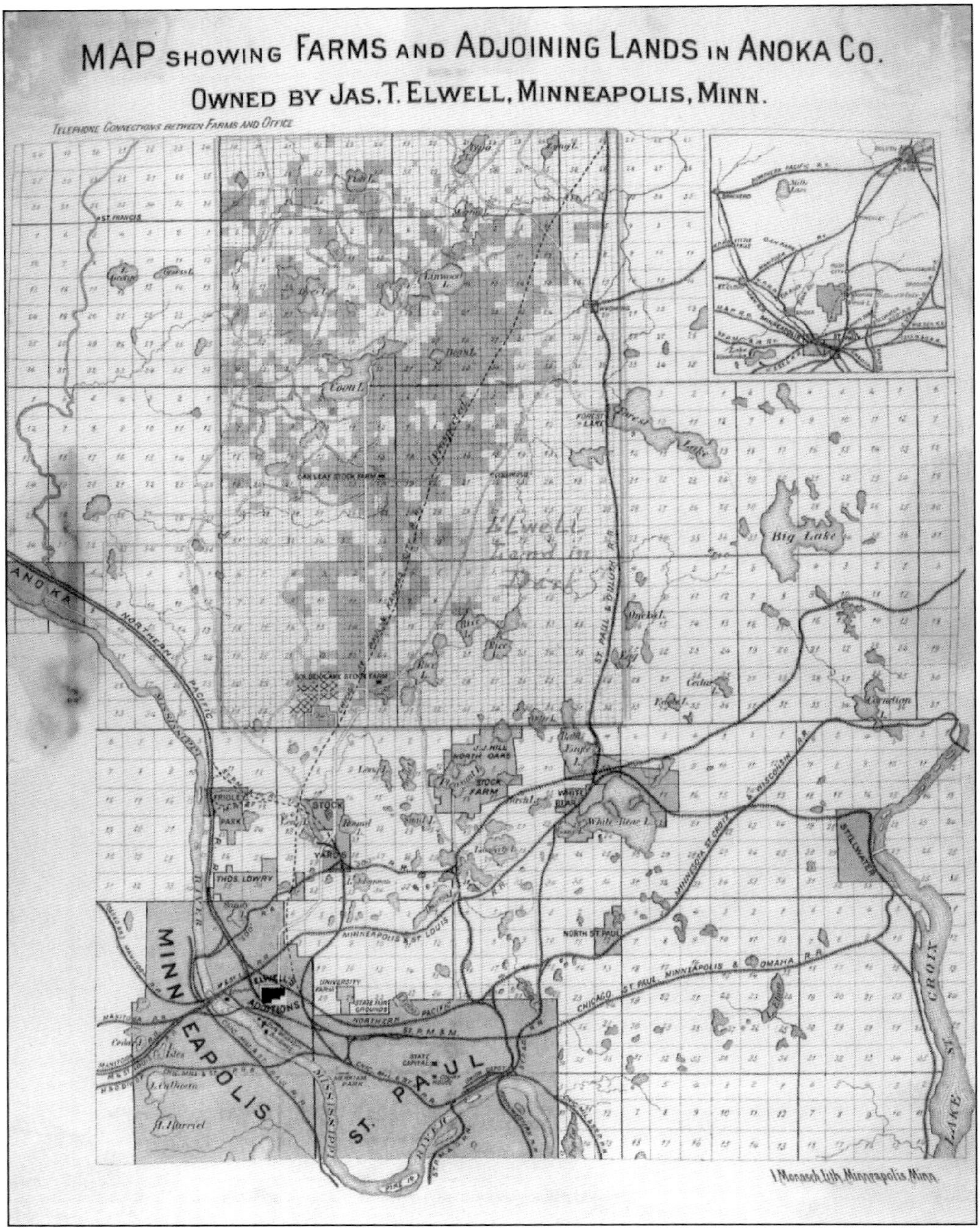

This is a map of James Elwell's extensive holdings in Anoka County, including nearly half of the township of Ham Lake. Beginning in 1886, Elwell invested in land in Anoka County, eventually totaling 52,700 acres. Much of it was wetlands, but he constructed over 200 miles of ditches, mostly in Ham Lake, to make those lands productive. Note the proposed Chicago, St. Paul & Kansas City Railroad line and two major Elwell farms: Golden Lake in Blaine and Oak Leaf Stock Farm in Ham Lake. (Courtesy of the Minnesota Historical Society.)

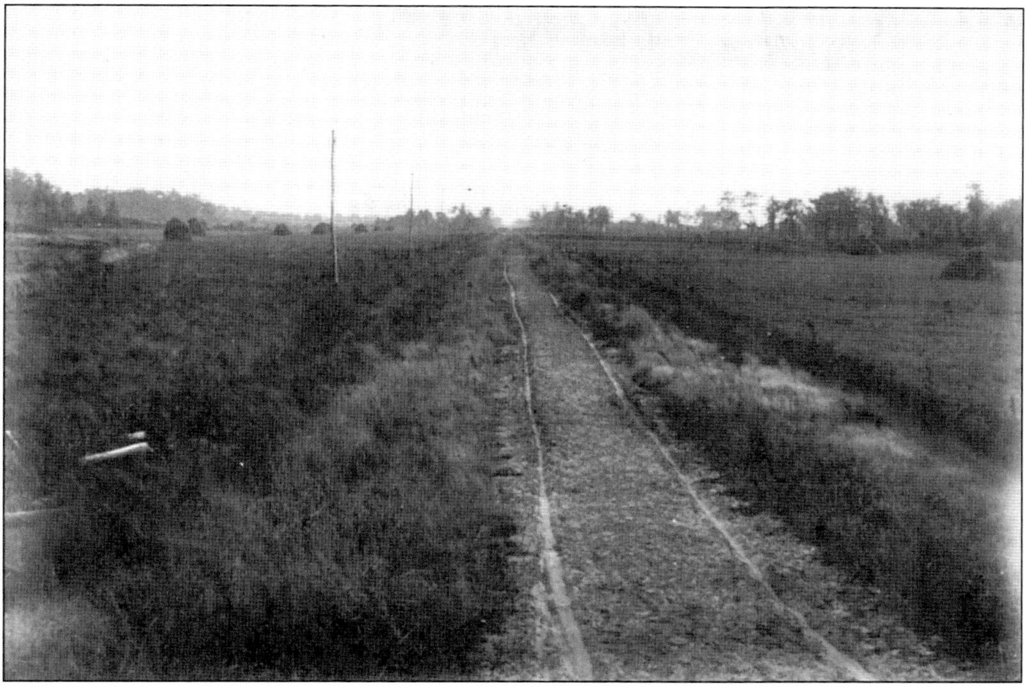

James Elwell needed transportation between the two farms and constructed an eight-mile-long road by piling the dirt from the drainage ditches on each side of the road. It was called for years "Elwell Grade" but is now known as Lexington Avenue. (Courtesy of the Minnesota Historical Society.)

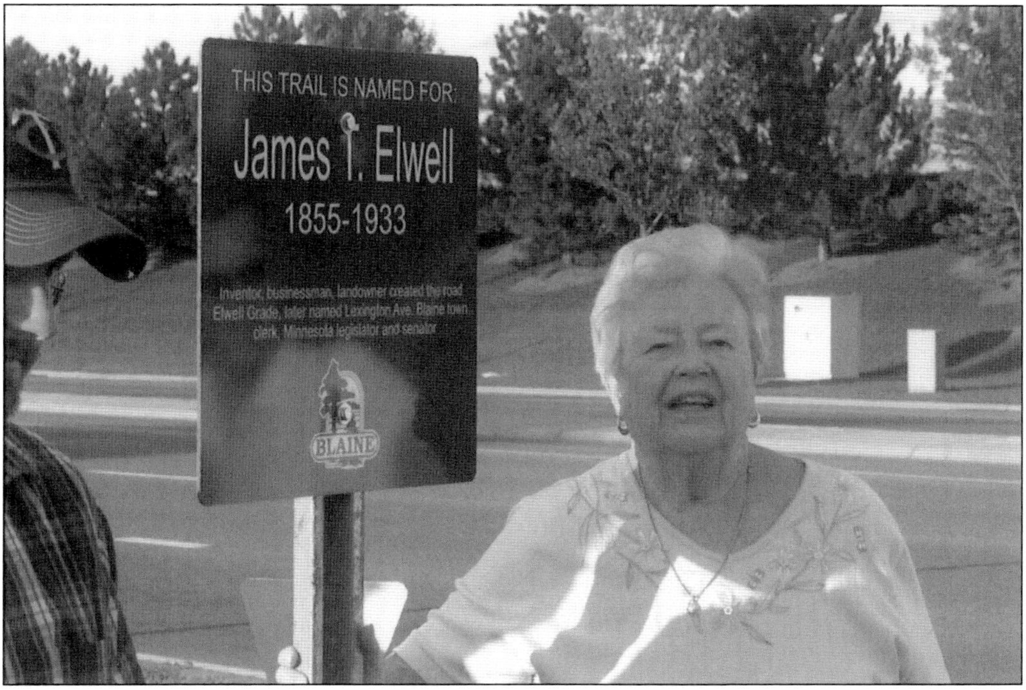

The walking trail along Lexington Avenue was dedicated to James Elwell. At the dedication are James's daughter-in-law Catherine and grandson Tom Elwell. (Courtesy of the Elwell family.)

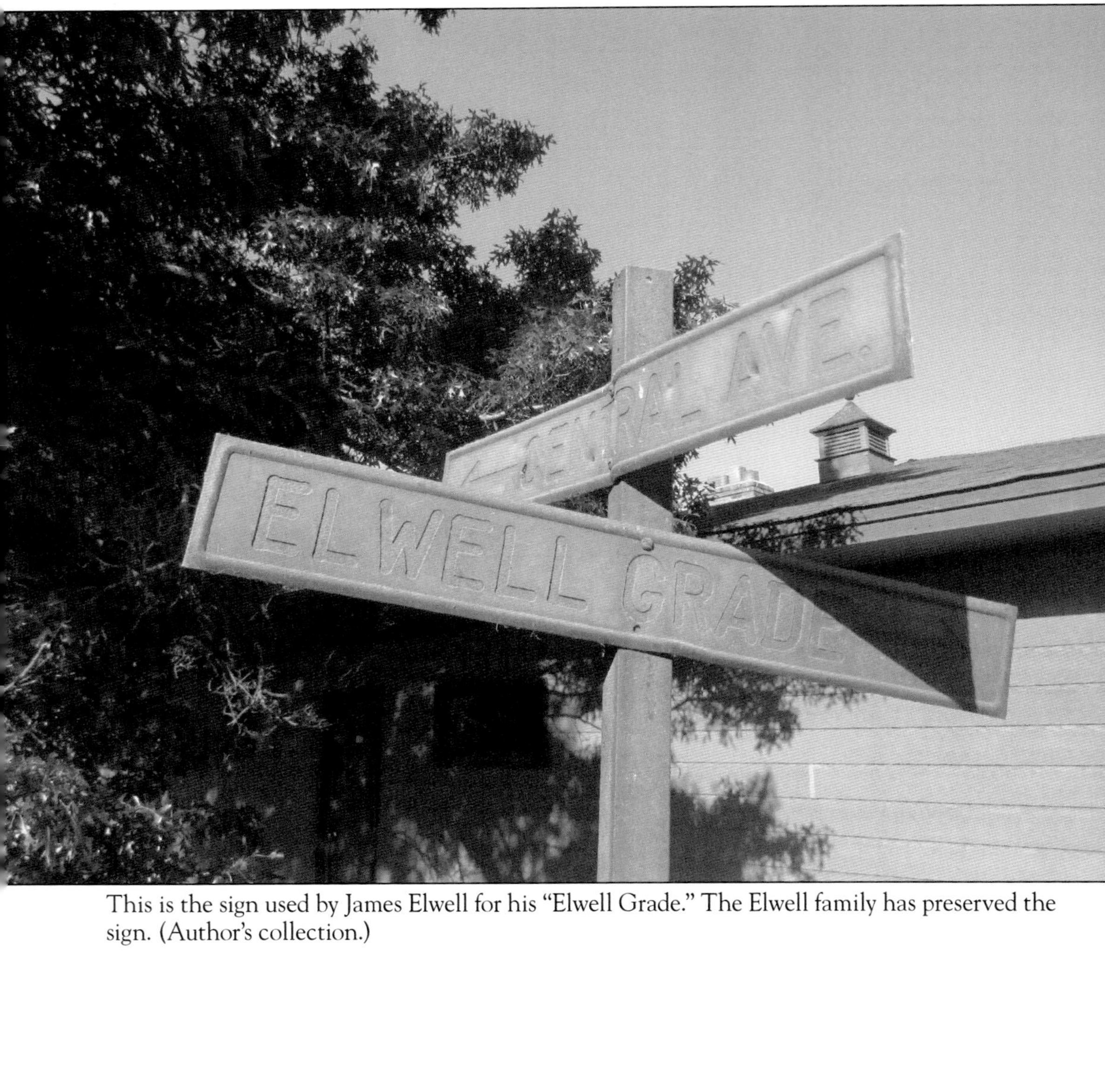

This is the sign used by James Elwell for his "Elwell Grade." The Elwell family has preserved the sign. (Author's collection.)

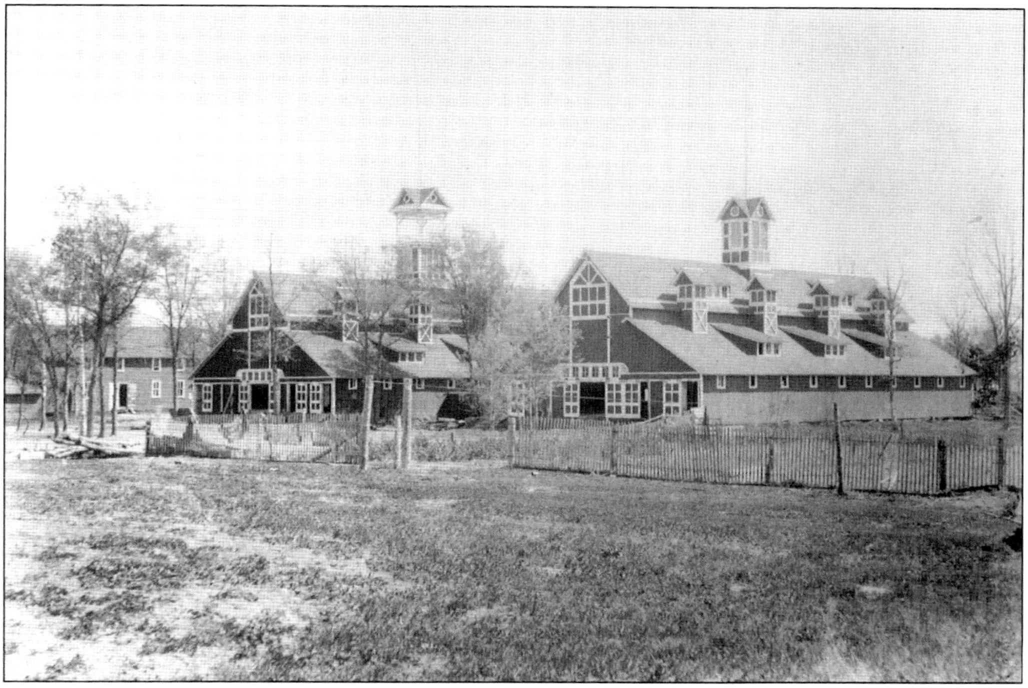

James Elwell created two stock farms: Golden Lake Farm in today's Blaine and Oak Leaf Farm in Ham Lake. In 1899, he was elected to a seat in the Minnesota House of Representatives representing Ham Lake and other neighboring communities. (Courtesy of the Elwell family.)

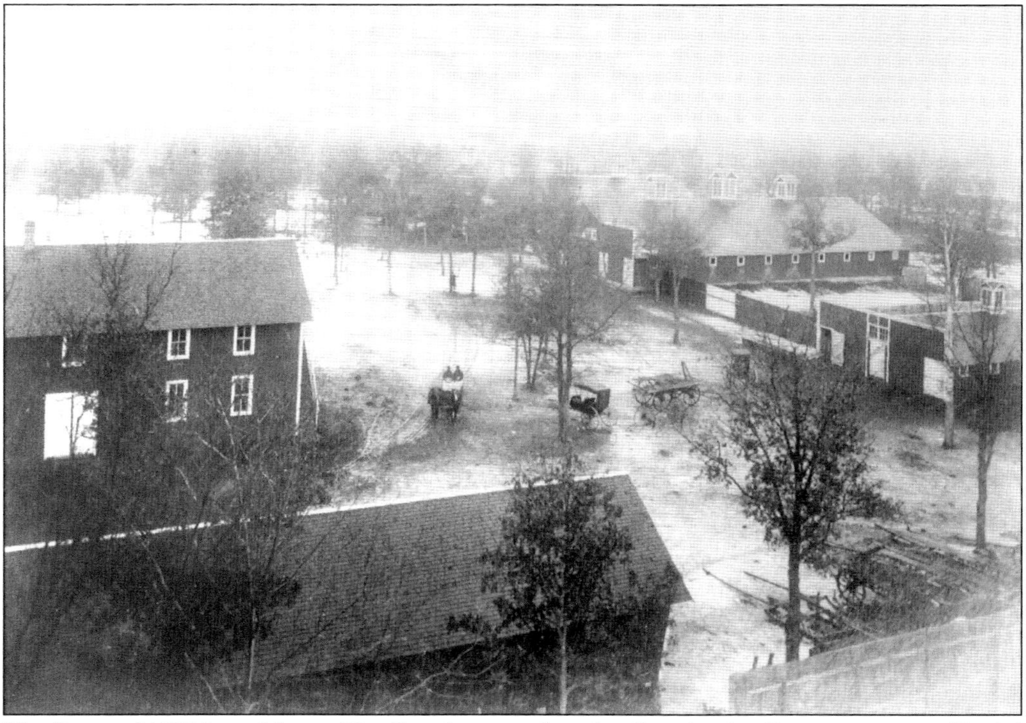

The Panic of 1893 forced James Elwell to dispose of much of his Anoka County property. He did keep the two major farms in Blaine and Ham Lake. (Courtesy of the Elwell family.)

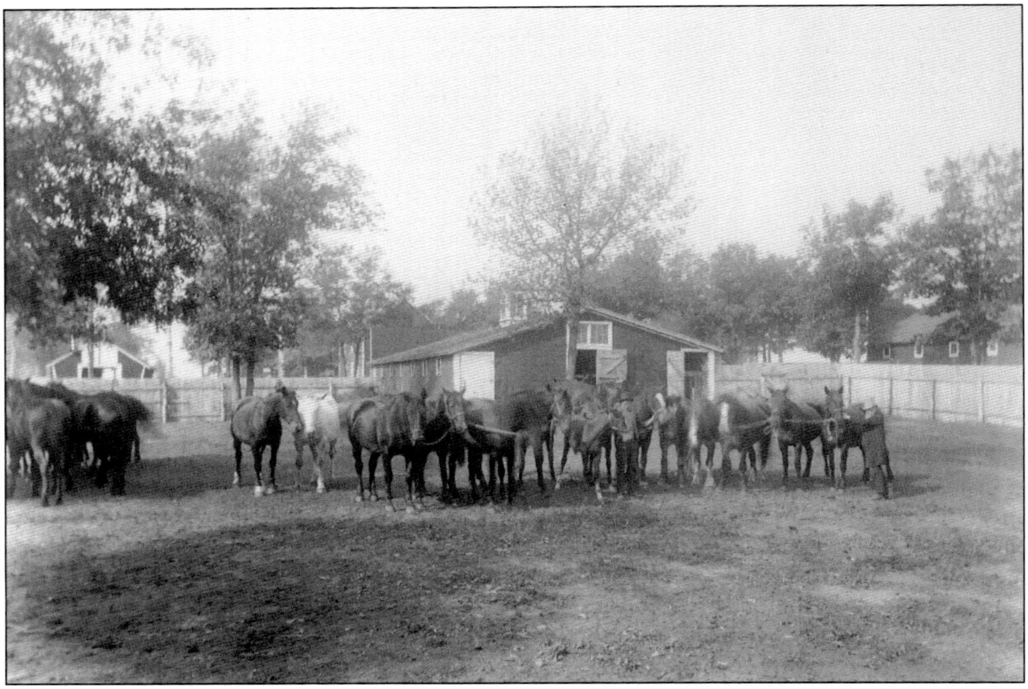

James Ewell gave up active farming in 1901 and moved the family back to Minneapolis. There, in 1906, he was elected to the Minnesota State Senate. He died in 1933. (Courtesy of the Elwell family.)

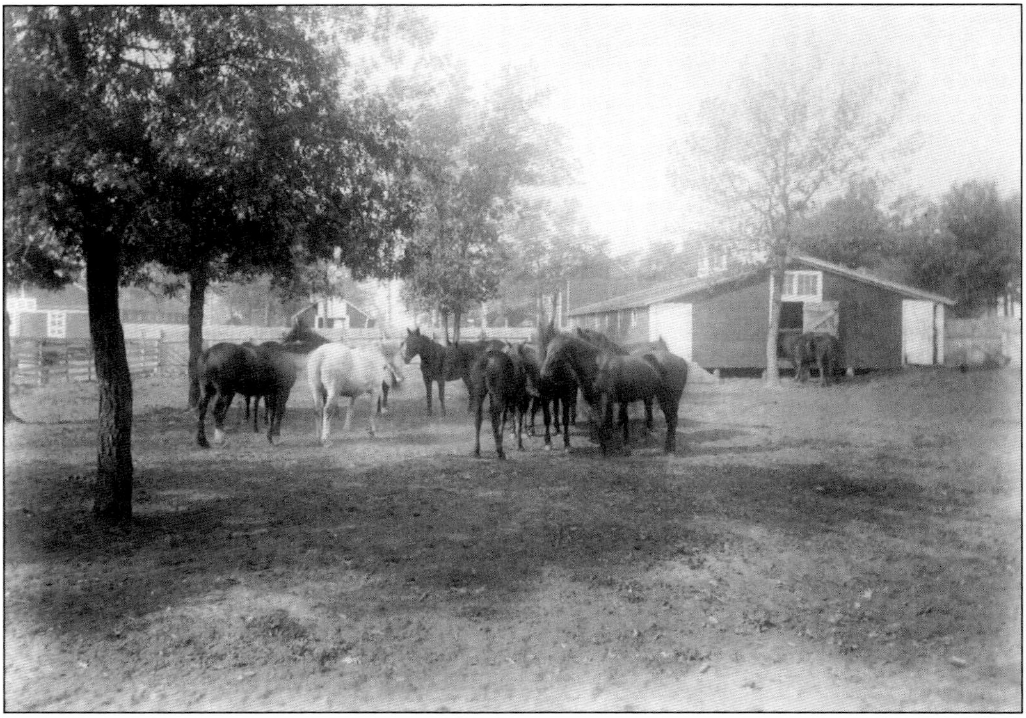

James Elwell was the largest breeder of horses in Anoka County. He bred both show horses and show cattle. (Courtesy of the Elwell family.)

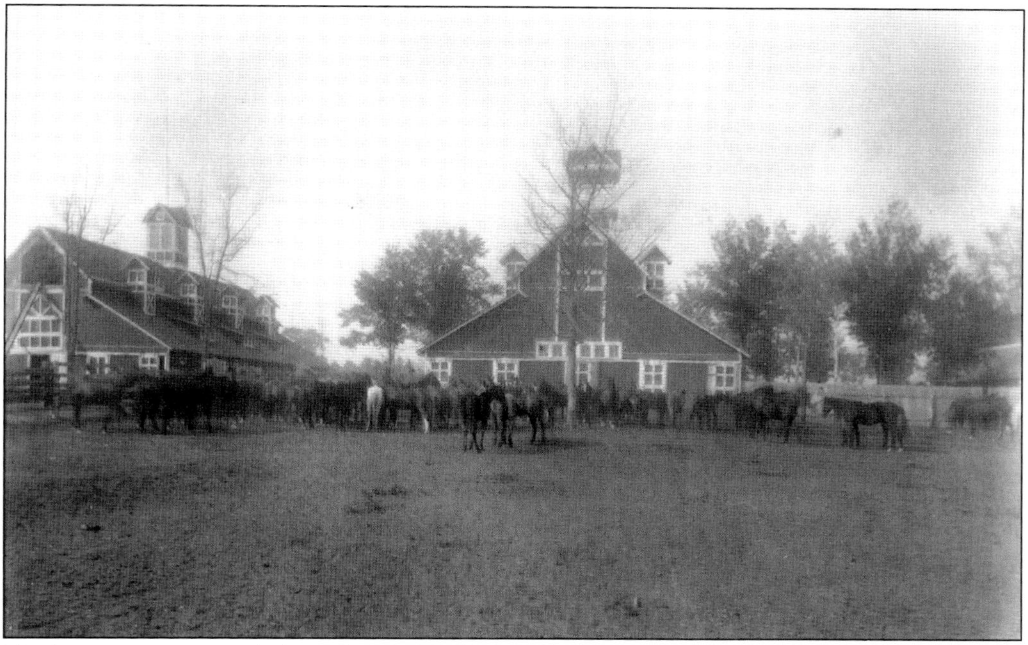

His farms were extremely large by Ham Lake standards. Pictured are more of the horses on the Elwell Farms. (Courtesy of the Elwell family.)

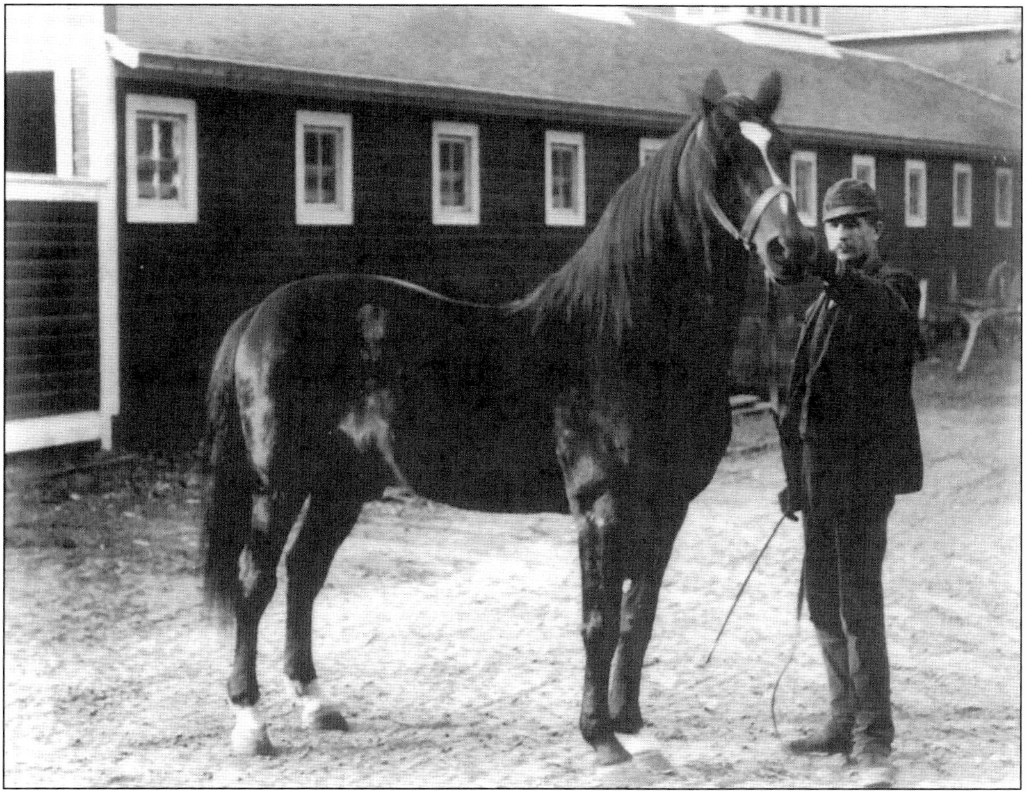

James Elwell bred award-winning cattle and horses. Pictured is the prizewinning Hambeltonian stallion Herschell. (Courtesy of the Minnesota Historical Society.)

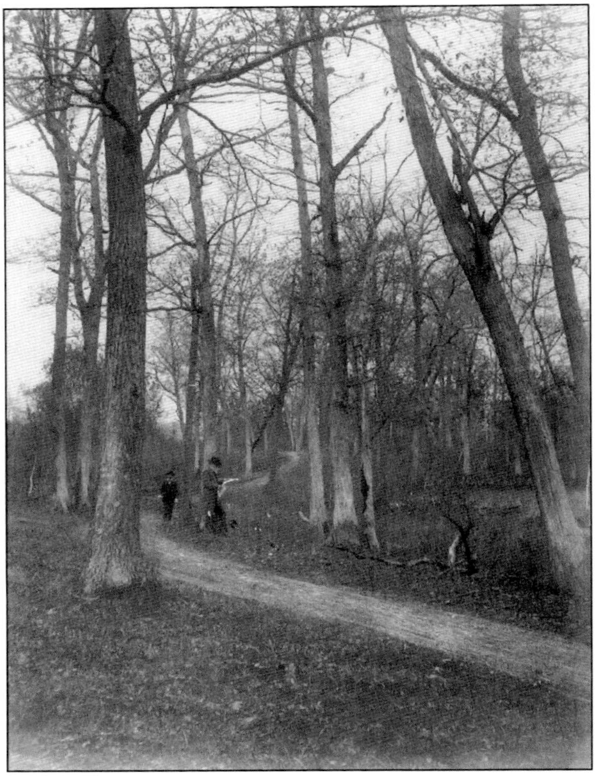

Like many farms in Ham Lake, wood had to be cut and sold. Pictured is James T. Elwell inspecting his woods at Oak Leaf Farm. (Courtesy of the Elwell family.)

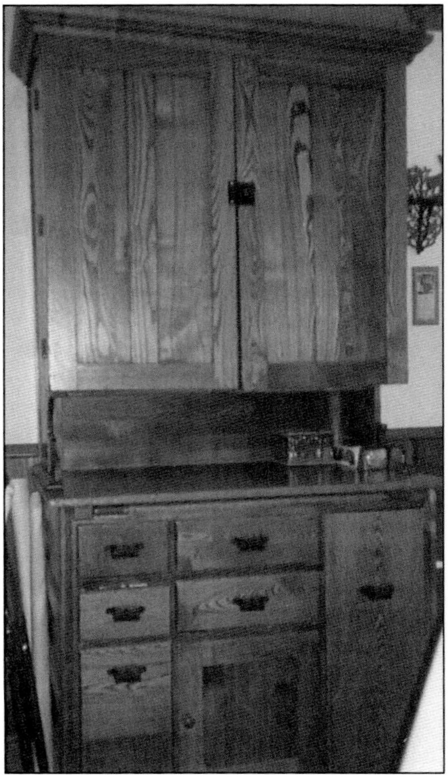

To finance his land purchases, James founded and then sold the Elwell Cabinet Company. Pictured is an example of products from the Elwell Cabinet Company. (Courtesy of the Elwell family.)

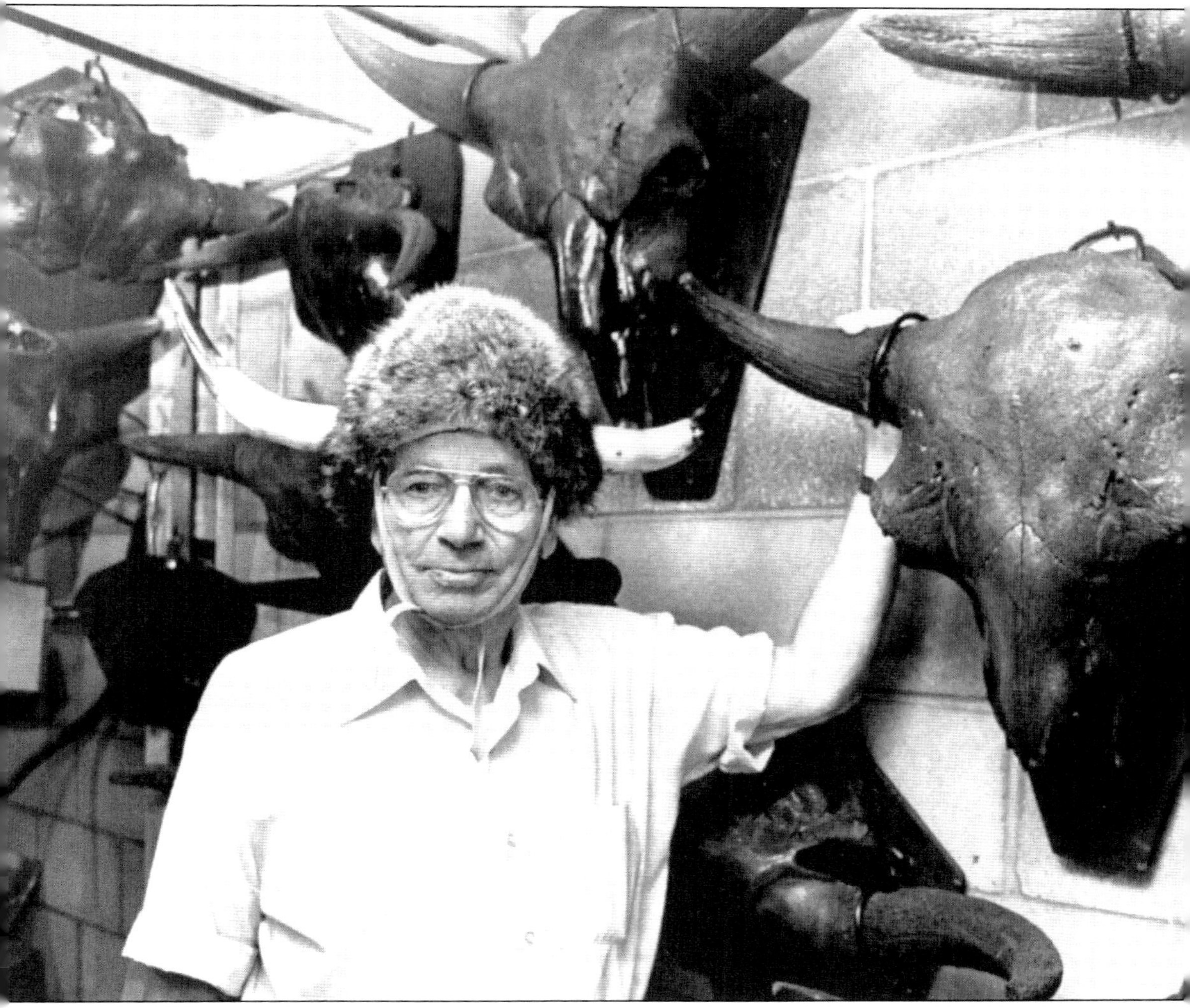

Morris Titterud was the son of Berger Titterud and Nellie Hanson and grandson of Halvor Titterud. In 1914, when the county was cutting-in Andover Boulevard near Coon Creek, bones were uncovered and discovered. Morris Titterud got wind of the bones and, not knowing what they were, took a few to the University of Minnesota and found that they were bones of the *bison antiquus*. (Courtesy of the *Minnesota Star Tribune*.)

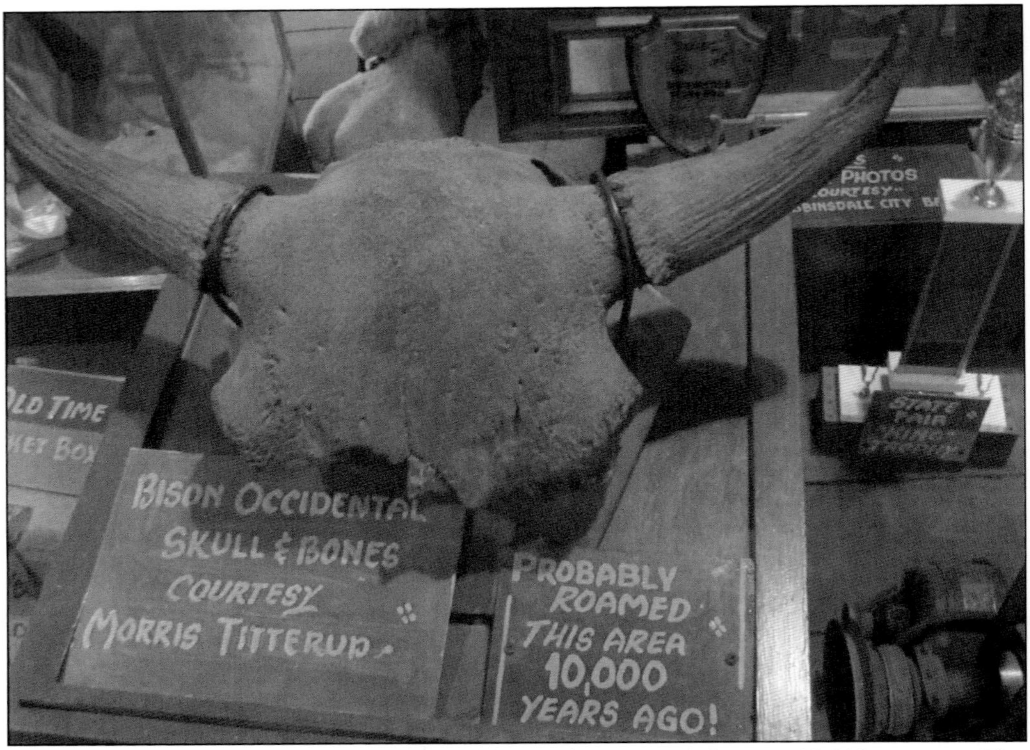

The *bison antiquus* is a 2,250-pound horned bison that roamed the area 10,000 year ago. The biggest horns measured six feet in length. There were so many bones that it was determined that what had been unearthed were from a butchering ground. Ice Age people would have driven the bison to this area where the footing was soggy. Morris got permission to dig out as many as he could find. No full animals were found, as normally the hindquarters were gone, but there were over 70 skulls, and Morris Titterud made a number of Viking-style hats from the horns. He gave most of the skulls and bones that he cleaned and put together to the Bell Museum, the University of Minnesota, the Minnesota State Fair, and a number of local high schools. This display is part of the Minnesota State Fair history exhibit. One must wonder what Morris's wife thought of this hobby. As late as 1961, he still had over 39 skulls on the wall of his shop. (Both, author's collection.)

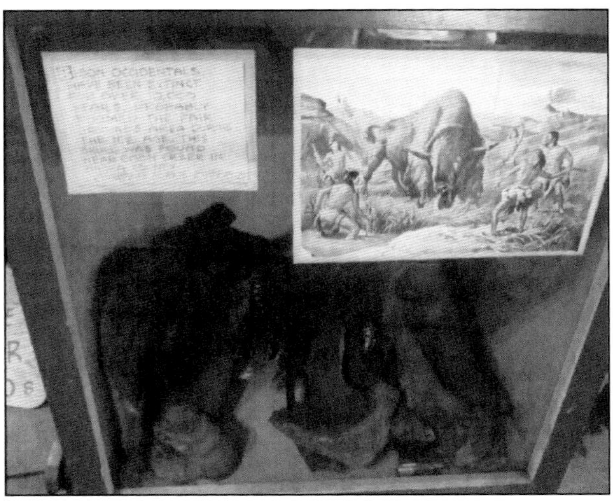

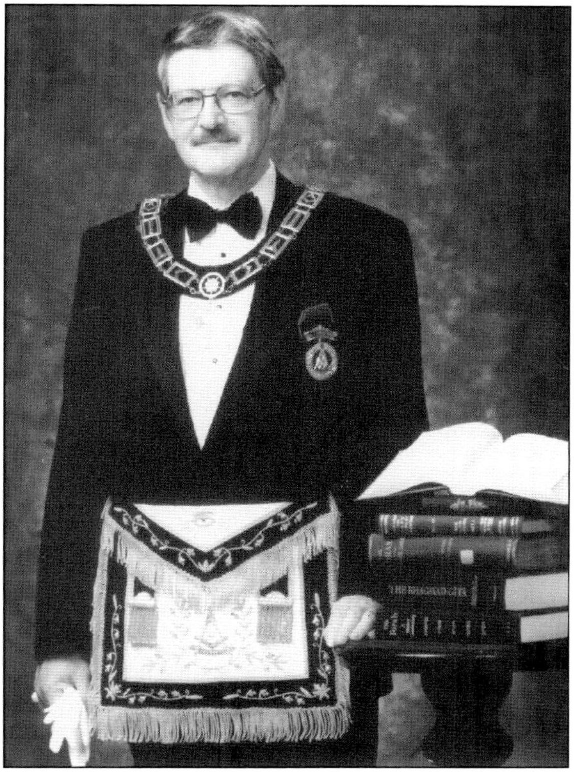

Rodney Larson was born in 1933 and lived most of his life in Ham Lake. He received his bachelor's degree in applied mathematics at the University of Minnesota and continued working on his master's and doctorate degrees in mathematics at the University of Minnesota. Rodney served as a captain in the US Air Force and worked for Minneapolis Honeywell for 28 years as a research fellow. Rodney served as master of the Anoka Masonic Lodge No. 30. He was elected grand master of Masons of Minnesota in 1994 and was a 33rd Degree Mason. Freemasonry is the oldest and the largest fraternal order in the world. (Courtesy of the Anoka County Historical Society.)

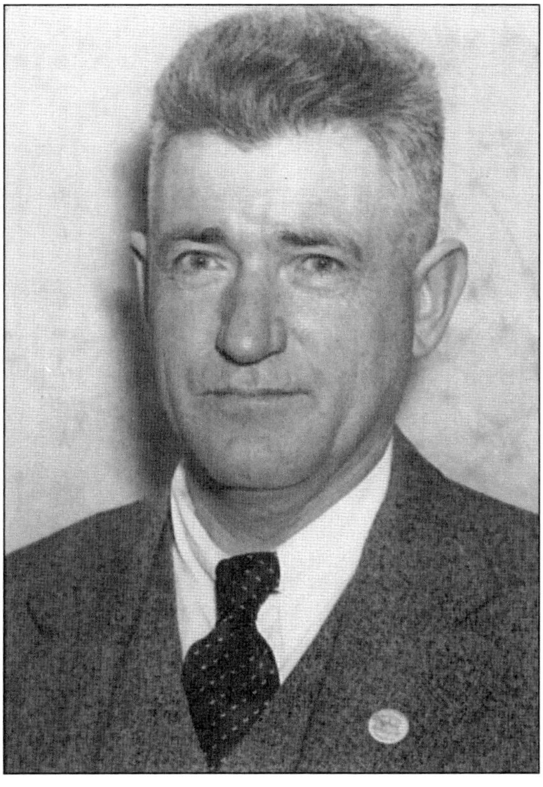

John Nordin was born in 1892 in Sweden. He came to the United States as an infant and was raised on a farm in South Dakota. He married in 1914 and moved to Minnesota in 1922. He settled in Columbia Heights in 1928, was elected to the Minnesota State Legislature in 1933, and served until 1938 when he was elected to the city council and then mayor of Columbia Heights. He moved to Ham Lake in 1947 and ran for and won another seat in the state legislature from 1947 to 1954 and again from 1957 to 1966, adding up to over 21 years as a state legislator. He was a member of the National Rivers and Harbors Congress and was appointed to its advisory committee in March 1934. He helped organize the Highway 65 Association to represent and lobby for the commercial interests along Highway 65. He also was a realtor and had a combination legislative and real estate office in the Soderville shopping area on the west side of Highway 65. (Courtesy of the Minnesota Historical Society.)

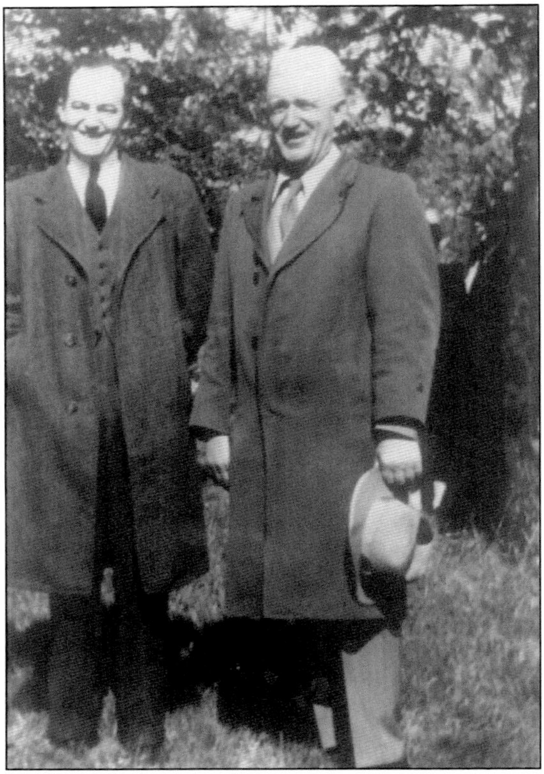

John Nordin (right) is pictured with Vice Pres. Hubert Humphrey. John was always a strong supporter of Anoka County. He had a strong Swedish accent, however, and once when he was seeking funding for the Anoka County jail, people asked when Anoka County joined the Ivy League because of course it came out as Anoka County "Yale." (Courtesy of the State Historical Society.)

Pictured are John Nordin and the Soderville Mothers Club. The ladies included Betty Nystorm, Norma Brellenthen, Lorraine Soderquist, Jennie Eugen, Abba Soderquist, and Agnes Broadbert on a capitol tour. (Courtesy of Lorraine Soderquist.)

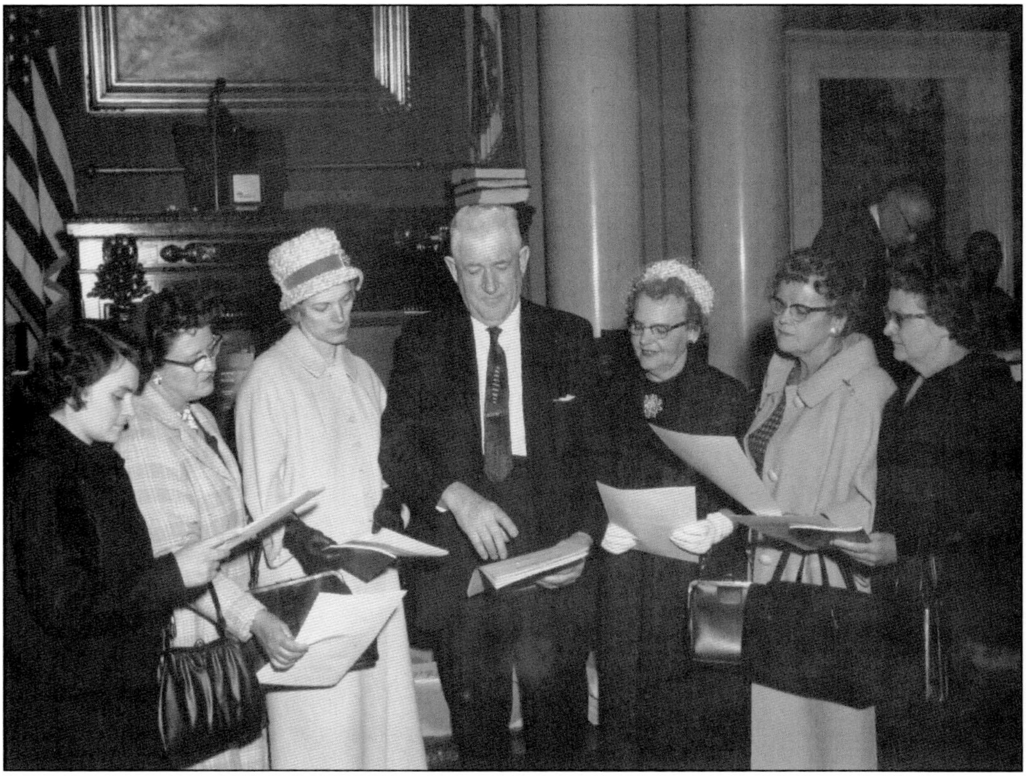

Seven

Government

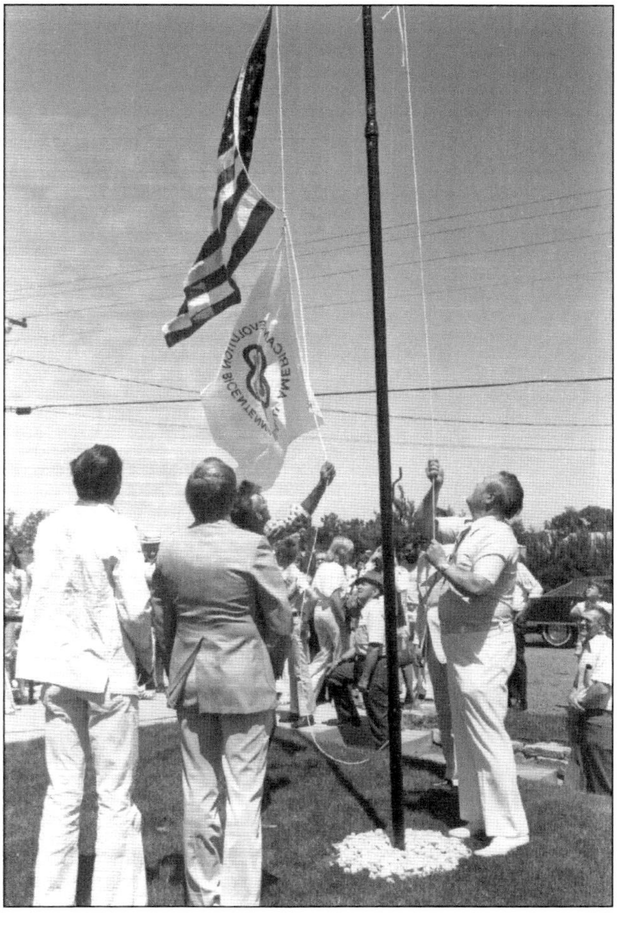

The township was organized in 1871 under the name Ham Lake. John Rowe was the chair of the board of supervisors, A.B. Livgard and C. Olson were supervisors, Charles Rowe was clerk, D.C. Money was treasurer, and Josiah Hart was justice of the peace. The population of Ham Lake grew from 235 in 1880 to 384 in 1890, to 505 in 1900, to 12,057 in 2000, and to 15,323 in 2010. Pictured at the new city hall and under the US bicentennial flag are, from left to right, David Sandstrom, Cordell Willman, Ken Braastad, and Bill Nelson. (Courtesy of Doris Nivala, the City of Ham Lake.)

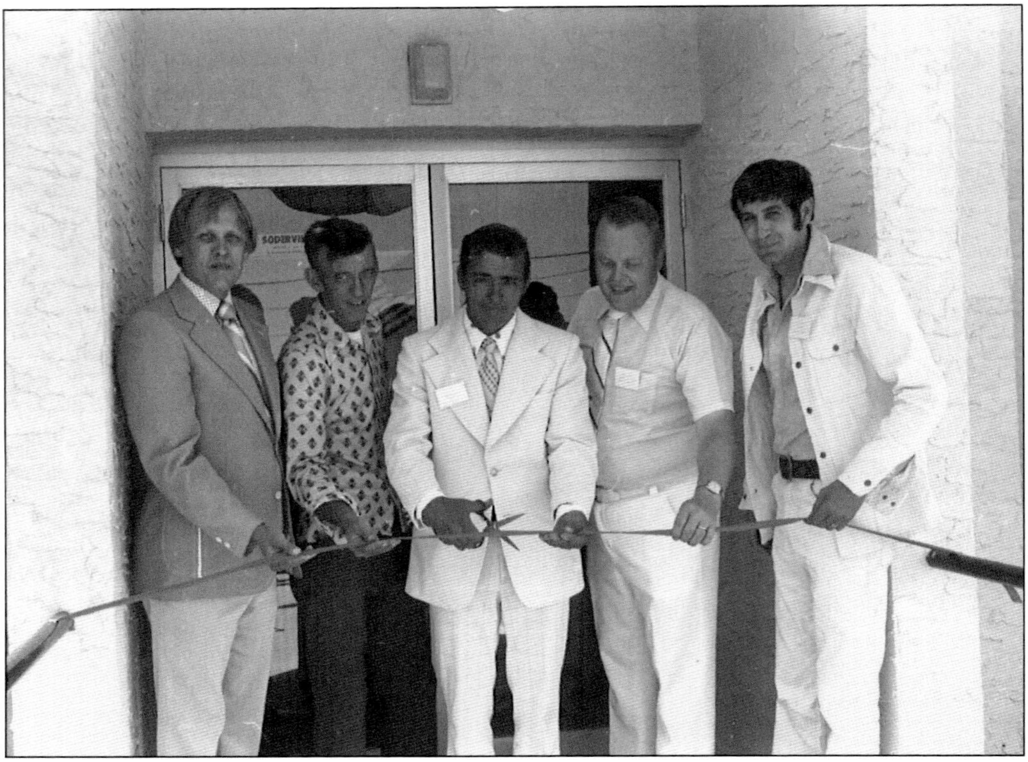

Members of the Ham Lake City Council in 1976 included, from left to right, Cordell Willman, Ken Braastad, Mayor Eldon Hentges, Bill Nelson, and David Sandstrom. (Courtesy of Doris Nivala, the City of Ham Lake.)

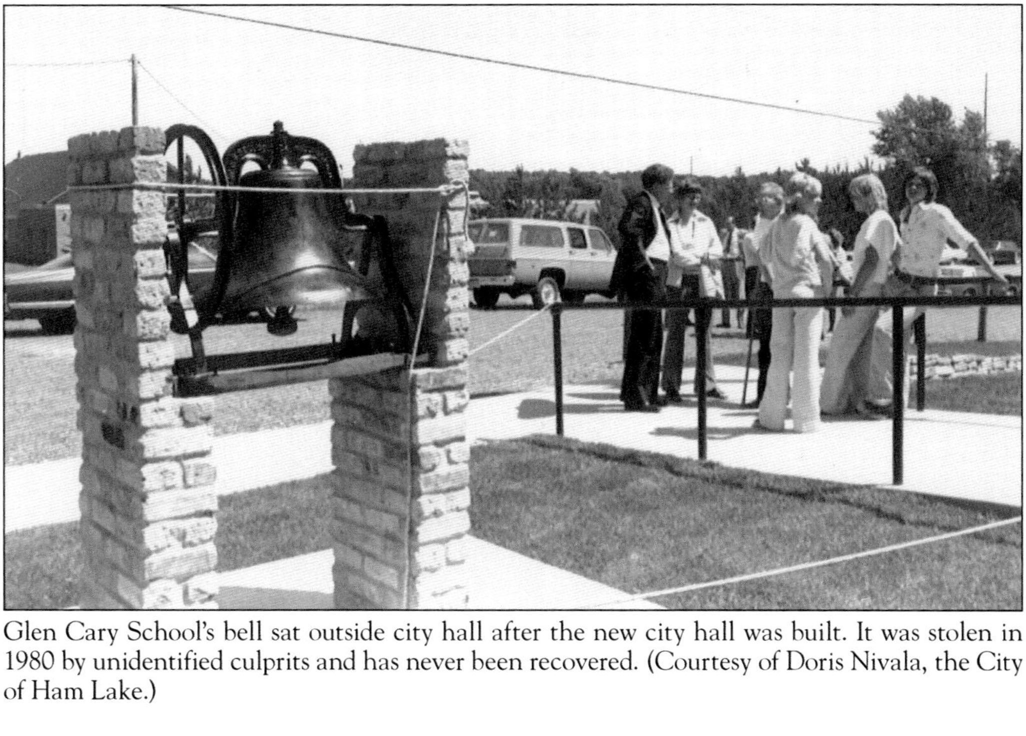

Glen Cary School's bell sat outside city hall after the new city hall was built. It was stolen in 1980 by unidentified culprits and has never been recovered. (Courtesy of Doris Nivala, the City of Ham Lake.)

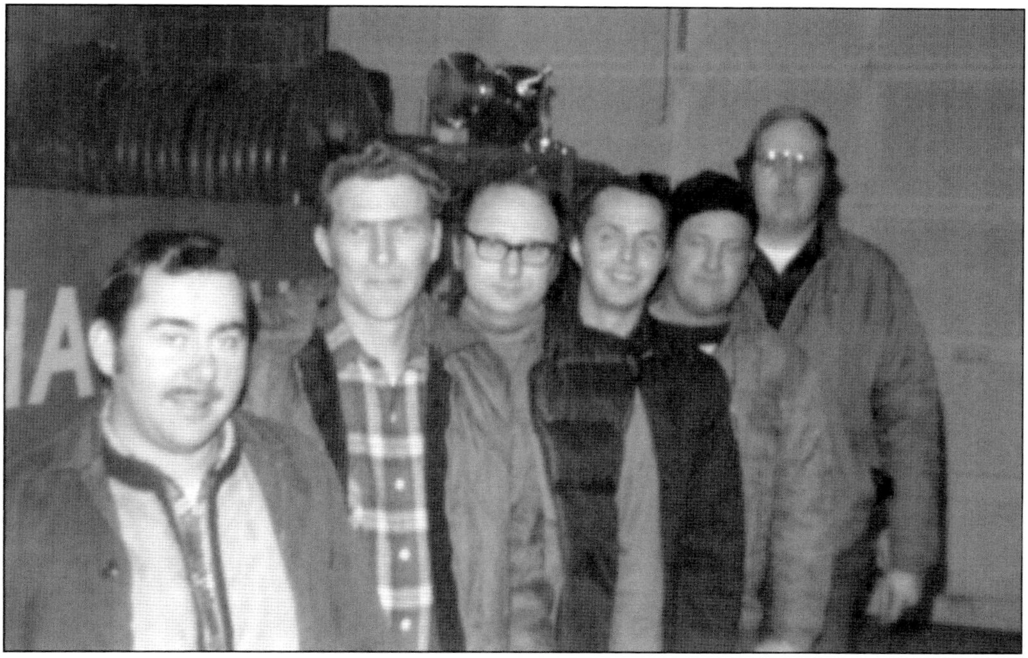

Although volunteers used the central garage to get water to fight fires as early as the 1920s, an official volunteer fire department did not begin until 1969. Pictured are, from left to right, early volunteers Roger Mechels, Gene Boelter, Marvin Buchhotz, Larry Hunt, Dick Schultz, and Terry Burtson. Buchhotz has been a volunteer fireman since its inception. (Courtesy of Marvin Buchhotz.)

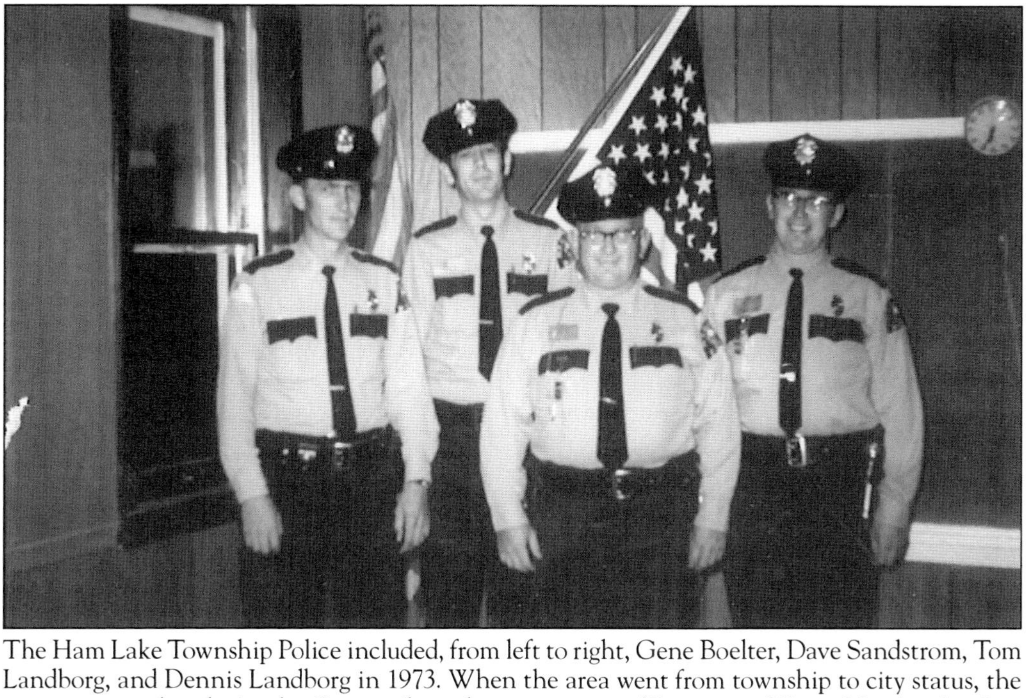

The Ham Lake Township Police included, from left to right, Gene Boelter, Dave Sandstrom, Tom Landborg, and Dennis Landborg in 1973. When the area went from township to city status, the city contracted with Anoka County for police protection. (Courtesy of Doris Nivala, the City of Ham Lake.)

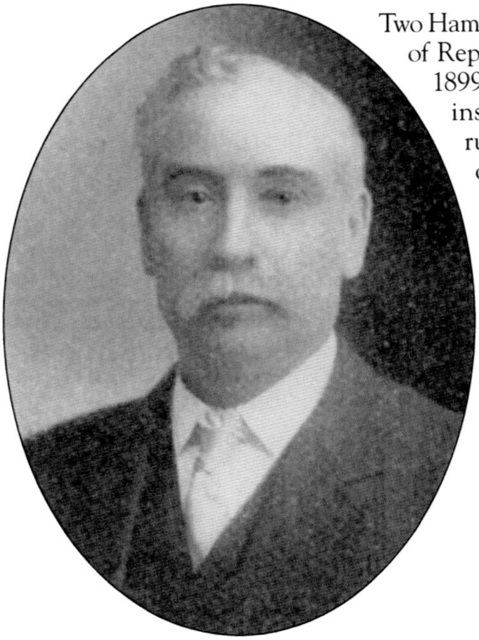

Two Ham Lake residents served in the Minnesota State House of Representatives. One was Rep. James T. Elwell, from 1899 to 1901. As a member of the legislature, he was instrumental in passing the "Elwell Law" supporting rural highway expansion and was an ardent supporter of the University of Minnesota. (Courtesy of the Minnesota State House of Representatives.)

Ham Lake City Council from the Move from Township to City to Present

Year	Mayor	Council 1
1974	Eldon Hentges	Kenneth Braastad
1976	Eldon Hentges	Kenneth Braastad
1978	Eldon Hentges	Kenneth Braastad
1980	Eldon Hentges	Kenneth Braastad
1981	Eldon Hentges	Kenneth Braastad
1982	William Nelson	Kenneth Braastad
1984	Dennis Landborg	Kenneth Braastad
1987	Marilyn Schultz	Kenneth Braastad
1989	Marilyn Schultz	Kenneth Braastad
1991	William Nelson	Kenneth Braastad
1993	William Nelson	Kenneth Braastad
1995	William Nelson	Kenneth Braastad
1997	Gary Kirkeide	Kenneth Braastad
1999	Gary Kirkeide	Kenneth Braastad
2001	Gary Kirkeide	Kenneth Braastad
2002	***Jacob Barthod	
2003	Gary Kirkeide	Jacob Barthod
2005	Gary Kirkeide	Jolynn Erikson
2007	Paul Meunier	Jolynn Erikson
2009	Paul Meunier	Tom Johnson
2011	Mike Van Kirk	Jim Doyle
2013	Mike Van Kirk	Jim Doyle
2015	Mike Van Kirk	Jim Doyle

* Appointed to fill a vacancy on the council from January 5, 1981, to February 31, 1983.
** Appointed to fill a vacancy on the council from August 14, 1989, to October 2, 1989, until William Nelson was elected at a special election.

Pictured is Rep. John Nordin, who served nonconsecutive terms of 1933–1938, 1947–1954, and 1957–1966. He supported funding for expansion of Highway 65, as well as those cities on Highway 65, and was a continuous advocate for Anoka County and its infrastructure. (Courtesy of the Minnesota State House of Representatives.)

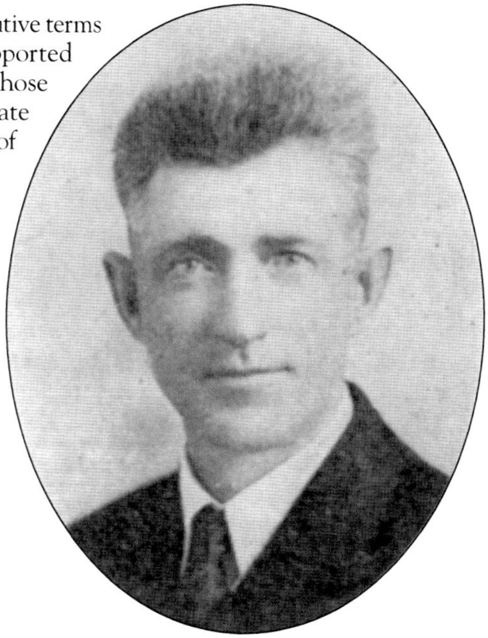

Council 2	Council 3	Council 4
William Nelson	Cordell Wellman	David Sandstrom
William Nelson	Cordell Wellman	David Sandstrom
William Nelson	Cordell Wellman	David Sandstrom
William Nelson	Jacob Barthold	Dick Lang
William Nelson	Jacob Barthold	Clarence Genz
Dennis Landborg	Jacob Barthold	Marilyn Schultz
*Gary Steen	Jacob Barthold	Marilyn Schultz
Gary Steen	Jacob Barthold	Merlyn Anderson
**Ernie Ruud	Jacob Barthold	Merlyn Anderson
William Larson	Jacob Barthold	Merlyn Anderson
William Larson	Jacob Barthold	Merlyn Anderson
William Larson	Jacob Barthold	Merlyn Anderson
William Larson	Jacob Barthold	Merlyn Anderson
William Larson	Jacob Barthold	Susie Thomas
William Larson	Christine Dahlman	Susie Thomas
William Larson	Christine Dahlman	Diane Theodorski
William Larson	Paul Meunier	Diane Theodorski
Julie Braastad	****Gary Kirkeide	Diane Theodorski
Julie Braastad	Gary Kirkeide	Diane Theodorski
Julie Braastad	Gary Kirkeide	Tom Johnson
*****Al Parranto	Gary Kirkeide	Tom Johnson
Al Parranto	Gary Kirkeide	Tom Johnson

*** Appointed on November 18, 2002, to fill vacancy of Kenneth Braastad.
**** Appointed to fill a vacancy on the council from January 2, 2007, to December 31, 2008.
***** Appointed to fill a vacancy on the council from February 4, 2013, to December 31, 2014.

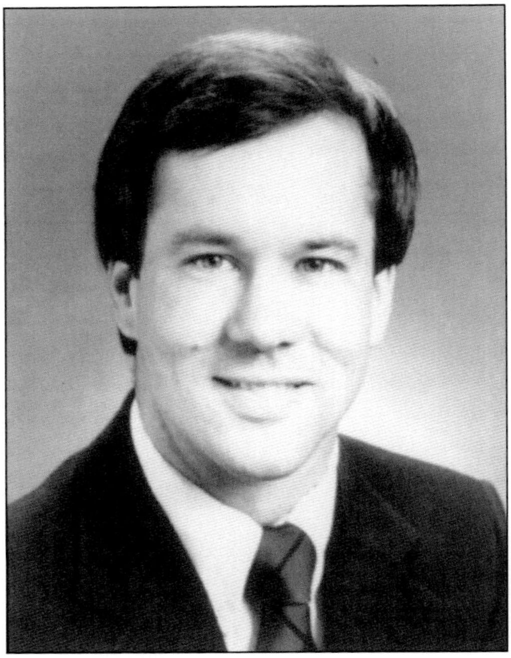 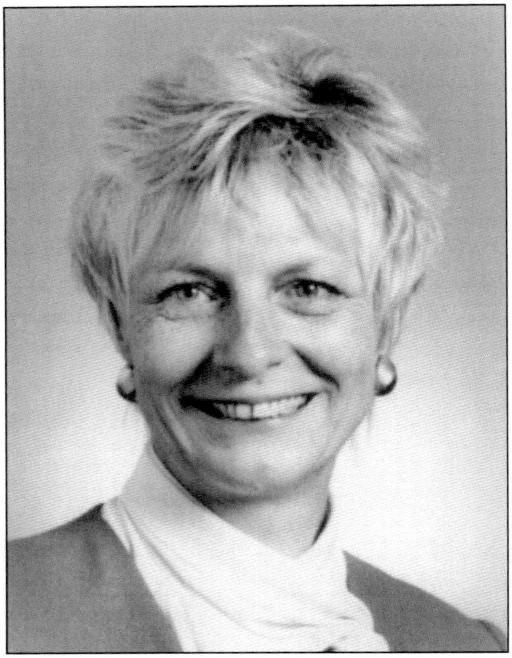
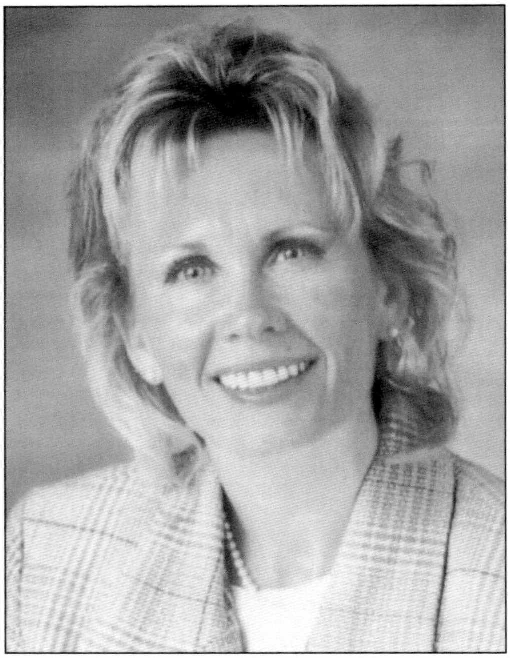 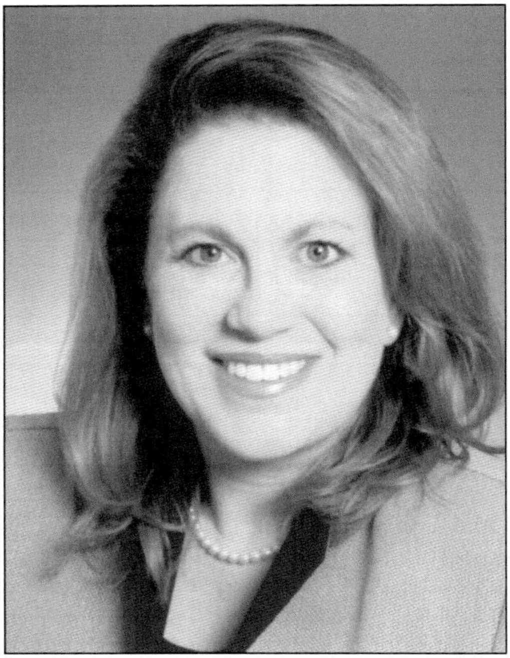

Four Ham Lake residents have served in the Minnesota State Senate. They include Sen. Gregory Dahl, who served from 1981 to 1991. He was the chair of the Senate Committees on Education Operation and Governance and Environmental Protection. Sen. Paula Hanson (upper right) served from 1993 to 2000. Her work concentrated on K-12 education and transportation. Sen. Debbie Johnson (lower left) served from 2001 to 2010. Her special legislative concerns were education, commerce, jobs, transportation, and taxes. Sen. Michelle Benson (lower right) has served since 2011. She has developed an expertise in health care policy and serves her caucus as an assistant leader. (All, courtesy of the Minnesota State Senate.)

Eight

Parks, Scouts, and Snowbowl

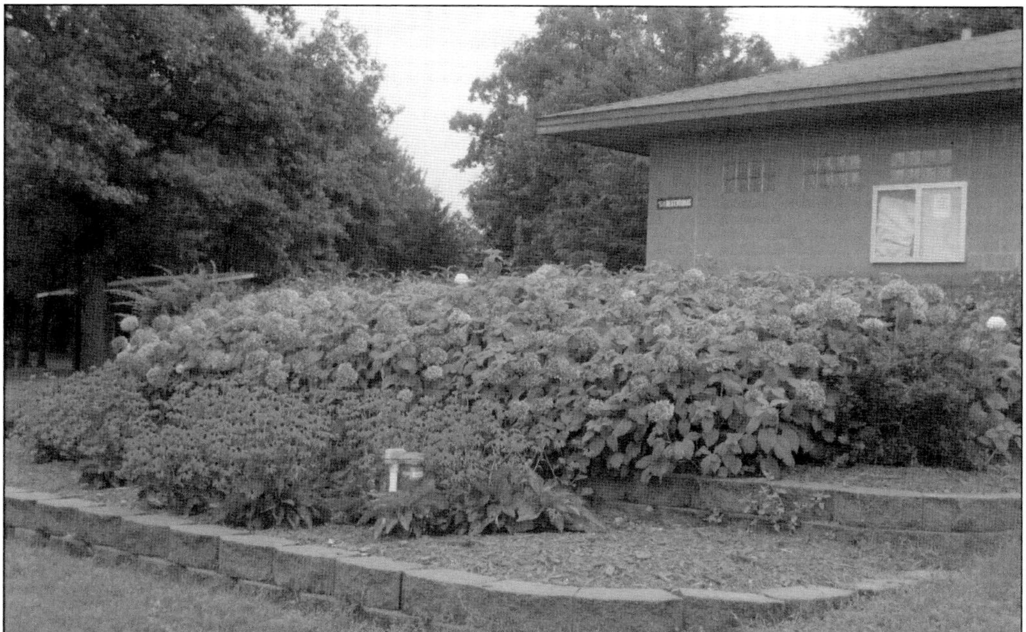

Ham Lake has developed an excellent park system with over 352 acres of land devoted to parks and recreation. The Eagle Scout rank is the highest achievement in the Boy Scout program. Among many other things, a Scout must perform a major community project. Because there were two Boy Scout leaders on the Ham Lake Park and Tree Commission, Ham Lake for many years was a haven for Eagle Scout projects. Boy Scouts from Ham Lake and many of the neighboring communities performed over 50 such projects in Ham Lake. This photograph is of a landscaping project at Lions Park. (Author's collection.)

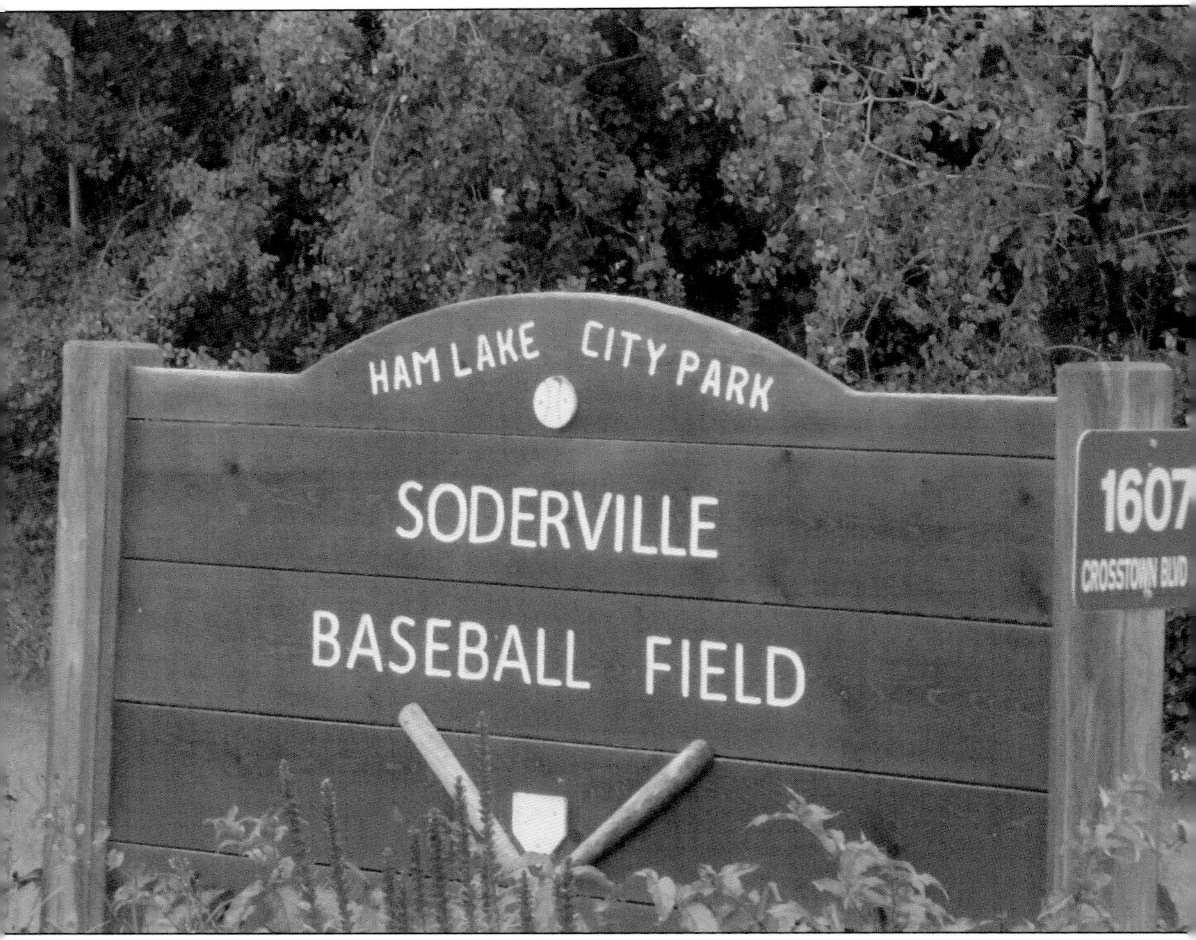

Each of the city's parks, except one, has had its sign designed and built by an Eagle Scout. Instead of having all the signs look the same, the city has decided that each park will have a distinctive sign by having Eagle Scout candidates design and build them. They meet the project portion of the Eagle Scout requirements, and the project allows them to be creative. (Author's collection.)

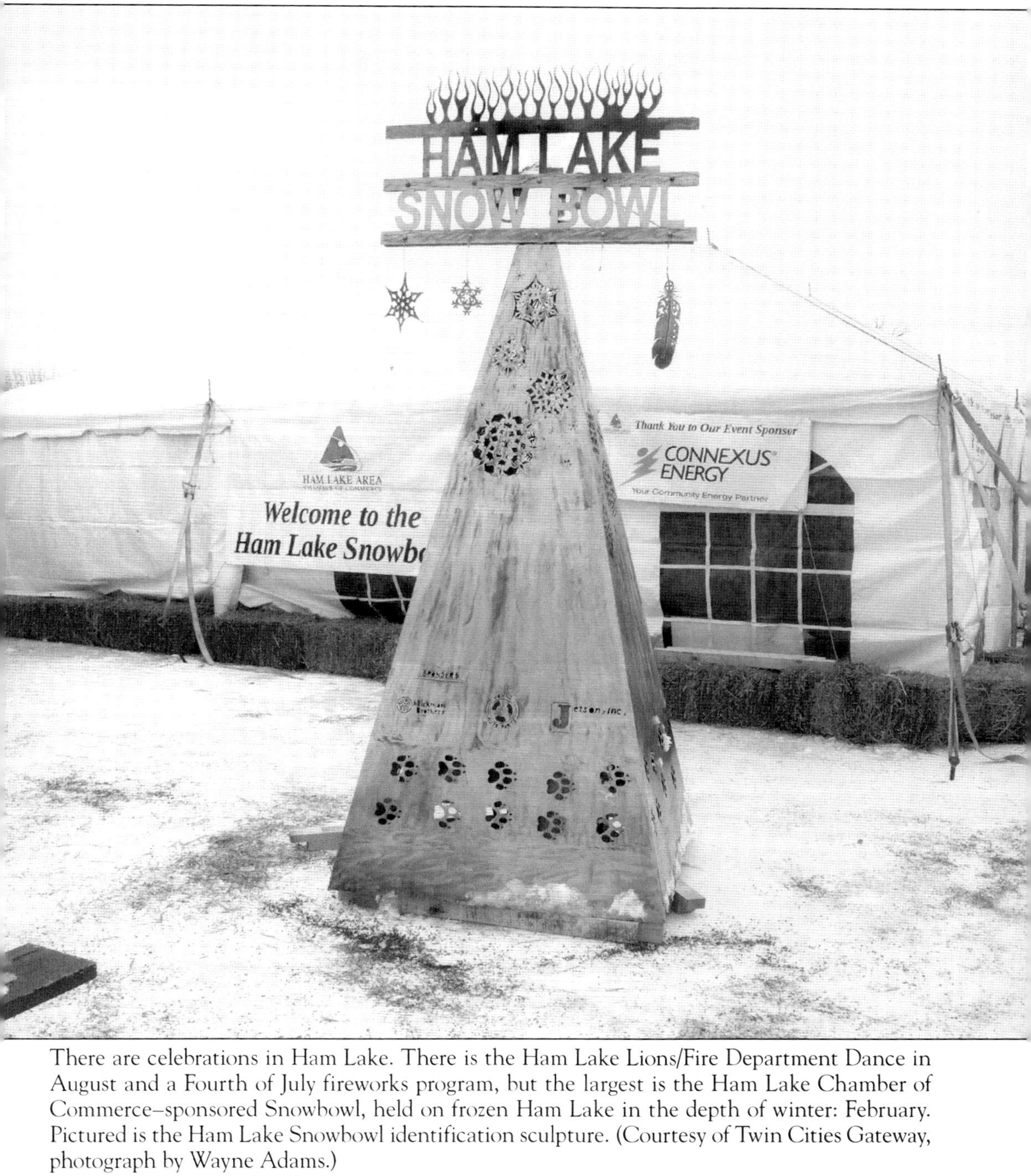

There are celebrations in Ham Lake. There is the Ham Lake Lions/Fire Department Dance in August and a Fourth of July fireworks program, but the largest is the Ham Lake Chamber of Commerce–sponsored Snowbowl, held on frozen Ham Lake in the depth of winter: February. Pictured is the Ham Lake Snowbowl identification sculpture. (Courtesy of Twin Cities Gateway, photograph by Wayne Adams.)

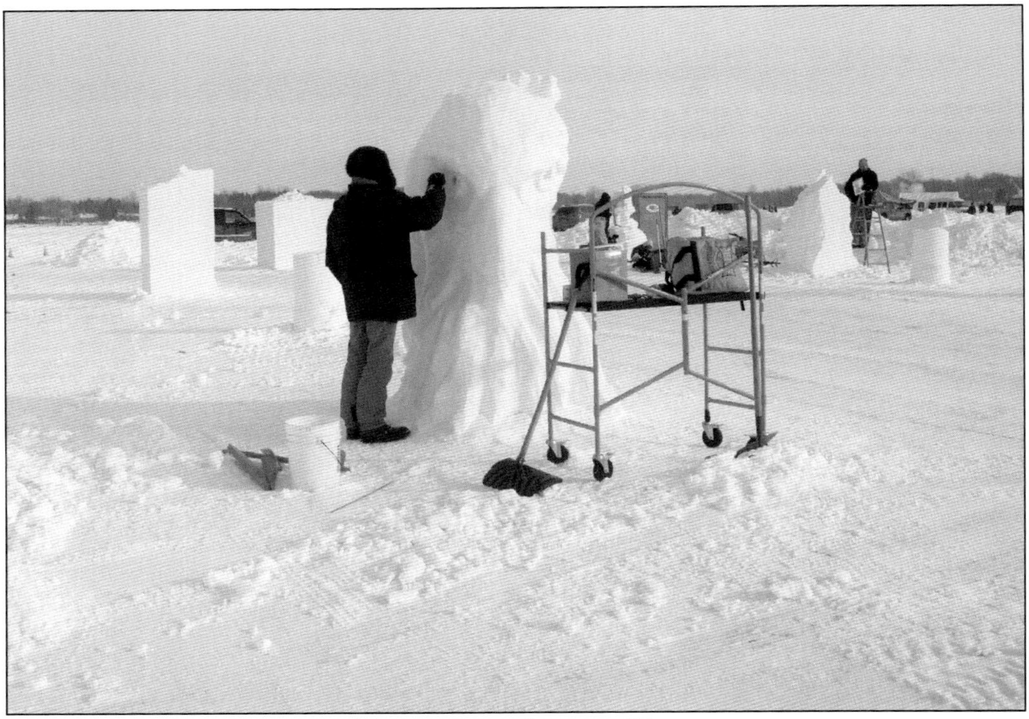

Among the many events on the lake is snow sculpturing. The event attracts many contestants, who compete for prizes and to show off their skills. (Courtesy of Twin Cities Gateway, photograph by Wayne Adams.)

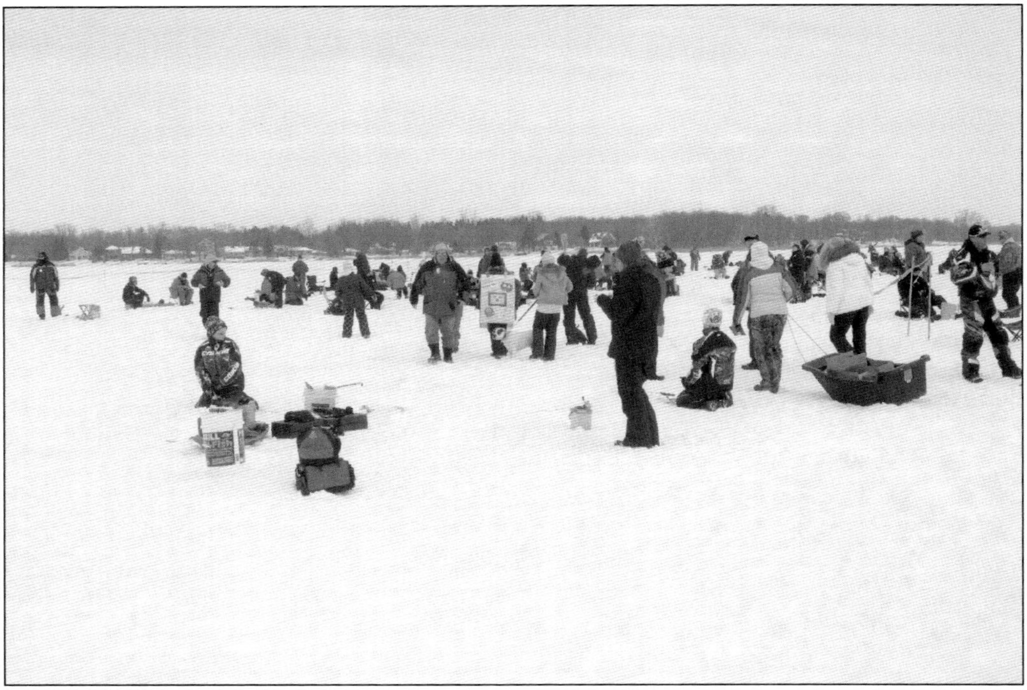

Hundreds of people participate in the ice-fishing contest. The local Boy Scouts Order of the Arrow chapter cosponsors the event. (Courtesy of Twin Cities Gateway, photograph by Wayne Adams.)

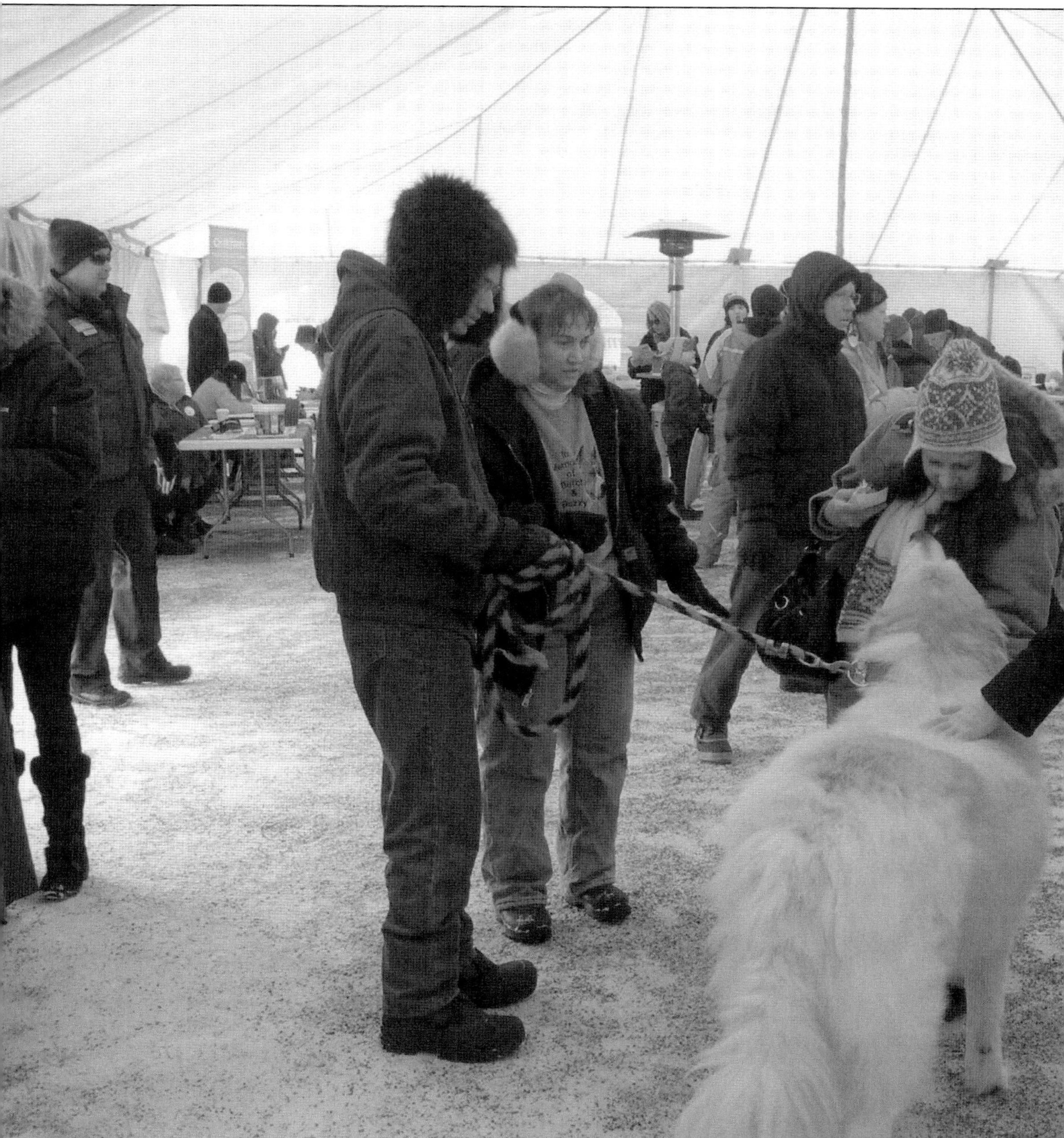

The event includes, but is not limited to, dog sled events, dog pulling, kids playgrounds sculpted out of snow and ice, and sporting events such as broomball. In the freezing temperatures, the event even has a business expo in a heated tent on the lake, where Ham Lake businesses can show their wares to the many people and their animals coming inside to get a little warmer. (Courtesy of Twin Cities Gateway, photograph by Wayne Adams.)

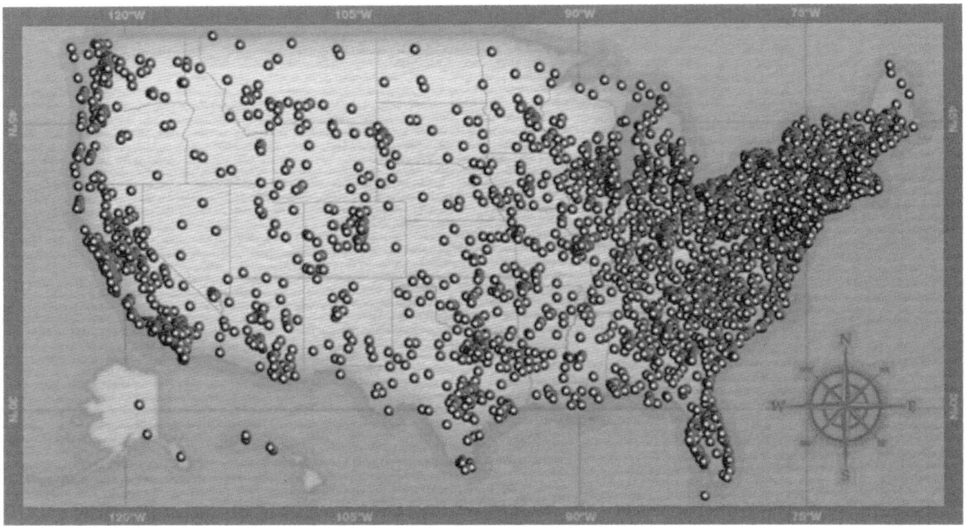